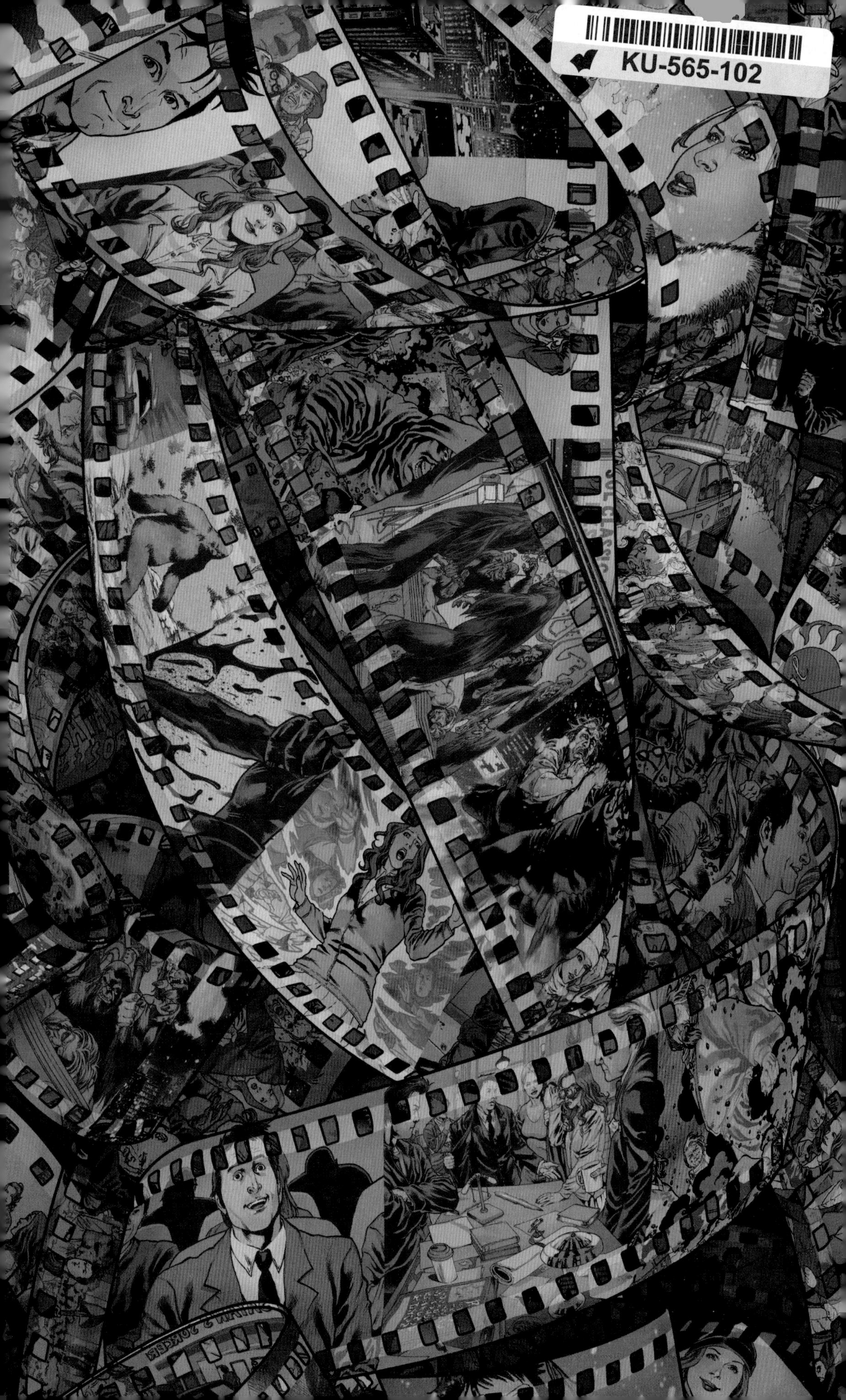

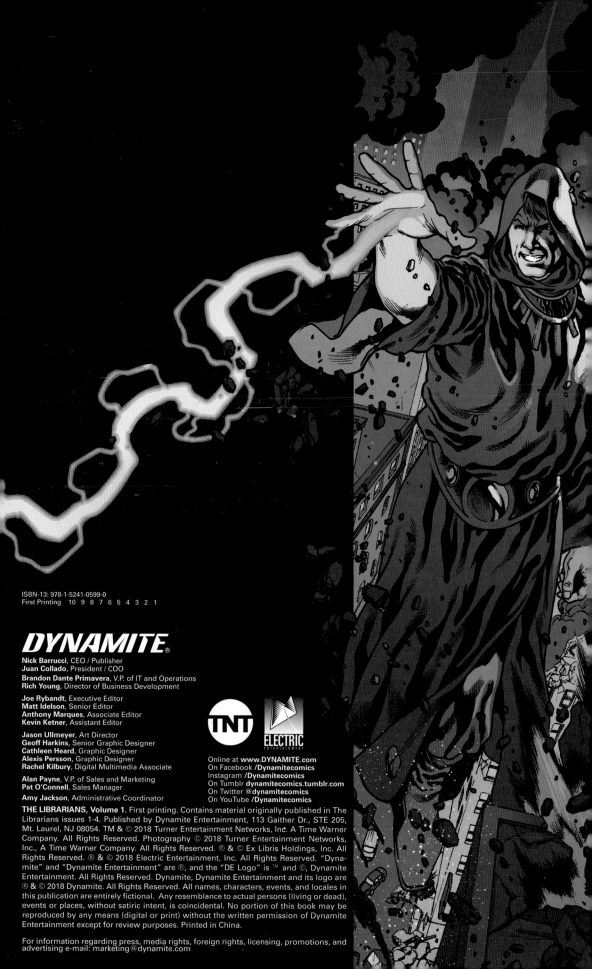

ISBN-13: 978-1-5241-0599-0
First Printing   10 9 8 7 6 5 4 3 2 1

DYNAMITE®

Nick Barrucci, CEO / Publisher
Juan Collado, President / COO
Brandon Dante Primavera, V.P. of IT and Operations
Rich Young, Director of Business Development

Joe Rybandt, Executive Editor
Matt Idelson, Senior Editor
Anthony Marques, Associate Editor
Kevin Ketner, Assistant Editor

Jason Ullmeyer, Art Director
Geoff Harkins, Senior Graphic Designer
Cathleen Heard, Graphic Designer
Alexis Persson, Graphic Designer
Rachel Kilbury, Digital Multimedia Associate

Alan Payne, V.P. of Sales and Marketing
Pat O'Connell, Sales Manager

Amy Jackson, Administrative Coordinator

Online at www.**DYNAMITE**.com
On Facebook /Dynamitecomics
Instagram /Dynamitecomics
On Tumblr dynamitecomics.tumblr.com
On Twitter @dynamitecomics
On YouTube /Dynamitecomics

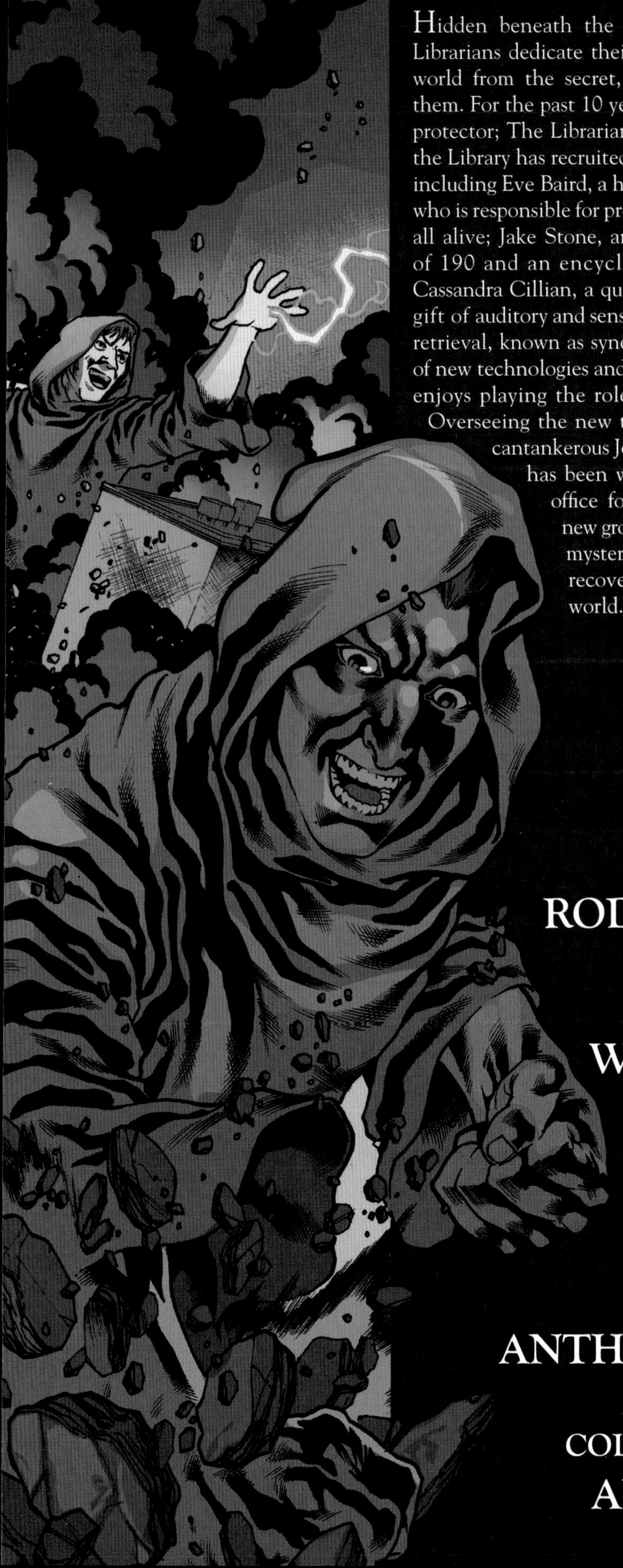

Hidden beneath the Metropolitan Public Library, The Librarians dedicate their lives to protecting an unknowing world from the secret, magical reality hidden all around them. For the past 10 years, Flynn Carsen has served as that protector; The Librarian and now, to aid him in his duties, the Library has recruited four people from around the world, including Eve Baird, a highly skilled counter-terrorism agent who is responsible for protecting the group and keeping them all alive; Jake Stone, an Oklahoma oil worker with an IQ of 190 and an encyclopedic knowledge of art history; Cassandra Cillian, a quirky young woman with the special gift of auditory and sensory hallucinations linked to memory retrieval, known as synesthesia; and Ezekiel Jones, a master of new technologies and aficionado of old classic crimes who enjoys playing the role of international man of mystery. Overseeing the new team of Librarians is the somewhat cantankerous Jenkins, an expert in ancient lore who has been working out of the Library's branch office for longer than anyone knows. This new group works together to solve impossible mysteries, fight supernatural threats and recover powerful artifacts from around the world.

WRITTEN BY
WILL PFEIFFER

ART BY
RODNEY BUCHEMI

COLORS BY
WESLEI MANUEL

LETTERS BY
TROY PETERI

EDITOR
ANTHONY MARQUES

COLLECTION DESIGNER
ALEXIS PERSSON

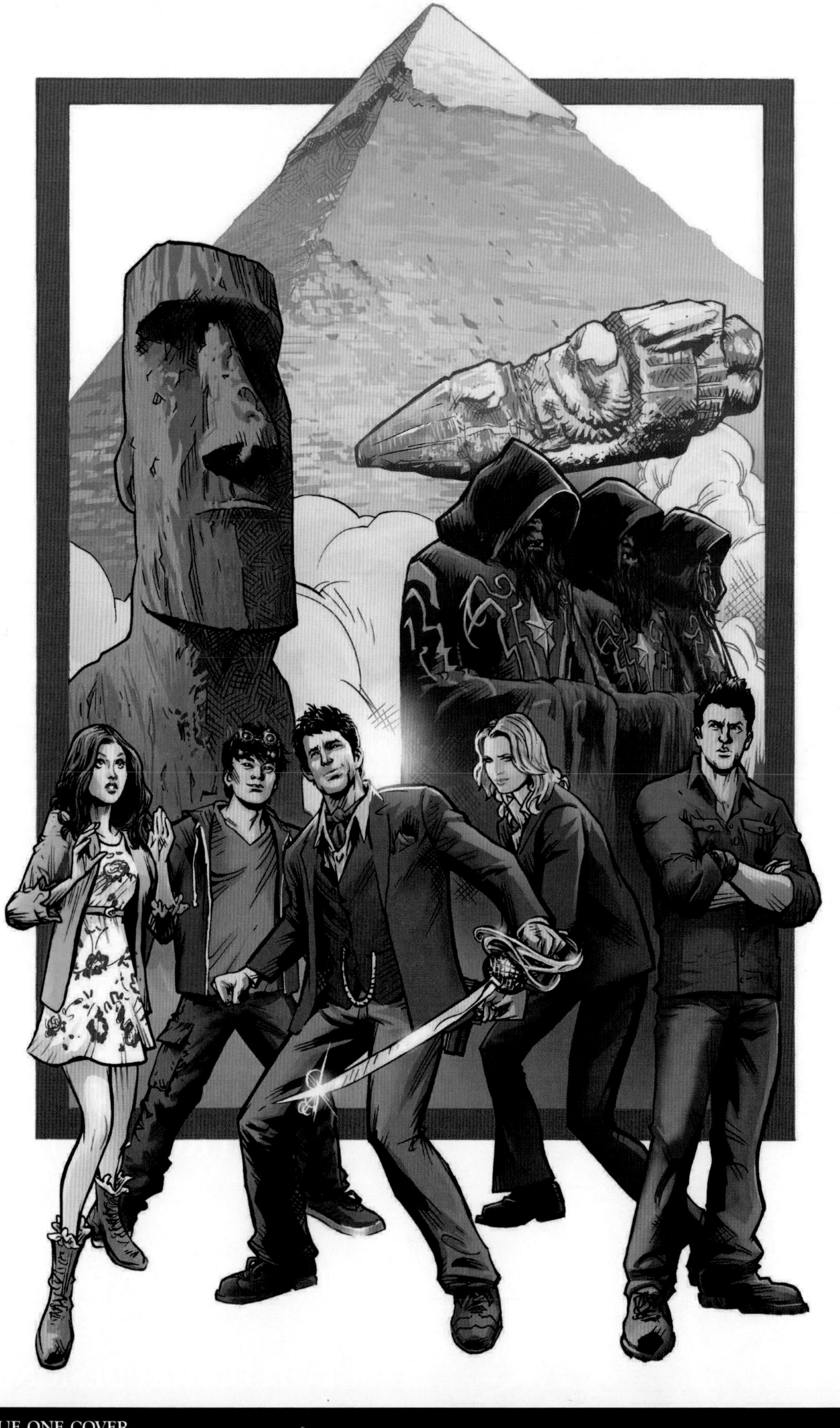

Issue one cover
art by KARL MOLINE

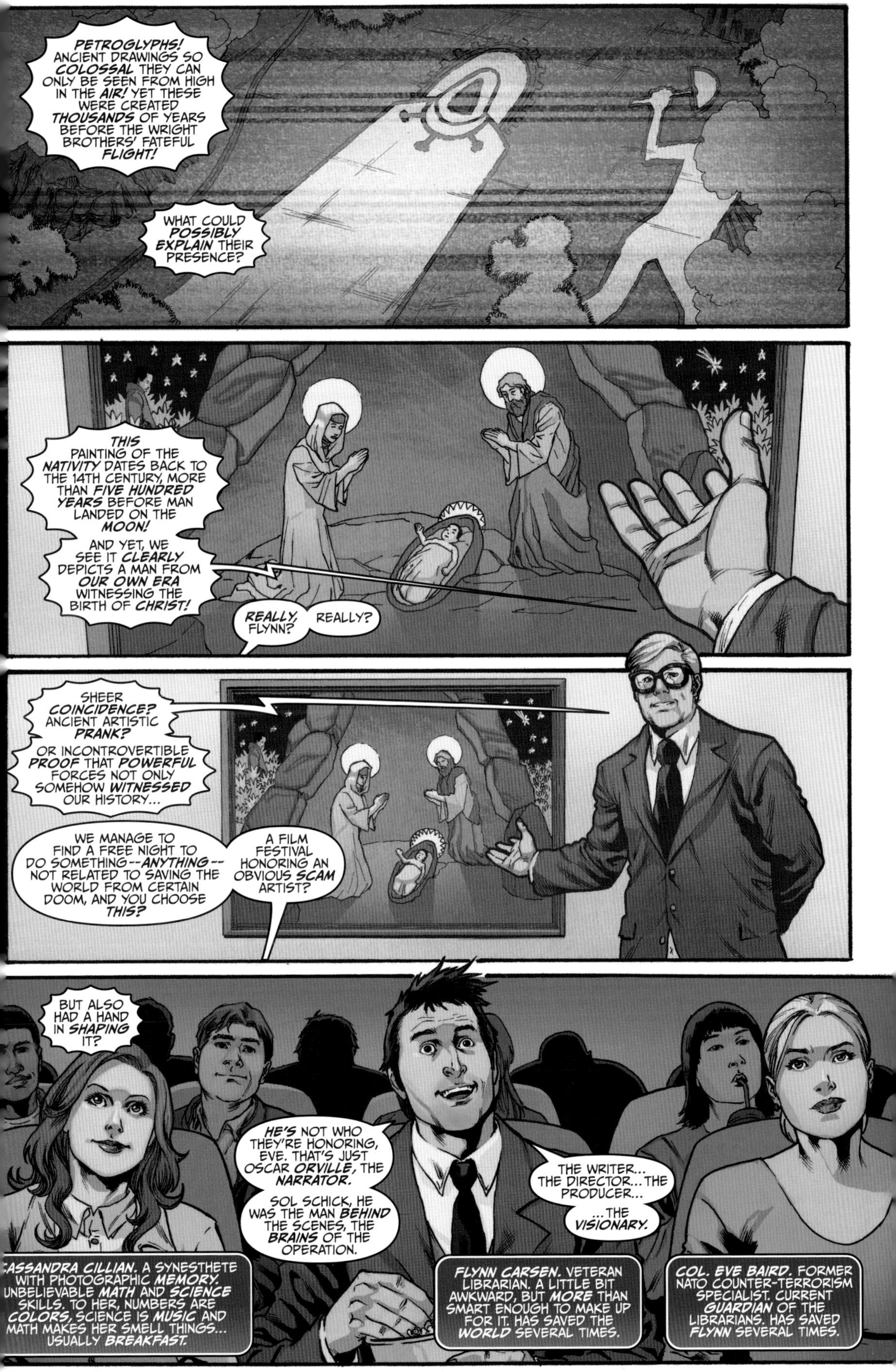
PETROGLYPHS! ANCIENT DRAWINGS SO COLOSSAL THEY CAN ONLY BE SEEN FROM HIGH IN THE AIR! YET THESE WERE CREATED THOUSANDS OF YEARS BEFORE THE WRIGHT BROTHERS' FATEFUL FLIGHT!
WHAT COULD POSSIBLY EXPLAIN THEIR PRESENCE?
THIS PAINTING OF THE NATIVITY DATES BACK TO THE 14TH CENTURY, MORE THAN FIVE HUNDRED YEARS BEFORE MAN LANDED ON THE MOON!
AND YET, WE SEE IT CLEARLY DEPICTS A MAN FROM OUR OWN ERA WITNESSING THE BIRTH OF CHRIST!
REALLY, FLYNN?
REALLY?
SHEER COINCIDENCE? ANCIENT ARTISTIC PRANK?
OR INCONTROVERTIBLE PROOF THAT POWERFUL FORCES NOT ONLY SOMEHOW WITNESSED OUR HISTORY...
WE MANAGE TO FIND A FREE NIGHT TO DO SOMETHING--ANYTHING--NOT RELATED TO SAVING THE WORLD FROM CERTAIN DOOM, AND YOU CHOOSE THIS?
A FILM FESTIVAL HONORING AN OBVIOUS SCAM ARTIST?
BUT ALSO HAD A HAND IN SHAPING IT?
HE'S NOT WHO THEY'RE HONORING, EVE. THAT'S JUST OSCAR ORVILLE, THE NARRATOR.
SOL SCHICK, HE WAS THE MAN BEHIND THE SCENES, THE BRAINS OF THE OPERATION.
THE WRITER... THE DIRECTOR... THE PRODUCER...
...THE VISIONARY.
CASSANDRA CILLIAN. A SYNESTHETE WITH PHOTOGRAPHIC MEMORY. UNBELIEVABLE MATH AND SCIENCE SKILLS. TO HER, NUMBERS ARE COLORS, SCIENCE IS MUSIC AND MATH MAKES HER SMELL THINGS... USUALLY BREAKFAST.
FLYNN CARSEN. VETERAN LIBRARIAN. A LITTLE BIT AWKWARD, BUT MORE THAN SMART ENOUGH TO MAKE UP FOR IT. HAS SAVED THE WORLD SEVERAL TIMES.
COL. EVE BAIRD. FORMER NATO COUNTER-TERRORISM SPECIALIST. CURRENT GUARDIAN OF THE LIBRARIANS. HAS SAVED FLYNN SEVERAL TIMES.

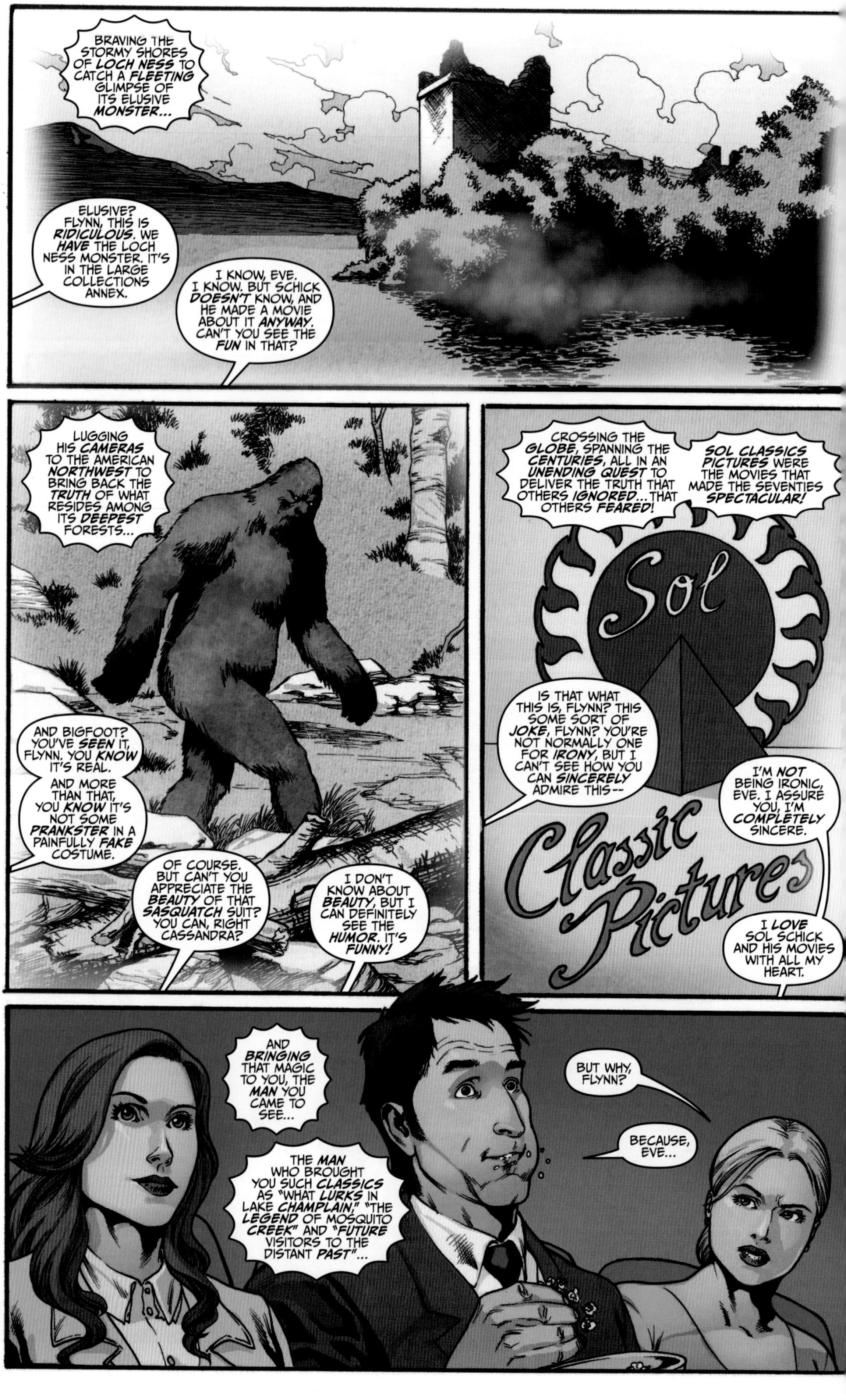
BRAVING THE STORMY SHORES OF LOCH NESS TO CATCH A FLEETING GLIMPSE OF ITS ELUSIVE MONSTER...
ELUSIVE? FLYNN, THIS IS RIDICULOUS. WE HAVE THE LOCH NESS MONSTER. IT'S IN THE LARGE COLLECTIONS ANNEX.
I KNOW, EVE. I KNOW. BUT SCHICK DOESN'T KNOW, AND HE MADE A MOVIE ABOUT IT ANYWAY. CAN'T YOU SEE THE FUN IN THAT?
LUGGING HIS CAMERAS TO THE AMERICAN NORTHWEST TO BRING BACK THE TRUTH OF WHAT RESIDES AMONG ITS DEEPEST FORESTS...
AND BIGFOOT? YOU'VE SEEN IT, FLYNN. YOU KNOW IT'S REAL.
AND MORE THAN THAT, YOU KNOW IT'S NOT SOME PRANKSTER IN A PAINFULLY FAKE COSTUME.
OF COURSE. BUT CAN'T YOU APPRECIATE THE BEAUTY OF THAT SASQUATCH SUIT? YOU CAN, RIGHT CASSANDRA?
I DON'T KNOW ABOUT BEAUTY, BUT I CAN DEFINITELY SEE THE HUMOR. IT'S FUNNY!
CROSSING THE GLOBE, SPANNING THE CENTURIES, ALL IN AN UNENDING QUEST TO DELIVER THE TRUTH THAT OTHERS IGNORED...THAT OTHERS FEARED!
SOL CLASSICS PICTURES WERE THE MOVIES THAT MADE THE SEVENTIES SPECTACULAR!
Sol
IS THAT WHAT THIS IS, FLYNN? THIS SOME SORT OF JOKE, FLYNN? YOU'RE NOT NORMALLY ONE FOR IRONY, BUT I CAN'T SEE HOW YOU CAN SINCERELY ADMIRE THIS--
I'M NOT BEING IRONIC, EVE. I ASSURE YOU, I'M COMPLETELY SINCERE.
Classic Pictures
I LOVE SOL SCHICK AND HIS MOVIES WITH ALL MY HEART.
AND BRINGING THAT MAGIC TO YOU, THE MAN YOU CAME TO SEE...
THE MAN WHO BROUGHT YOU SUCH CLASSICS AS "WHAT LURKS IN LAKE CHAMPLAIN," "THE LEGEND OF MOSQUITO CREEK" AND "FUTURE VISITORS TO THE DISTANT PAST"...
BUT WHY, FLYNN?
BECAUSE, EVE...

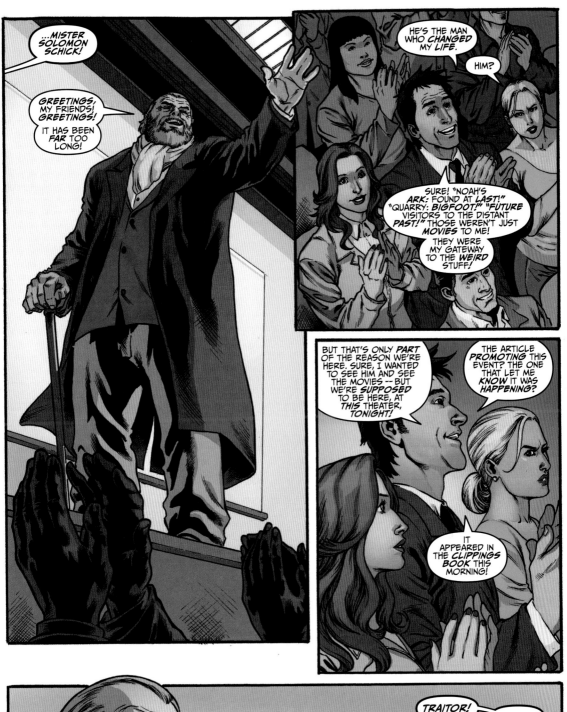

...MISTER SOLOMON SCHICK!

GREETINGS, MY FRIENDS! GREETINGS! IT HAS BEEN *FAR* TOO LONG!

HE'S THE MAN WHO *CHANGED* MY *LIFE.*

HIM?

SURE! "NOAH'S *ARK:* FOUND AT *LAST!*" "QUARRY: *BIGFOOT!*" "*FUTURE* VISITORS TO THE DISTANT *PAST!*" THOSE WEREN'T JUST *MOVIES* TO ME!

THEY WERE MY GATEWAY TO THE *WEIRD* STUFF!

BUT THAT'S ONLY *PART* OF THE REASON WE'RE HERE. SURE, I WANTED TO SEE HIM AND SEE THE MOVIES -- BUT WE'RE *SUPPOSED* TO BE HERE, AT *THIS* THEATER, TONIGHT!

THE ARTICLE *PROMOTING* THIS EVENT? THE ONE THAT LET ME *KNOW* IT WAS *HAPPENING?*

IT APPEARED IN THE *CLIPPINGS BOOK* THIS MORNING!

TRAITOR!

JUDAS!

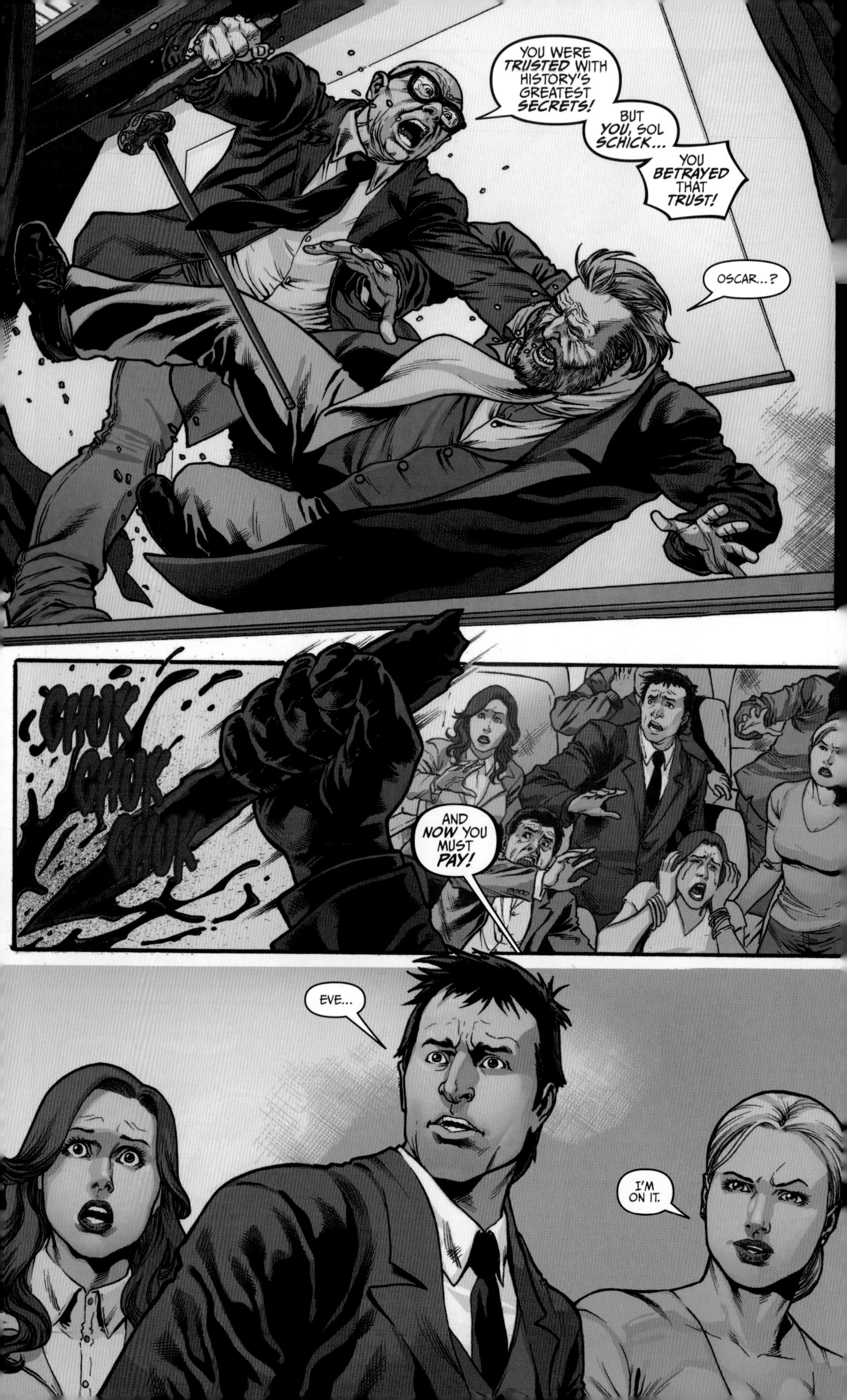
YOU WERE TRUSTED WITH HISTORY'S GREATEST SECRETS!
BUT YOU, SOL SCHICK...
YOU BETRAYED THAT TRUST!
OSCAR...?
CHUK CHUK CHUK
AND NOW YOU MUST PAY!
EVE...
I'M ON IT.

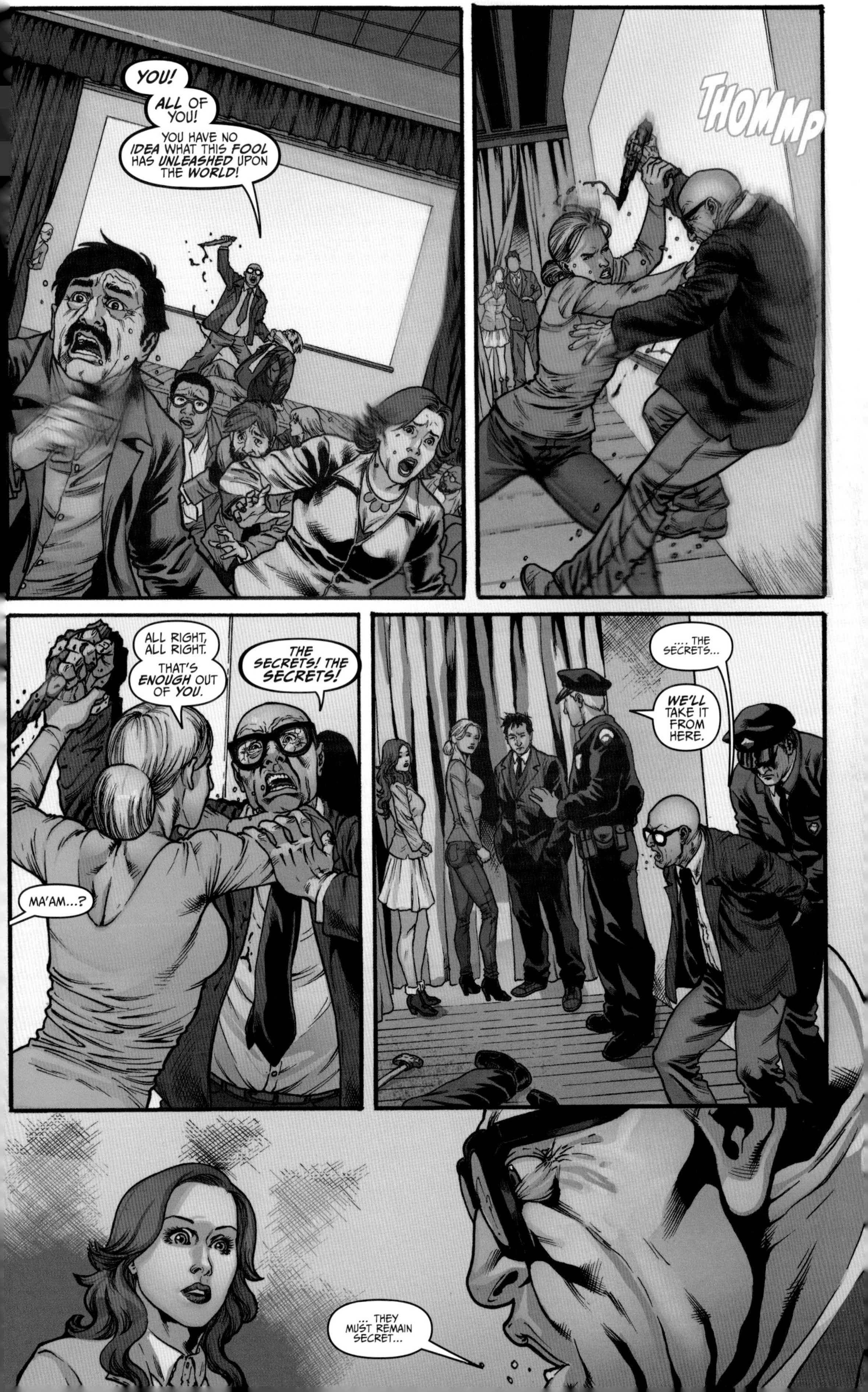
YOU!
ALL OF YOU!
YOU HAVE NO IDEA WHAT THIS FOOL HAS UNLEASHED UPON THE WORLD!
THOMMP
ALL RIGHT, ALL RIGHT.
THAT'S ENOUGH OUT OF YOU.
THE SECRETS! THE SECRETS!
MA'AM...?
.... THE SECRETS...
WE'LL TAKE IT FROM HERE.
... THEY MUST REMAIN SECRET...

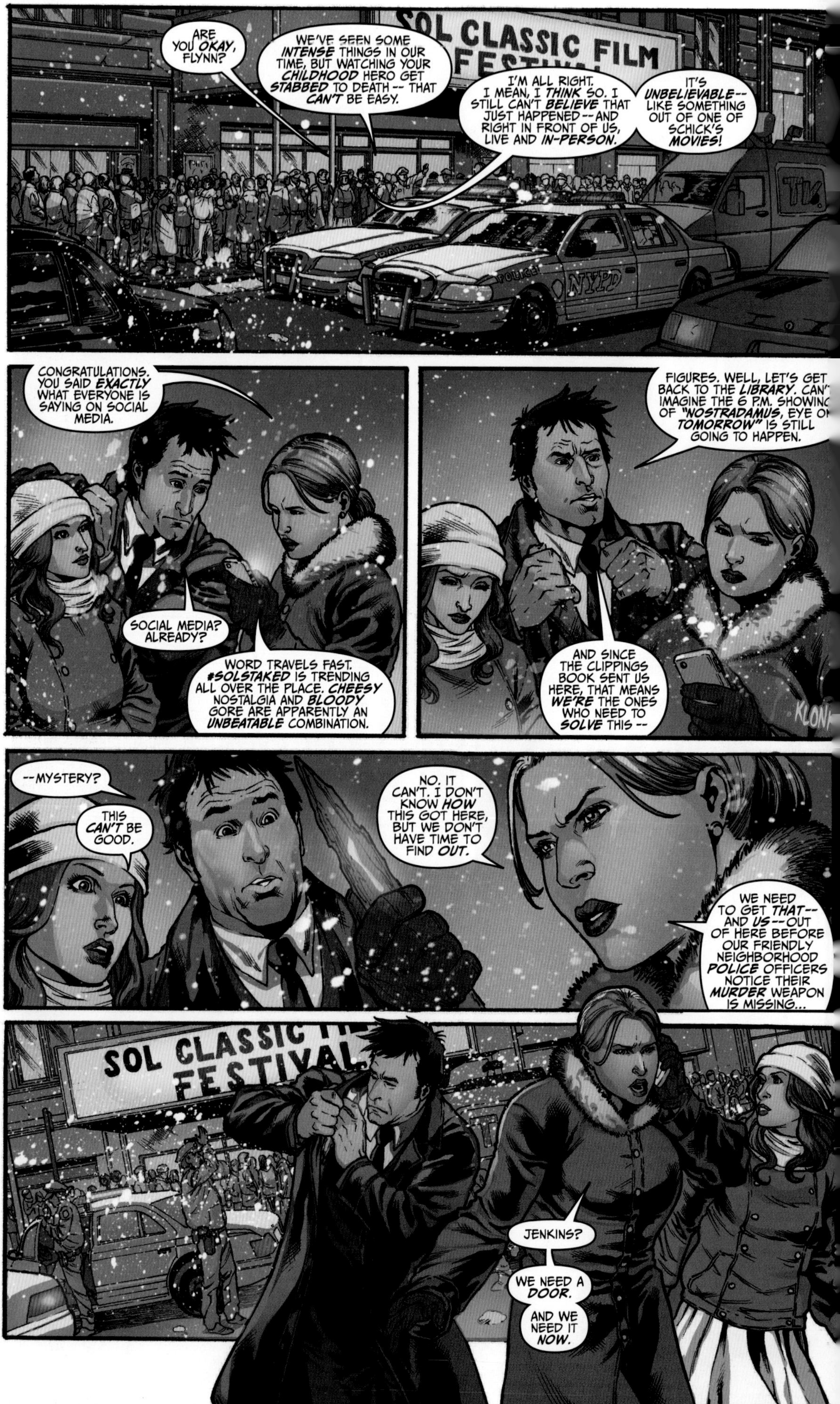
SOL CLASSIC FILM
ARE YOU OKAY, FLYNN?
WE'VE SEEN SOME INTENSE THINGS IN OUR TIME, BUT WATCHING YOUR CHILDHOOD HERO GET STABBED TO DEATH -- THAT CAN'T BE EASY.
I'M ALL RIGHT. I MEAN, I THINK SO. I STILL CAN'T BELIEVE THAT JUST HAPPENED -- AND RIGHT IN FRONT OF US, LIVE AND IN-PERSON.
IT'S UNBELIEVABLE -- LIKE SOMETHING OUT OF ONE OF SCHICK'S MOVIES!
POLICE
NYPD
CONGRATULATIONS. YOU SAID EXACTLY WHAT EVERYONE IS SAYING ON SOCIAL MEDIA.
SOCIAL MEDIA? ALREADY?
WORD TRAVELS FAST. #SOLSTAKED IS TRENDING ALL OVER THE PLACE. CHEESY NOSTALGIA AND BLOODY GORE ARE APPARENTLY AN UNBEATABLE COMBINATION.
FIGURES. WELL, LET'S GET BACK TO THE LIBRARY. CAN'T IMAGINE THE 6 P.M. SHOWING OF "NOSTRADAMUS, EYE ON TOMORROW" IS STILL GOING TO HAPPEN.
AND SINCE THE CLIPPINGS BOOK SENT US HERE, THAT MEANS WE'RE THE ONES WHO NEED TO SOLVE THIS --
--MYSTERY?
THIS CAN'T BE GOOD.
NO. IT CAN'T. I DON'T KNOW HOW THIS GOT HERE, BUT WE DON'T HAVE TIME TO FIND OUT.
WE NEED TO GET THAT -- AND US -- OUT OF HERE BEFORE OUR FRIENDLY NEIGHBORHOOD POLICE OFFICERS NOTICE THEIR MURDER WEAPON IS MISSING...
SOL CLASSIC
FESTIVAL
JENKINS?
WE NEED A DOOR.
AND WE NEED IT NOW.

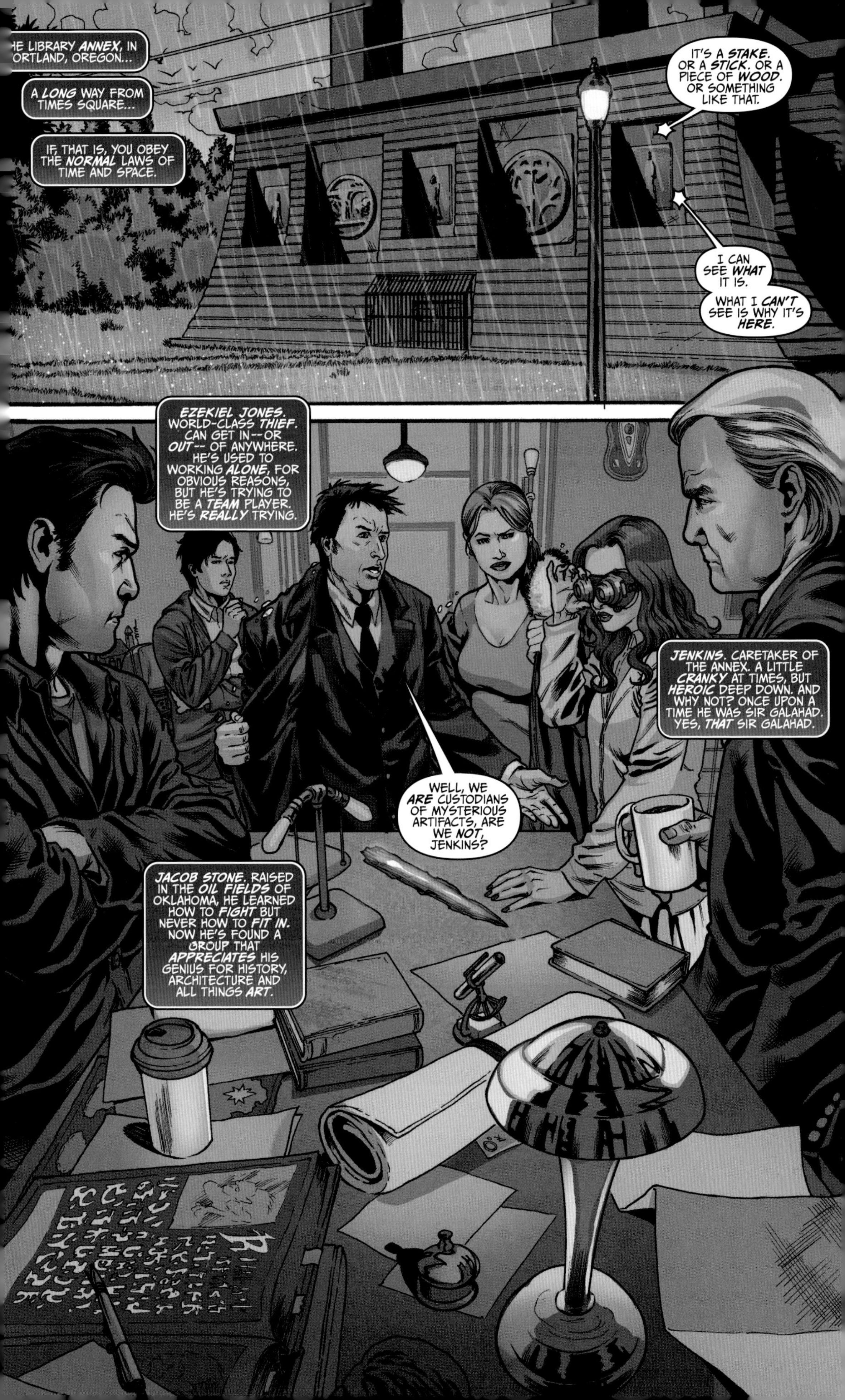
HE LIBRARY ANNEX, IN
ORTLAND, OREGON...
A LONG WAY FROM TIMES SQUARE...
IF, THAT IS, YOU OBEY THE NORMAL LAWS OF TIME AND SPACE.
IT'S A STAKE. OR A STICK. OR A PIECE OF WOOD. OR SOMETHING LIKE THAT.
I CAN SEE WHAT IT IS.
WHAT I CAN'T SEE IS WHY IT'S HERE.
EZEKIEL JONES. WORLD-CLASS THIEF. CAN GET IN--OR OUT-- OF ANYWHERE. HE'S USED TO WORKING ALONE, FOR OBVIOUS REASONS, BUT HE'S TRYING TO BE A TEAM PLAYER. HE'S REALLY TRYING.
JENKINS. CARETAKER OF THE ANNEX. A LITTLE CRANKY AT TIMES, BUT HEROIC DEEP DOWN. AND WHY NOT? ONCE UPON A TIME HE WAS SIR GALAHAD. YES, THAT SIR GALAHAD.
WELL, WE ARE CUSTODIANS OF MYSTERIOUS ARTIFACTS, ARE WE NOT, JENKINS?
JACOB STONE. RAISED IN THE OIL FIELDS OF OKLAHOMA, HE LEARNED HOW TO FIGHT BUT NEVER HOW TO FIT IN. NOW HE'S FOUND A GROUP THAT APPRECIATES HIS GENIUS FOR HISTORY, ARCHITECTURE AND ALL THINGS ART.

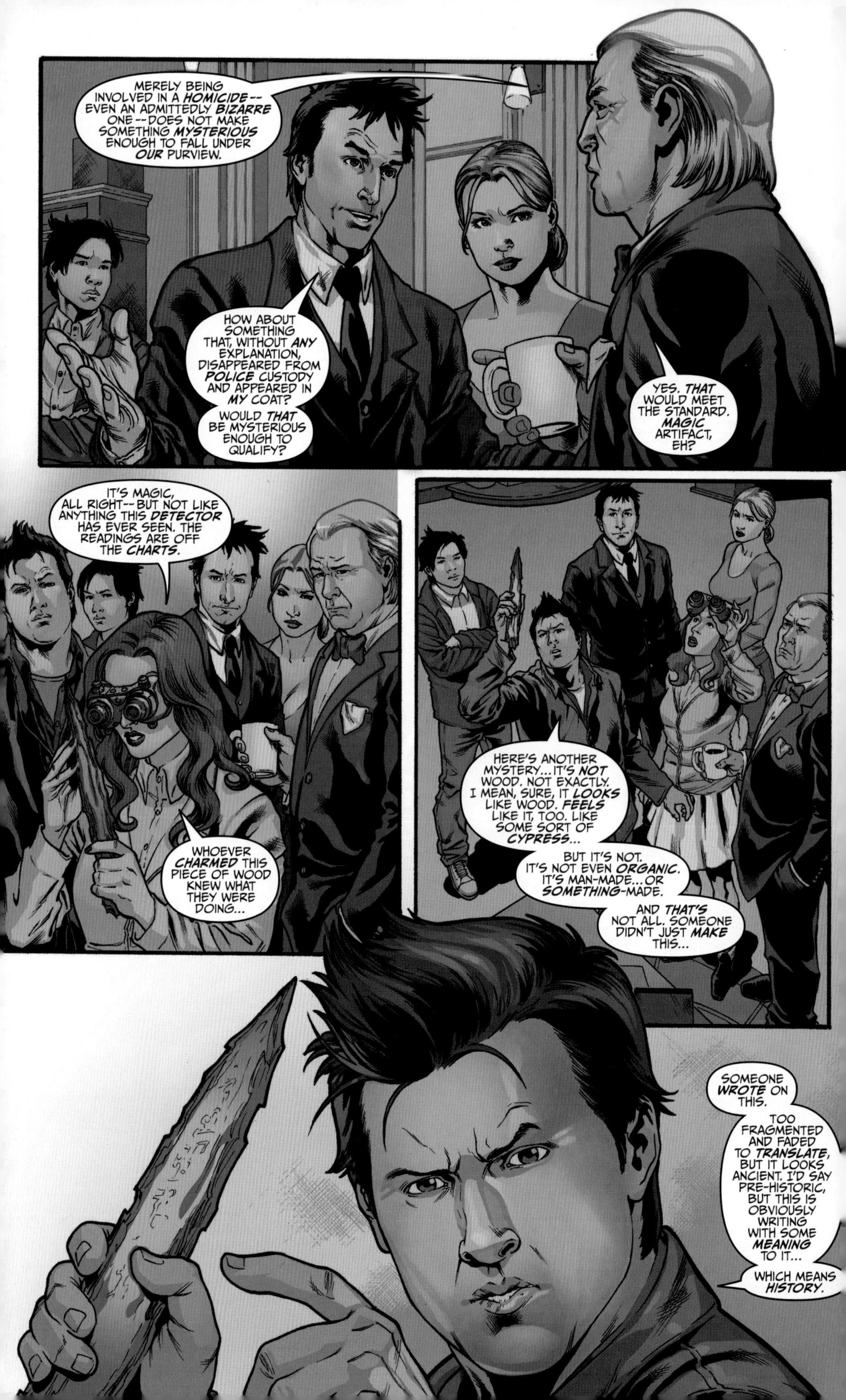
MERELY BEING INVOLVED IN A HOMICIDE-- EVEN AN ADMITTEDLY BIZARRE ONE--DOES NOT MAKE SOMETHING MYSTERIOUS ENOUGH TO FALL UNDER OUR PURVIEW.
HOW ABOUT SOMETHING THAT, WITHOUT ANY EXPLANATION, DISAPPEARED FROM POLICE CUSTODY AND APPEARED IN MY COAT?
WOULD THAT BE MYSTERIOUS ENOUGH TO QUALIFY?
YES. THAT WOULD MEET THE STANDARD. MAGIC ARTIFACT, EH?
IT'S MAGIC, ALL RIGHT--BUT NOT LIKE ANYTHING THIS DETECTOR HAS EVER SEEN. THE READINGS ARE OFF THE CHARTS.
WHOEVER CHARMED THIS PIECE OF WOOD KNEW WHAT THEY WERE DOING...
HERE'S ANOTHER MYSTERY... IT'S NOT WOOD. NOT EXACTLY. I MEAN, SURE, IT LOOKS LIKE WOOD. FEELS LIKE IT, TOO. LIKE SOME SORT OF CYPRESS...
BUT IT'S NOT. IT'S NOT EVEN ORGANIC. IT'S MAN-MADE... OR SOMETHING-MADE.
AND THAT'S NOT ALL. SOMEONE DIDN'T JUST MAKE THIS...
SOMEONE WROTE ON THIS.
TOO FRAGMENTED AND FADED TO TRANSLATE, BUT IT LOOKS ANCIENT. I'D SAY PRE-HISTORIC, BUT THIS IS OBVIOUSLY WRITING WITH SOME MEANING TO IT...
WHICH MEANS HISTORY.

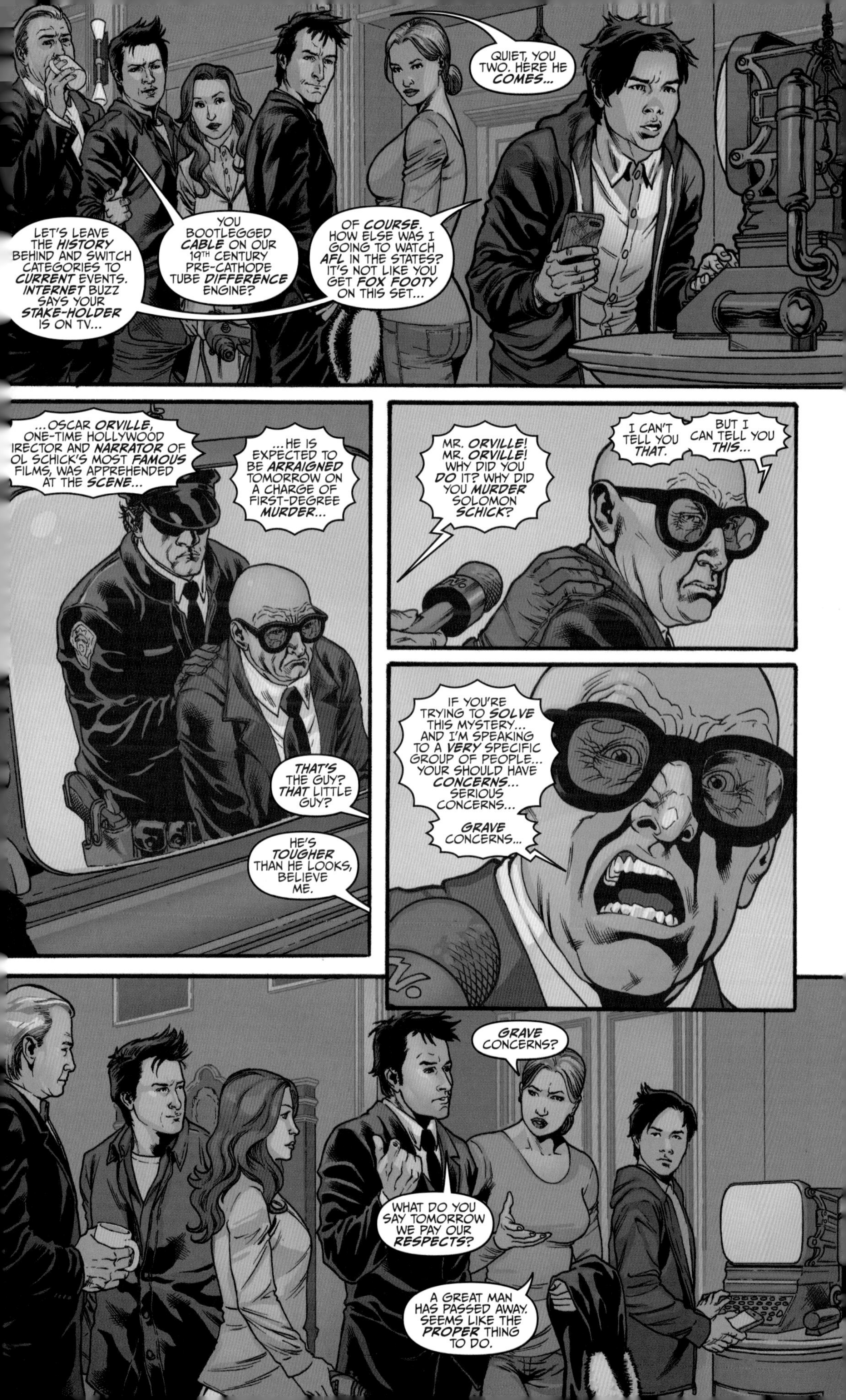
QUIET, YOU TWO. HERE HE COMES...
LET'S LEAVE THE HISTORY BEHIND AND SWITCH CATEGORIES TO CURRENT EVENTS. INTERNET BUZZ SAYS YOUR STAKE-HOLDER IS ON TV...
YOU BOOTLEGGED CABLE ON OUR 19TH CENTURY PRE-CATHODE TUBE DIFFERENCE ENGINE?
OF COURSE. HOW ELSE WAS I GOING TO WATCH AFL IN THE STATES? IT'S NOT LIKE YOU GET FOX FOOTY ON THIS SET...
...OSCAR ORVILLE, ONE-TIME HOLLYWOOD IRECTOR AND NARRATOR OF OL SCHICK'S MOST FAMOUS FILMS, WAS APPREHENDED AT THE SCENE...
...HE IS EXPECTED TO BE ARRAIGNED TOMORROW ON A CHARGE OF FIRST-DEGREE MURDER...
THAT'S THE GUY? THAT LITTLE GUY?
HE'S TOUGHER THAN HE LOOKS, BELIEVE ME.
MR. ORVILLE! MR. ORVILLE! WHY DID YOU DO IT? WHY DID YOU MURDER SOLOMON SCHICK?
I CAN'T TELL YOU THAT.
BUT I CAN TELL YOU THIS...
IF YOU'RE TRYING TO SOLVE THIS MYSTERY... AND I'M SPEAKING TO A VERY SPECIFIC GROUP OF PEOPLE... YOUR SHOULD HAVE CONCERNS... SERIOUS CONCERNS...
GRAVE CONCERNS...
GRAVE CONCERNS?
WHAT DO YOU SAY TOMORROW WE PAY OUR RESPECTS?
A GREAT MAN HAS PASSED AWAY. SEEMS LIKE THE PROPER THING TO DO.

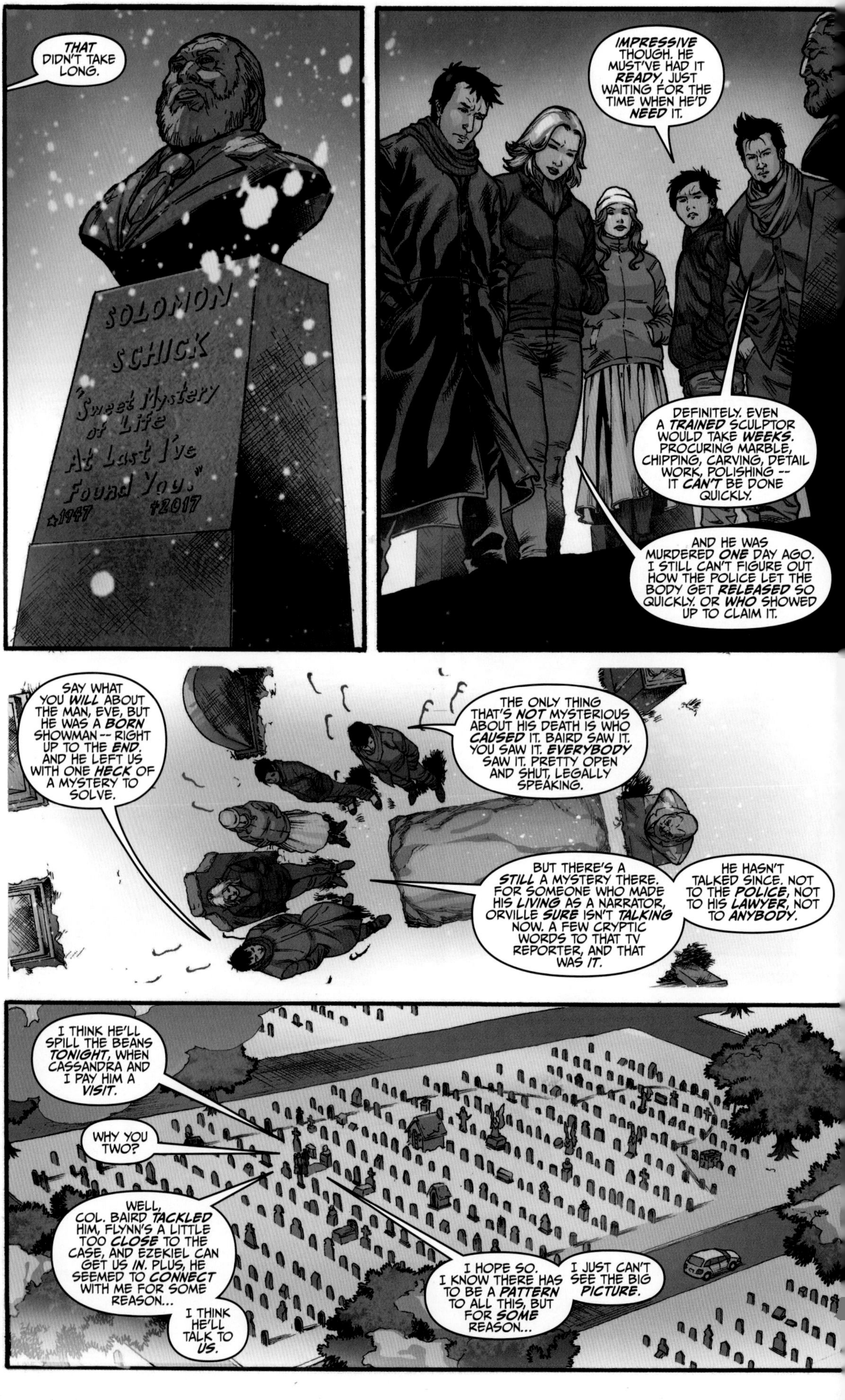
THAT DIDN'T TAKE LONG.
SOLOMON SCHICK
"Sweet Mystery of Life At Last I've Found You."
1947 2017
IMPRESSIVE THOUGH. HE MUST'VE HAD IT READY, JUST WAITING FOR THE TIME WHEN HE'D NEED IT.
DEFINITELY. EVEN A TRAINED SCULPTOR WOULD TAKE WEEKS. PROCURING MARBLE, CHIPPING, CARVING, DETAIL WORK, POLISHING -- IT CAN'T BE DONE QUICKLY.
AND HE WAS MURDERED ONE DAY AGO. I STILL CAN'T FIGURE OUT HOW THE POLICE LET THE BODY GET RELEASED SO QUICKLY. OR WHO SHOWED UP TO CLAIM IT.
SAY WHAT YOU WILL ABOUT THE MAN, EVE, BUT HE WAS A BORN SHOWMAN -- RIGHT UP TO THE END. AND HE LEFT US WITH ONE HECK OF A MYSTERY TO SOLVE.
THE ONLY THING THAT'S NOT MYSTERIOUS ABOUT HIS DEATH IS WHO CAUSED IT. BAIRD SAW IT. YOU SAW IT. EVERYBODY SAW IT. PRETTY OPEN AND SHUT, LEGALLY SPEAKING.
BUT THERE'S A STILL A MYSTERY THERE. FOR SOMEONE WHO MADE HIS LIVING AS A NARRATOR, ORVILLE SURE ISN'T TALKING NOW. A FEW CRYPTIC WORDS TO THAT TV REPORTER, AND THAT WAS IT.
HE HASN'T TALKED SINCE. NOT TO THE POLICE, NOT TO HIS LAWYER, NOT TO ANYBODY.
I THINK HE'LL SPILL THE BEANS TONIGHT, WHEN CASSANDRA AND I PAY HIM A VISIT.
WHY YOU TWO?
WELL, COL. BAIRD TACKLED HIM, FLYNN'S A LITTLE TOO CLOSE TO THE CASE, AND EZEKIEL CAN GET US IN. PLUS, HE SEEMED TO CONNECT WITH ME FOR SOME REASON...
I THINK HE'LL TALK TO US.
I HOPE SO. I KNOW THERE HAS TO BE A PATTERN TO ALL THIS, BUT FOR SOME REASON...
I JUST CAN'T SEE THE BIG PICTURE.

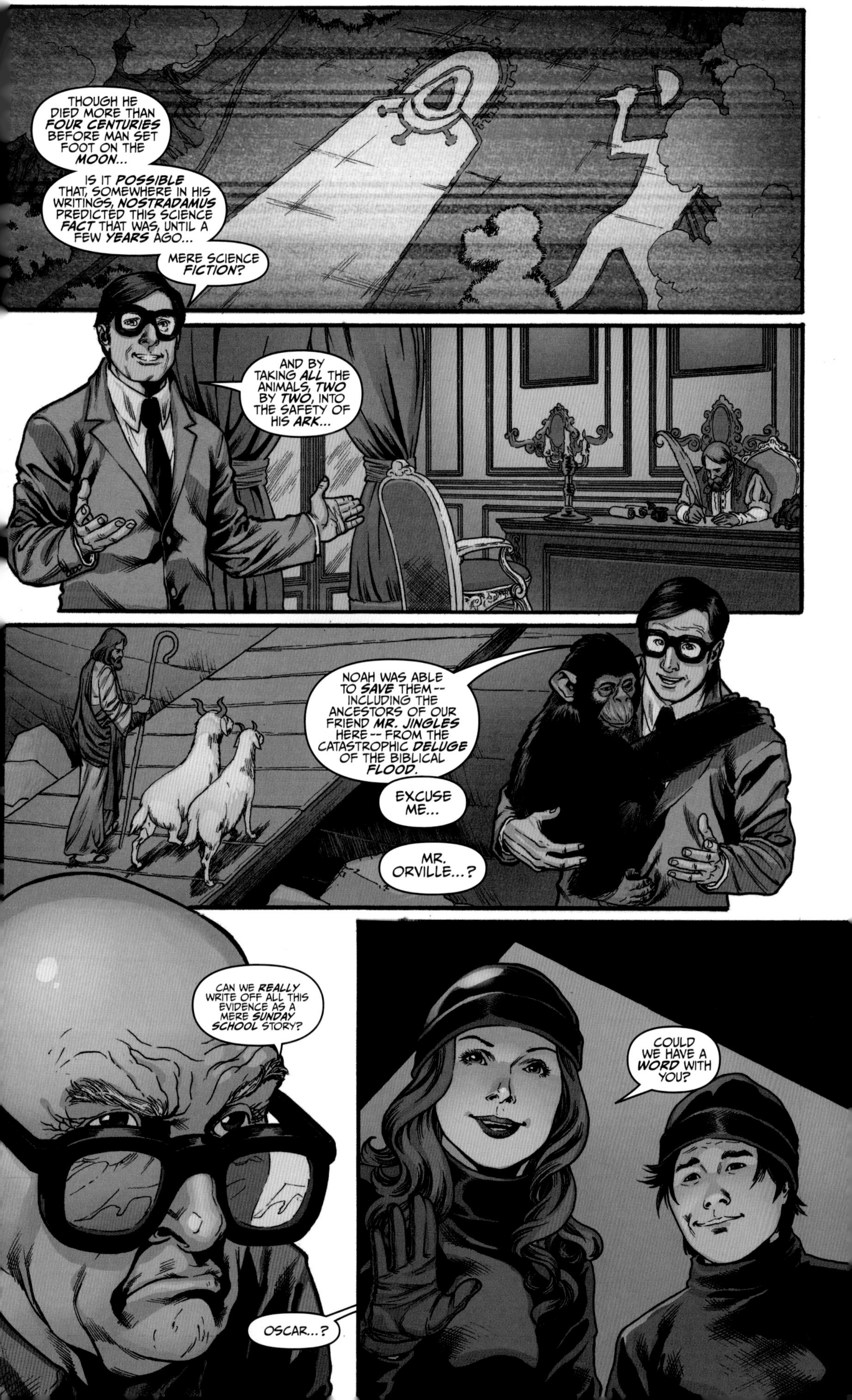
THOUGH HE DIED MORE THAN FOUR CENTURIES BEFORE MAN SET FOOT ON THE MOON...
IS IT POSSIBLE THAT, SOMEWHERE IN HIS WRITINGS, NOSTRADAMUS PREDICTED THIS SCIENCE FACT THAT WAS, UNTIL A FEW YEARS AGO...
MERE SCIENCE FICTION?
AND BY TAKING ALL THE ANIMALS, TWO BY TWO, INTO THE SAFETY OF HIS ARK...
NOAH WAS ABLE TO SAVE THEM -- INCLUDING THE ANCESTORS OF OUR FRIEND MR. JINGLES HERE -- FROM THE CATASTROPHIC DELUGE OF THE BIBLICAL FLOOD.
EXCUSE ME...
MR. ORVILLE...?
CAN WE REALLY WRITE OFF ALL THIS EVIDENCE AS A MERE SUNDAY SCHOOL STORY?
COULD WE HAVE A WORD WITH YOU?
OSCAR...?

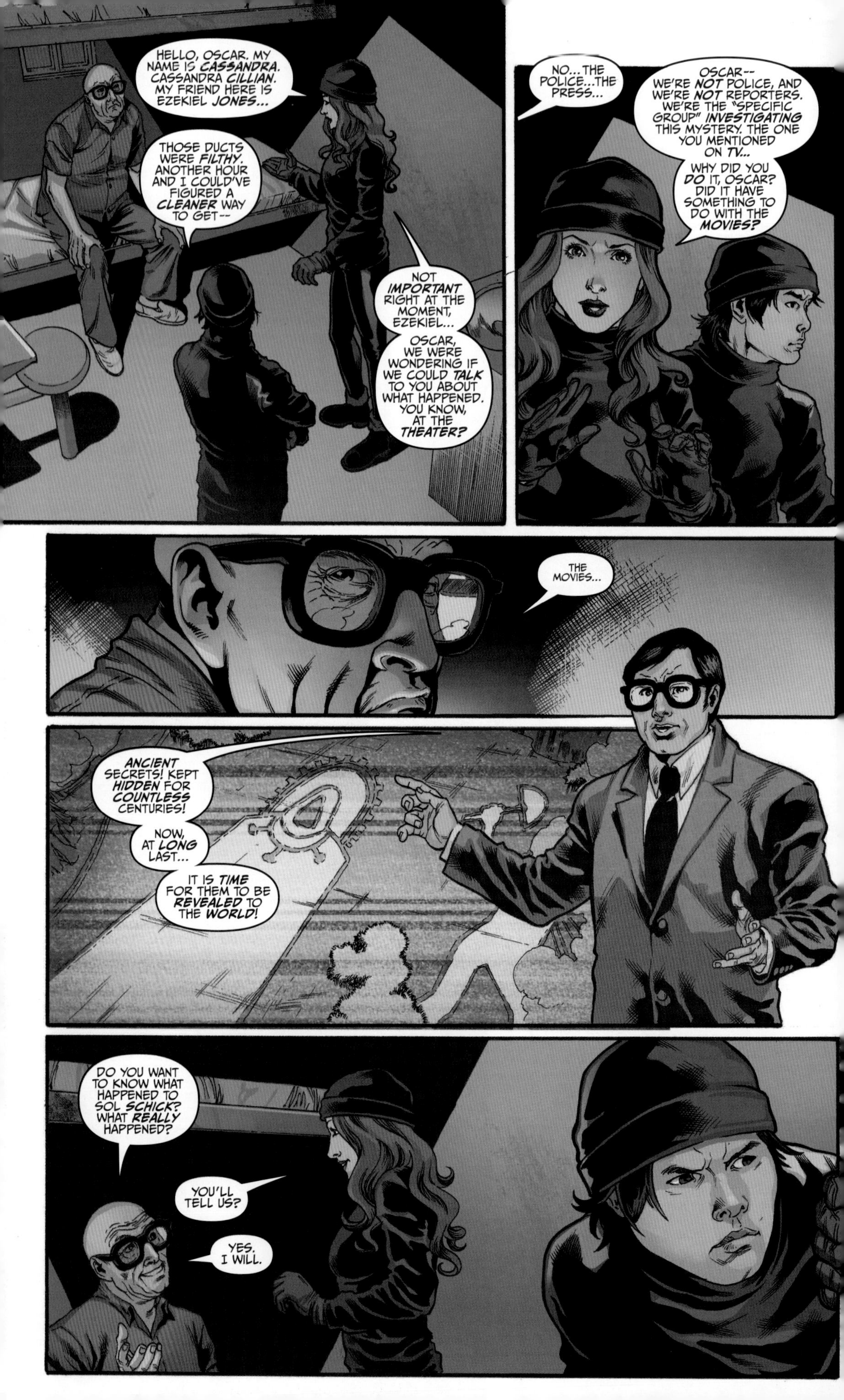
HELLO, OSCAR. MY NAME IS CASSANDRA. CASSANDRA CILLIAN. MY FRIEND HERE IS EZEKIEL JONES...
THOSE DUCTS WERE FILTHY. ANOTHER HOUR AND I COULD'VE FIGURED A CLEANER WAY TO GET--
NOT IMPORTANT RIGHT AT THE MOMENT, EZEKIEL...
OSCAR, WE WERE WONDERING IF WE COULD TALK TO YOU ABOUT WHAT HAPPENED. YOU KNOW, AT THE THEATER?
NO...THE POLICE...THE PRESS...
OSCAR-- WE'RE NOT POLICE, AND WE'RE NOT REPORTERS. WE'RE THE "SPECIFIC GROUP" INVESTIGATING THIS MYSTERY. THE ONE YOU MENTIONED ON TV...
WHY DID YOU DO IT, OSCAR? DID IT HAVE SOMETHING TO DO WITH THE MOVIES?
THE MOVIES...
ANCIENT SECRETS! KEPT HIDDEN FOR COUNTLESS CENTURIES!
NOW, AT LONG LAST...
IT IS TIME FOR THEM TO BE REVEALED TO THE WORLD!
DO YOU WANT TO KNOW WHAT HAPPENED TO SOL SCHICK? WHAT REALLY HAPPENED?
YOU'LL TELL US?
YES. I WILL.

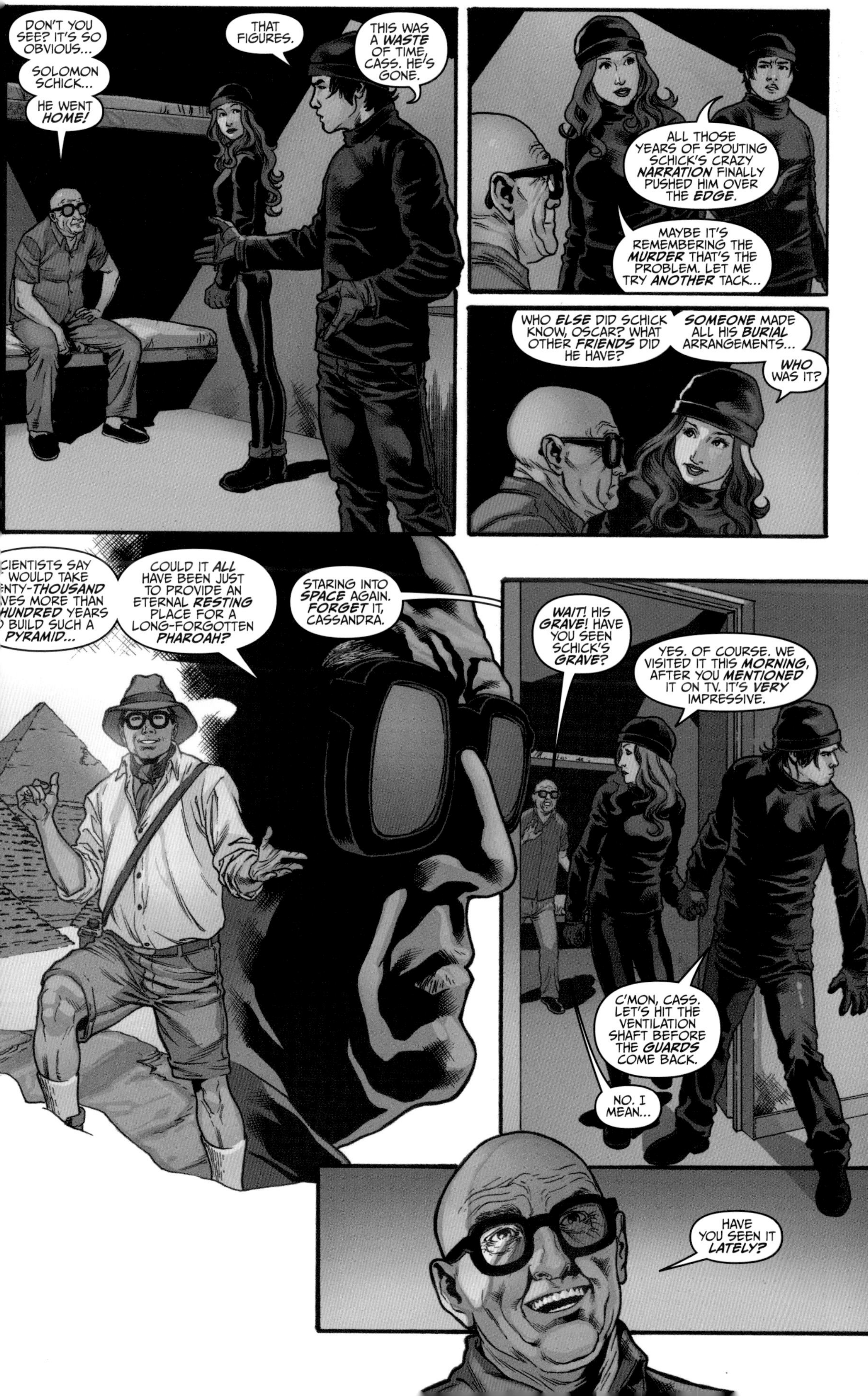
DON'T YOU SEE? IT'S SO OBVIOUS...
SOLOMON SCHICK...
HE WENT HOME!
THAT FIGURES.
THIS WAS A WASTE OF TIME, CASS. HE'S GONE.
ALL THOSE YEARS OF SPOUTING SCHICK'S CRAZY NARRATION FINALLY PUSHED HIM OVER THE EDGE.
MAYBE IT'S REMEMBERING THE MURDER THAT'S THE PROBLEM. LET ME TRY ANOTHER TACK...
WHO ELSE DID SCHICK KNOW, OSCAR? WHAT OTHER FRIENDS DID HE HAVE?
SOMEONE MADE ALL HIS BURIAL ARRANGEMENTS...
WHO WAS IT?
CIENTISTS SAY WOULD TAKE ENTY-THOUSAND AVES MORE THAN HUNDRED YEARS D BUILD SUCH A PYRAMID...
COULD IT ALL HAVE BEEN JUST TO PROVIDE AN ETERNAL RESTING PLACE FOR A LONG-FORGOTTEN PHAROAH?
STARING INTO SPACE AGAIN. FORGET IT, CASSANDRA.
WAIT! HIS GRAVE! HAVE YOU SEEN SCHICK'S GRAVE?
YES. OF COURSE. WE VISITED IT THIS MORNING, AFTER YOU MENTIONED IT ON TV. IT'S VERY IMPRESSIVE.
C'MON, CASS. LET'S HIT THE VENTILATION SHAFT BEFORE THE GUARDS COME BACK.
NO. I MEAN...
HAVE YOU SEEN IT LATELY?

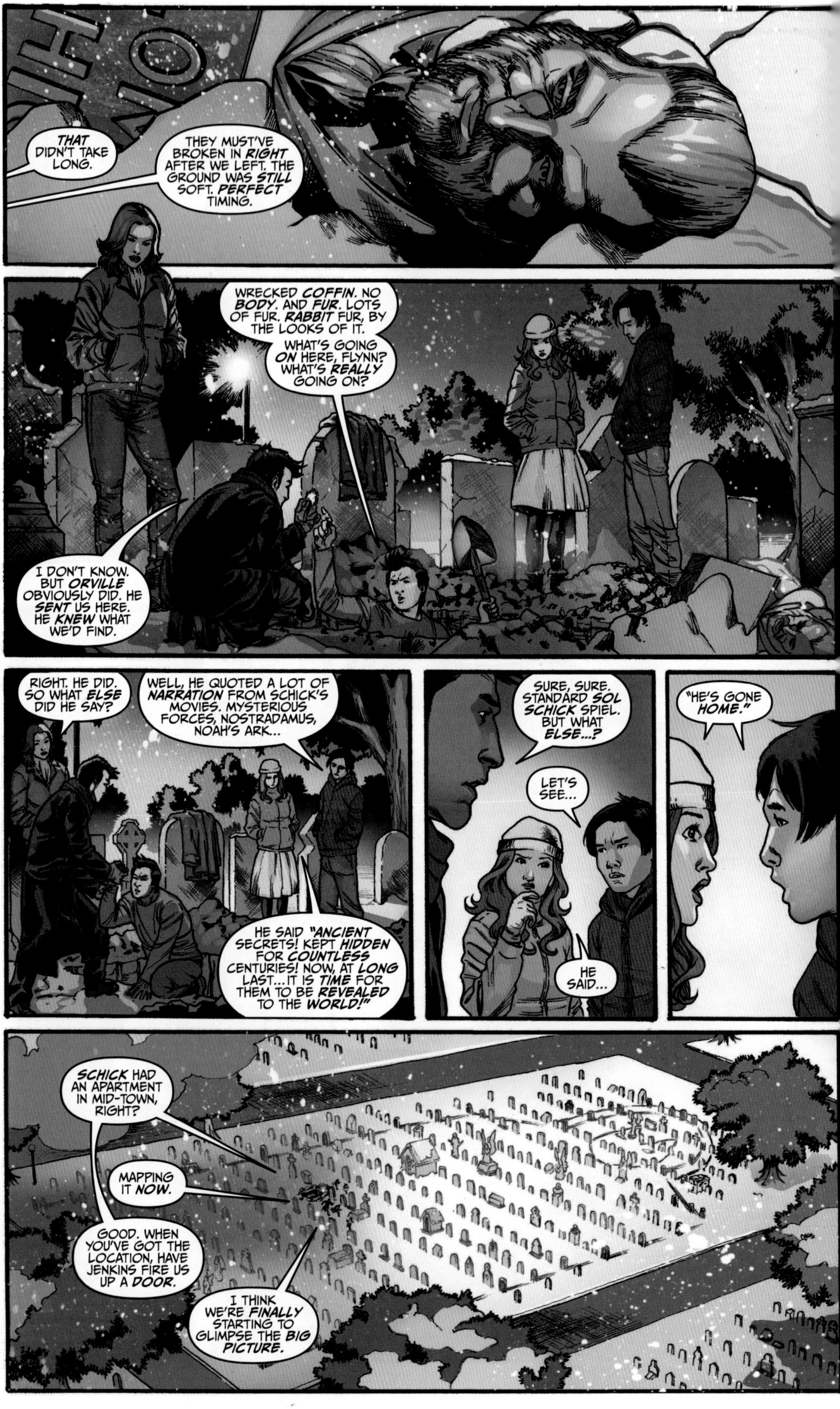
THAT DIDN'T TAKE LONG.
THEY MUST'VE BROKEN IN RIGHT AFTER WE LEFT. THE GROUND WAS STILL SOFT. PERFECT TIMING.
WRECKED COFFIN. NO BODY. AND FUR. LOTS OF FUR. RABBIT FUR, BY THE LOOKS OF IT.
WHAT'S GOING ON HERE, FLYNN? WHAT'S REALLY GOING ON?
I DON'T KNOW. BUT ORVILLE OBVIOUSLY DID. HE SENT US HERE. HE KNEW WHAT WE'D FIND.
RIGHT. HE DID. SO WHAT ELSE DID HE SAY?
WELL, HE QUOTED A LOT OF NARRATION FROM SCHICK'S MOVIES. MYSTERIOUS FORCES, NOSTRADAMUS, NOAH'S ARK...
HE SAID "ANCIENT SECRETS! KEPT HIDDEN FOR COUNTLESS CENTURIES! NOW, AT LONG LAST...IT IS TIME FOR THEM TO BE REVEALED TO THE WORLD!"
SURE, SURE. STANDARD SOL SCHICK SPIEL. BUT WHAT ELSE...?
LET'S SEE...
HE SAID...
"HE'S GONE HOME."
SCHICK HAD AN APARTMENT IN MID-TOWN, RIGHT?
MAPPING IT NOW.
GOOD. WHEN YOU'VE GOT THE LOCATION, HAVE JENKINS FIRE US UP A DOOR.
I THINK WE'RE FINALLY STARTING TO GLIMPSE THE BIG PICTURE.

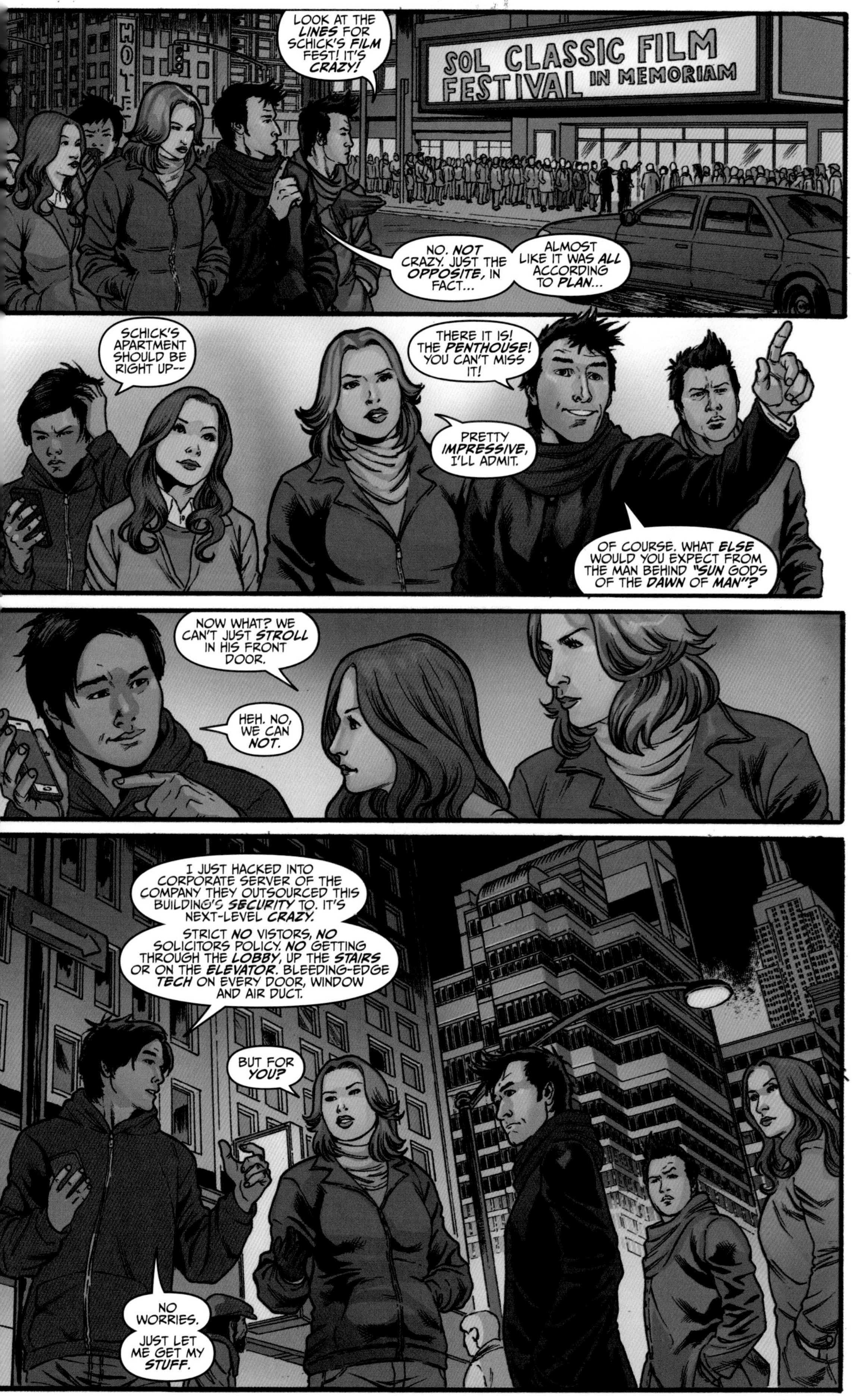
SOL CLASSIC FILM FESTIVAL IN MEMORIAM
HOTEL
LOOK AT THE LINES FOR SCHICK'S FILM FEST! IT'S CRAZY!
NO. NOT CRAZY. JUST THE OPPOSITE, IN FACT...
ALMOST LIKE IT WAS ALL ACCORDING TO PLAN...
SCHICK'S APARTMENT SHOULD BE RIGHT UP--
THERE IT IS! THE PENTHOUSE! YOU CAN'T MISS IT!
PRETTY IMPRESSIVE, I'LL ADMIT.
OF COURSE. WHAT ELSE WOULD YOU EXPECT FROM THE MAN BEHIND "SUN GODS OF THE DAWN OF MAN"?
NOW WHAT? WE CAN'T JUST STROLL IN HIS FRONT DOOR.
HEH. NO, WE CAN NOT.
I JUST HACKED INTO CORPORATE SERVER OF THE COMPANY THEY OUTSOURCED THIS BUILDING'S SECURITY TO. IT'S NEXT-LEVEL CRAZY.
STRICT NO VISTORS, NO SOLICITORS POLICY. NO GETTING THROUGH THE LOBBY, UP THE STAIRS OR ON THE ELEVATOR. BLEEDING-EDGE TECH ON EVERY DOOR, WINDOW AND AIR DUCT.
BUT FOR YOU?
NO WORRIES.
JUST LET ME GET MY STUFF.

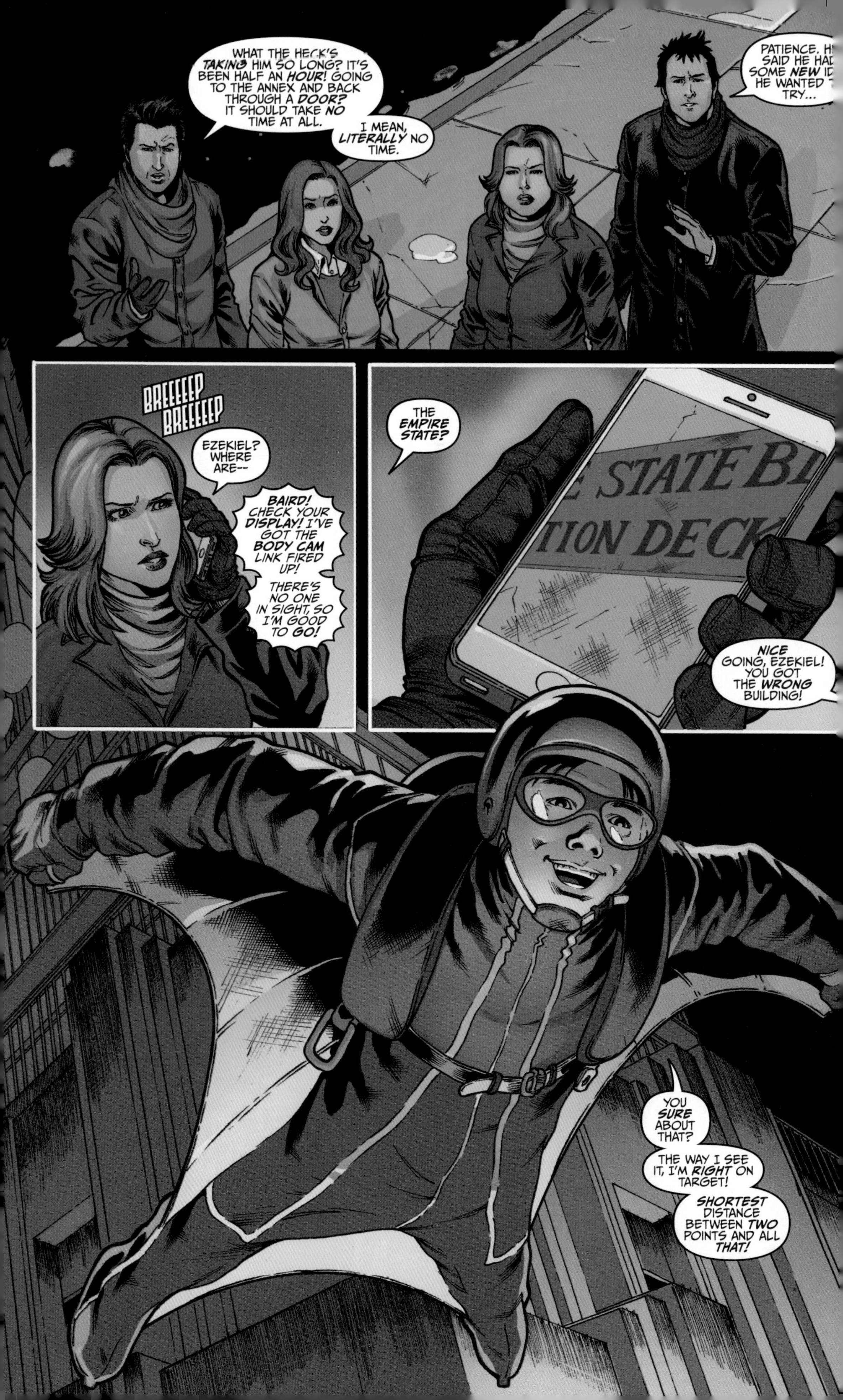

WHAT THE HECK'S TAKING HIM SO LONG? IT'S BEEN HALF AN HOUR! GOING TO THE ANNEX AND BACK THROUGH A DOOR? IT SHOULD TAKE NO TIME AT ALL.
I MEAN, LITERALLY NO TIME.
PATIENCE. H SAID HE HAD SOME NEW ID HE WANTED TRY...
BREEEEEP BREEEEEP
EZEKIEL? WHERE ARE--
BAIRD! CHECK YOUR DISPLAY! I'VE GOT THE BODY CAM LINK FIRED UP!
THERE'S NO ONE IN SIGHT, SO I'M GOOD TO GO!
THE EMPIRE STATE?
E STATE BL
TION DECK
NICE GOING, EZEKIEL! YOU GOT THE WRONG BUILDING!
YOU SURE ABOUT THAT?
THE WAY I SEE IT, I'M RIGHT ON TARGET!
SHORTEST DISTANCE BETWEEN TWO POINTS AND ALL THAT!

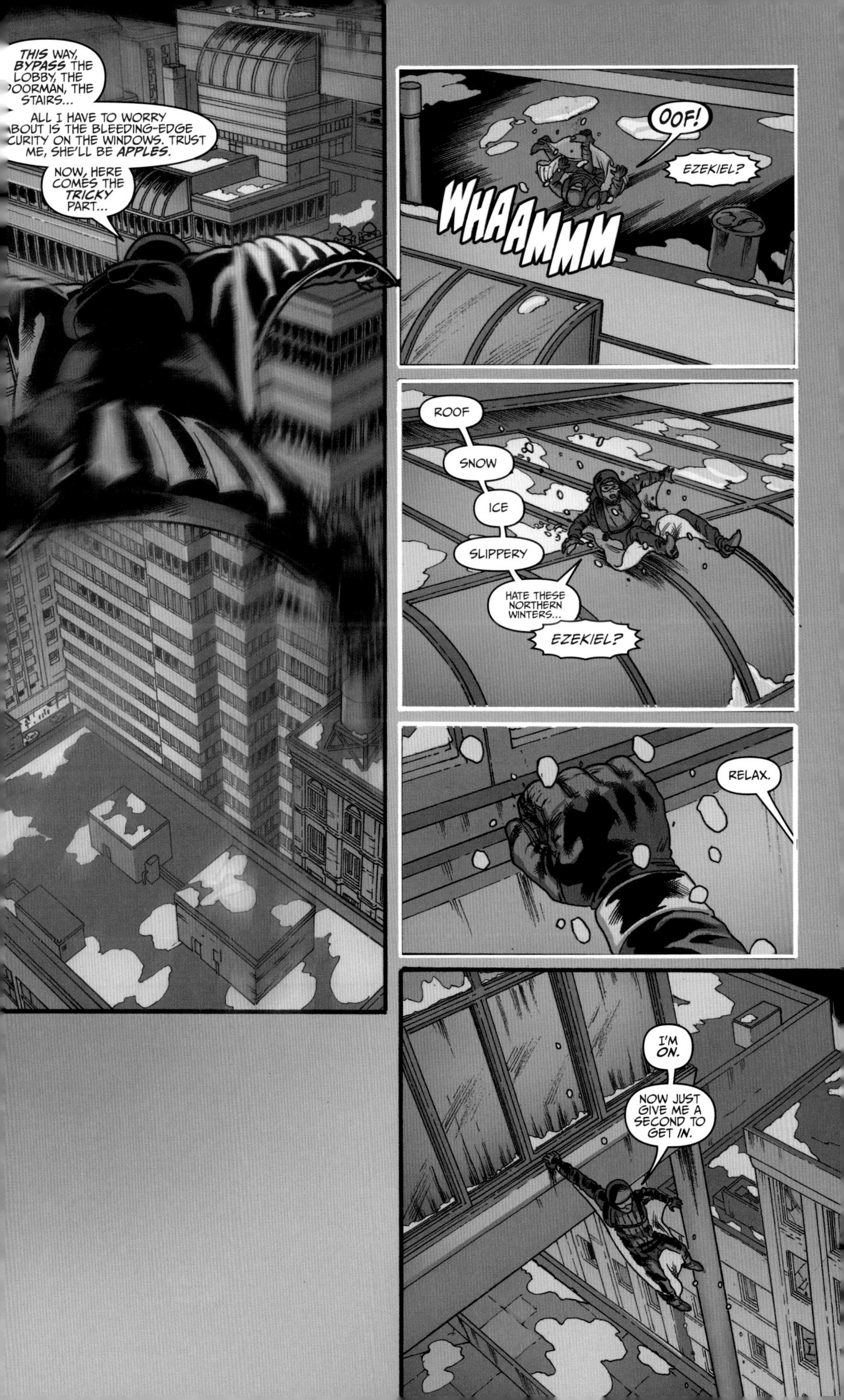

THIS WAY, BYPASS THE LOBBY, THE OORMAN, THE STAIRS...
ALL I HAVE TO WORRY ABOUT IS THE BLEEDING-EDGE CURITY ON THE WINDOWS. TRUST ME, SHE'LL BE APPLES.
NOW, HERE COMES THE TRICKY PART...
OOF!
EZEKIEL?
WHAAMMM
ROOF
SNOW
ICE
SLIPPERY
HATE THESE NORTHERN WINTERS...
EZEKIEL?
RELAX.
I'M ON.
NOW JUST GIVE ME A SECOND TO GET IN.

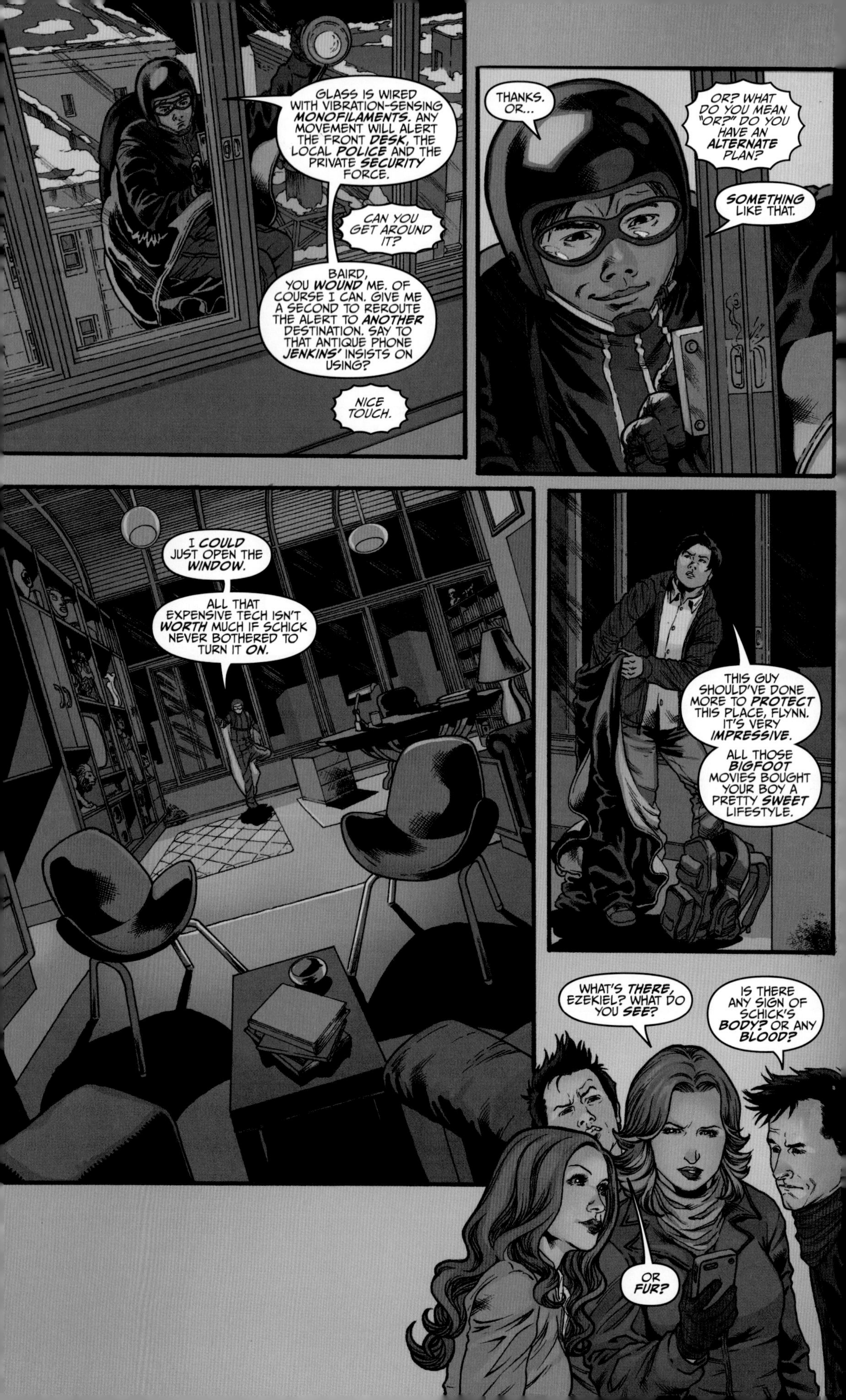
GLASS IS WIRED WITH VIBRATION-SENSING MONOFILAMENTS. ANY MOVEMENT WILL ALERT THE FRONT DESK, THE LOCAL POLICE AND THE PRIVATE SECURITY FORCE.
CAN YOU GET AROUND IT?
BAIRD, YOU WOUND ME. OF COURSE I CAN. GIVE ME A SECOND TO REROUTE THE ALERT TO ANOTHER DESTINATION. SAY TO THAT ANTIQUE PHONE JENKINS' INSISTS ON USING?
NICE TOUCH.
THANKS. OR...
OR? WHAT DO YOU MEAN "OR?" DO YOU HAVE AN ALTERNATE PLAN?
SOMETHING LIKE THAT.
I COULD JUST OPEN THE WINDOW.
ALL THAT EXPENSIVE TECH ISN'T WORTH MUCH IF SCHICK NEVER BOTHERED TO TURN IT ON.
THIS GUY SHOULD'VE DONE MORE TO PROTECT THIS PLACE, FLYNN. IT'S VERY IMPRESSIVE.
ALL THOSE BIGFOOT MOVIES BOUGHT YOUR BOY A PRETTY SWEET LIFESTYLE.
WHAT'S THERE, EZEKIEL? WHAT DO YOU SEE?
IS THERE ANY SIGN OF SCHICK'S BODY? OR ANY BLOOD?
OR FUR?

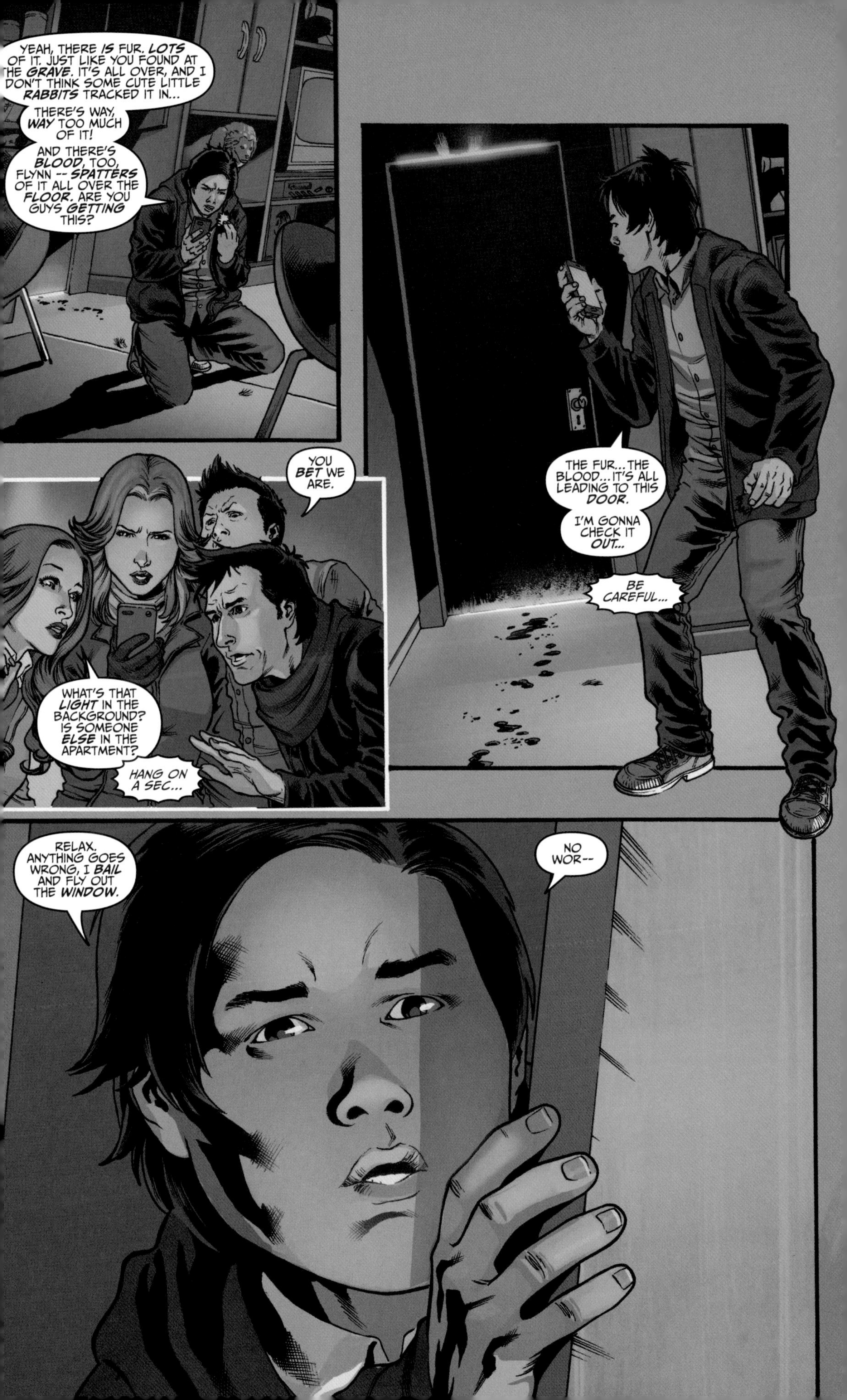
YEAH, THERE IS FUR. LOTS OF IT. JUST LIKE YOU FOUND AT THE GRAVE. IT'S ALL OVER, AND I DON'T THINK SOME CUTE LITTLE RABBITS TRACKED IT IN...
THERE'S WAY, WAY TOO MUCH OF IT!
AND THERE'S BLOOD, TOO, FLYNN -- SPATTERS OF IT ALL OVER THE FLOOR. ARE YOU GUYS GETTING THIS?
YOU BET WE ARE.
WHAT'S THAT LIGHT IN THE BACKGROUND? IS SOMEONE ELSE IN THE APARTMENT?
HANG ON A SEC...
THE FUR... THE BLOOD... IT'S ALL LEADING TO THIS DOOR.
I'M GONNA CHECK IT OUT...
BE CAREFUL...
RELAX. ANYTHING GOES WRONG, I BAIL AND FLY OUT THE WINDOW.
NO WOR--

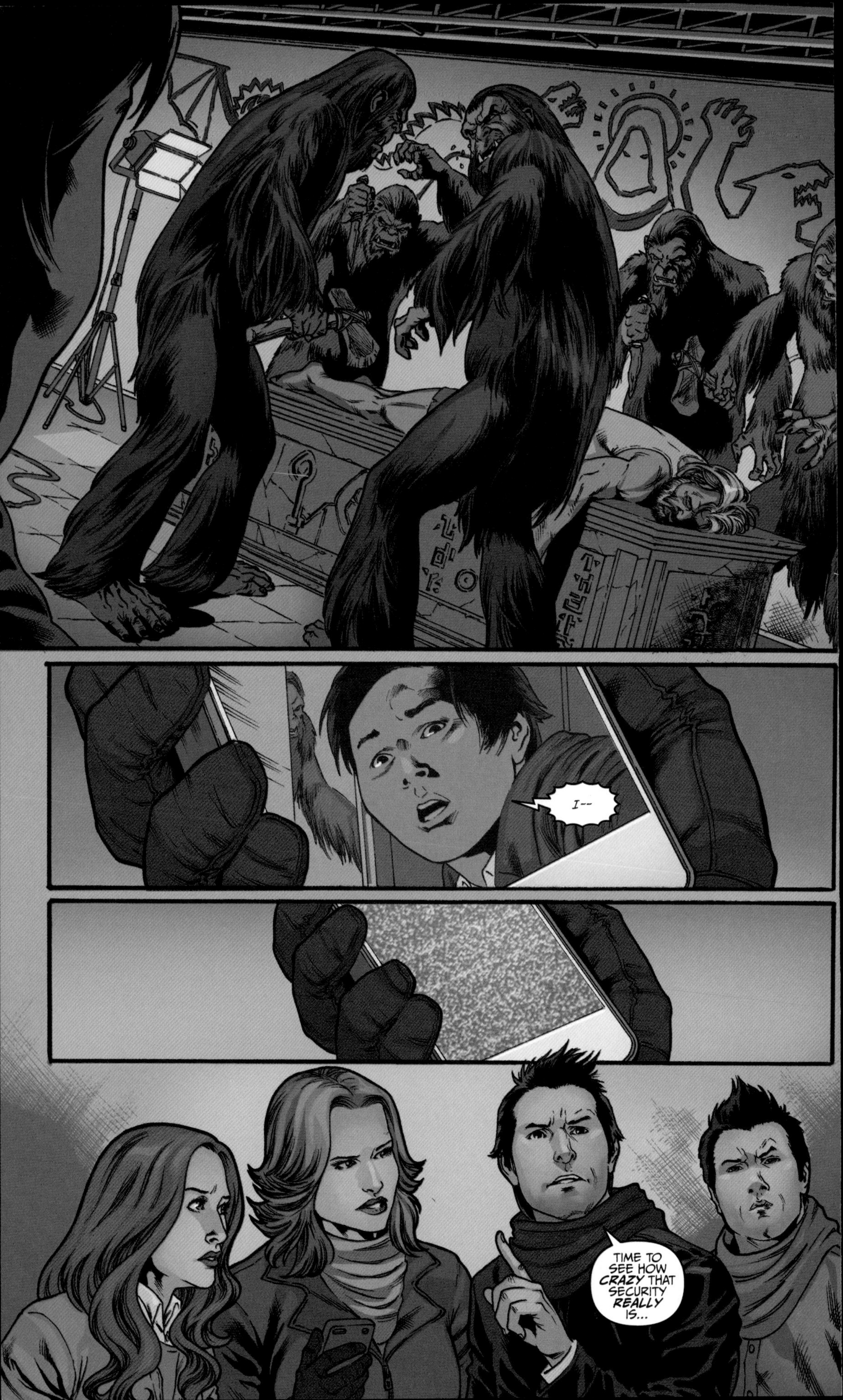
I--
TIME TO SEE HOW CRAZY THAT SECURITY REALLY IS...

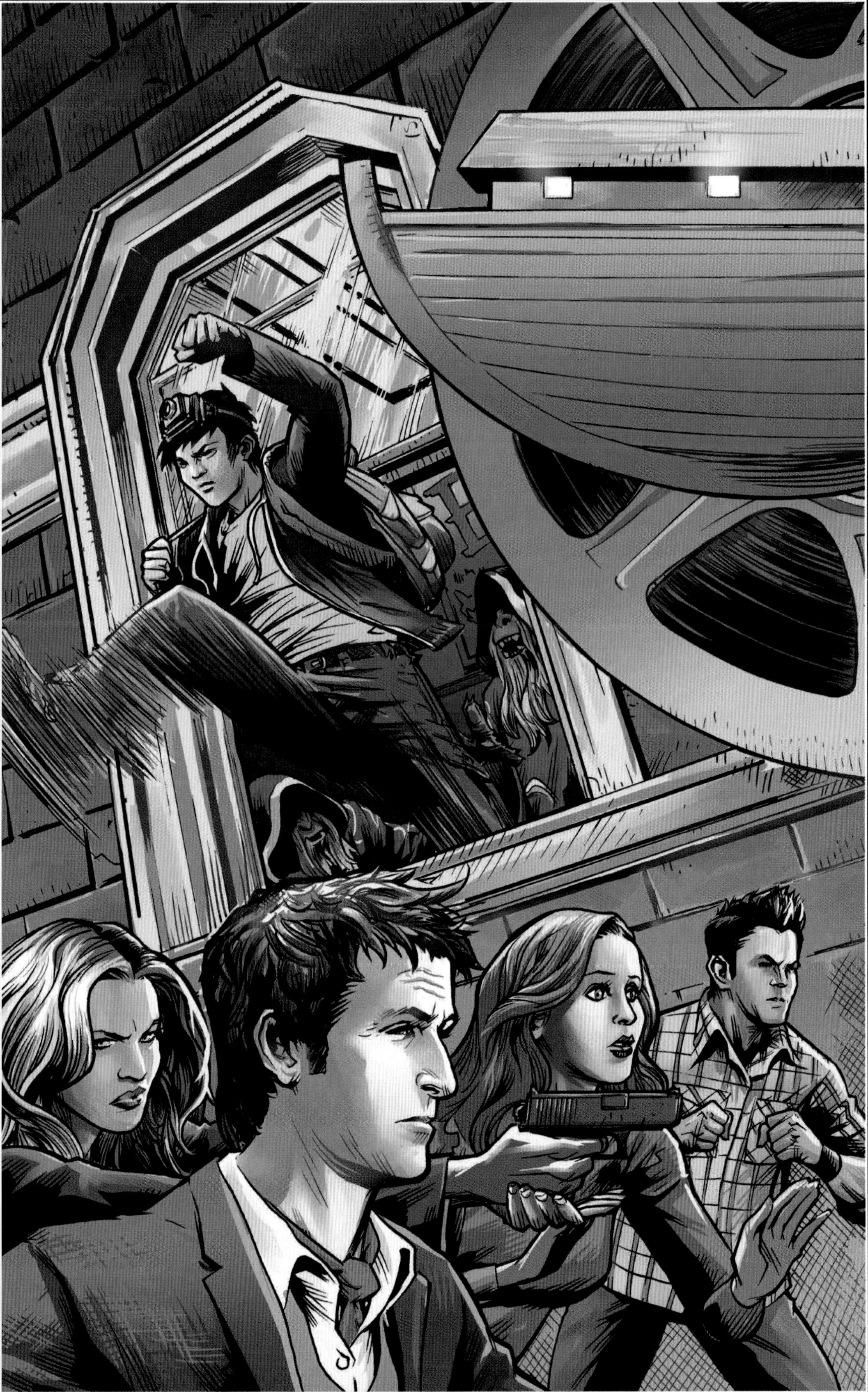

Issue two cover
art by KARL MOLINE

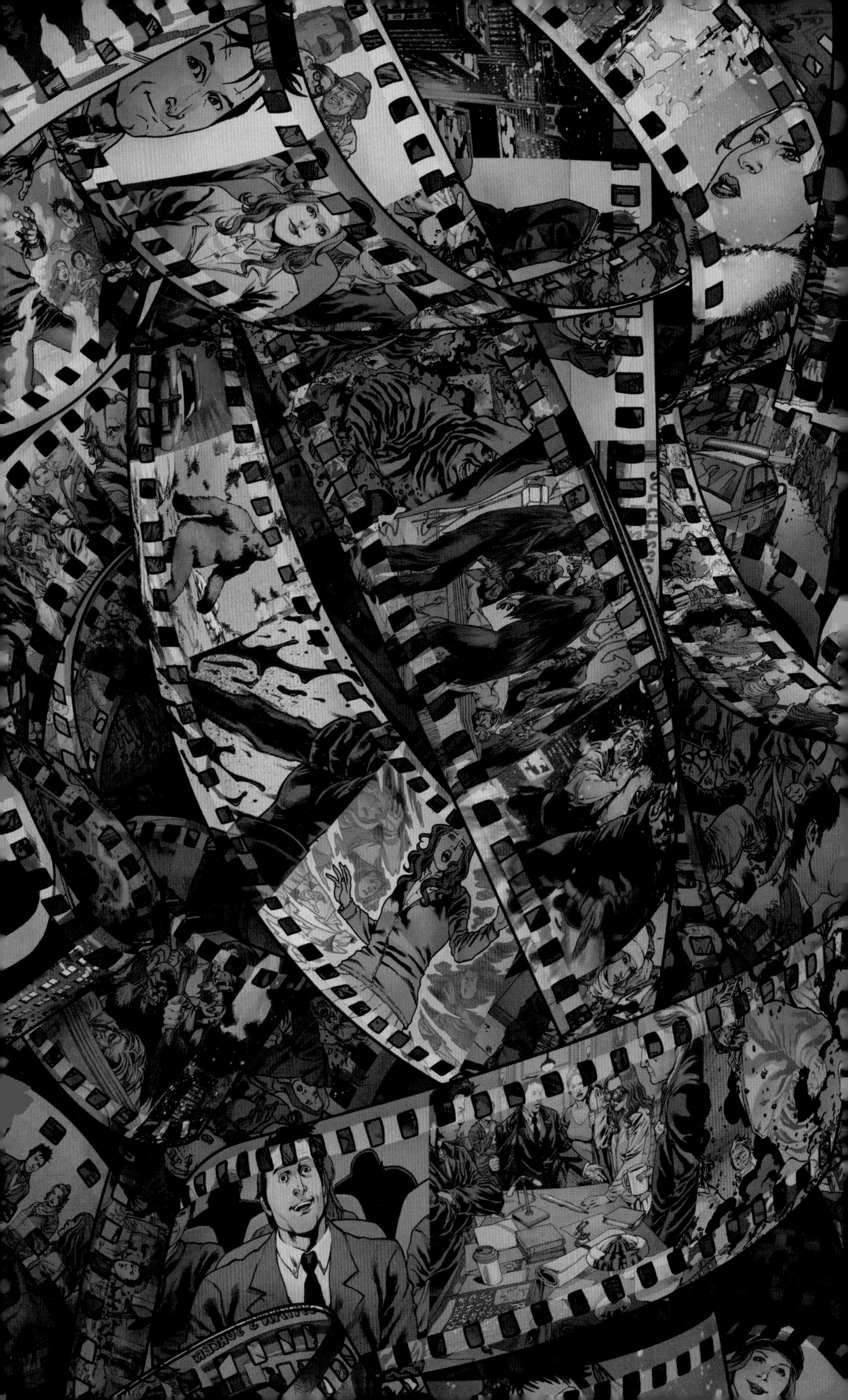

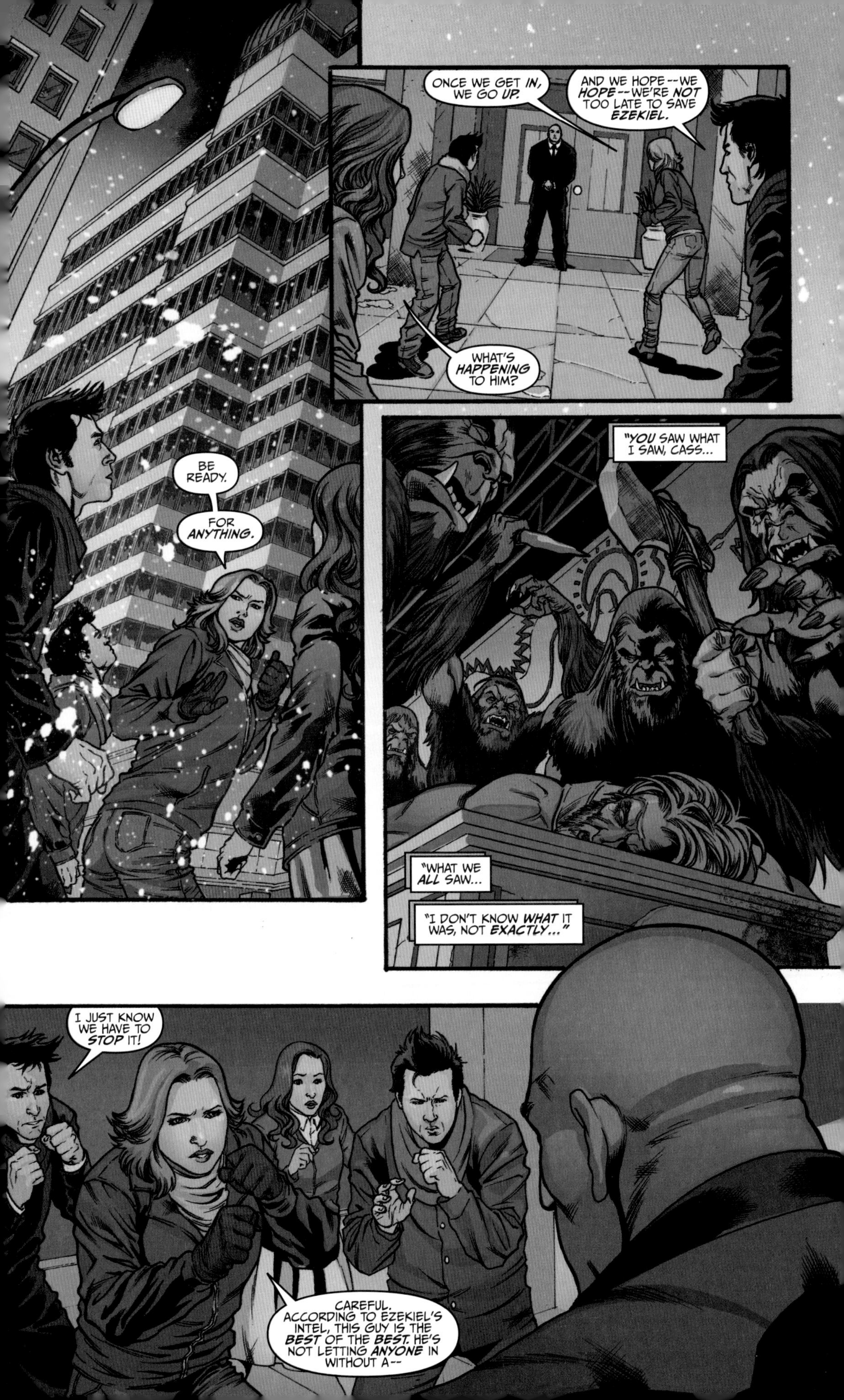

ONCE WE GET IN, WE GO UP.
AND WE HOPE--WE HOPE--WE'RE NOT TOO LATE TO SAVE EZEKIEL.
WHAT'S HAPPENING TO HIM?
BE READY.
FOR ANYTHING.
"YOU SAW WHAT I SAW, CASS...
"WHAT WE ALL SAW...
"I DON'T KNOW WHAT IT WAS, NOT EXACTLY..."
I JUST KNOW WE HAVE TO STOP IT!
CAREFUL. ACCORDING TO EZEKIEL'S INTEL, THIS GUY IS THE BEST OF THE BEST. HE'S NOT LETTING ANYONE IN WITHOUT A--

COL. *BAIRD*. MS. *CILLIAN*.

MISTER *CARSEN*. MISTER *STONE*.

WELCOME TO THE LANDSBURG ARMS. THE ELEVATOR TO THE PENTHOUSE IS TO YOUR *LEFT*.

MISTER SCHICK IS *EXPECTING* YOU.

ENJOY YOUR *VISIT*!

WHAT THE...?

A *TRAP*. CLEARLY THE *FIRST* STEP IN A TRAP.

BE ON YOUR *TOES*. ON YOUR *TIP* TOES.

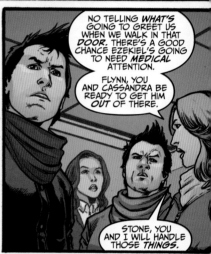

NO TELLING *WHAT'S* GOING TO GREET US WHEN WE WALK IN THAT *DOOR*. THERE'S A GOOD CHANCE EZEKIEL'S GOING TO NEED *MEDICAL* ATTENTION.

FLYNN, YOU AND CASSANDRA BE READY TO GET HIM *OUT* OF THERE.

STONE, YOU AND I WILL HANDLE THOSE *THINGS*.

OK...

LIKE I SAID, BE READY FOR *ANYTHING*.

THIS COULD BE A *NIGHTMARE* SCENARIO OF THE *FIRST* ORDER.

STONE, *KICK* IT IN ON ONE...

TWO...

KLIK

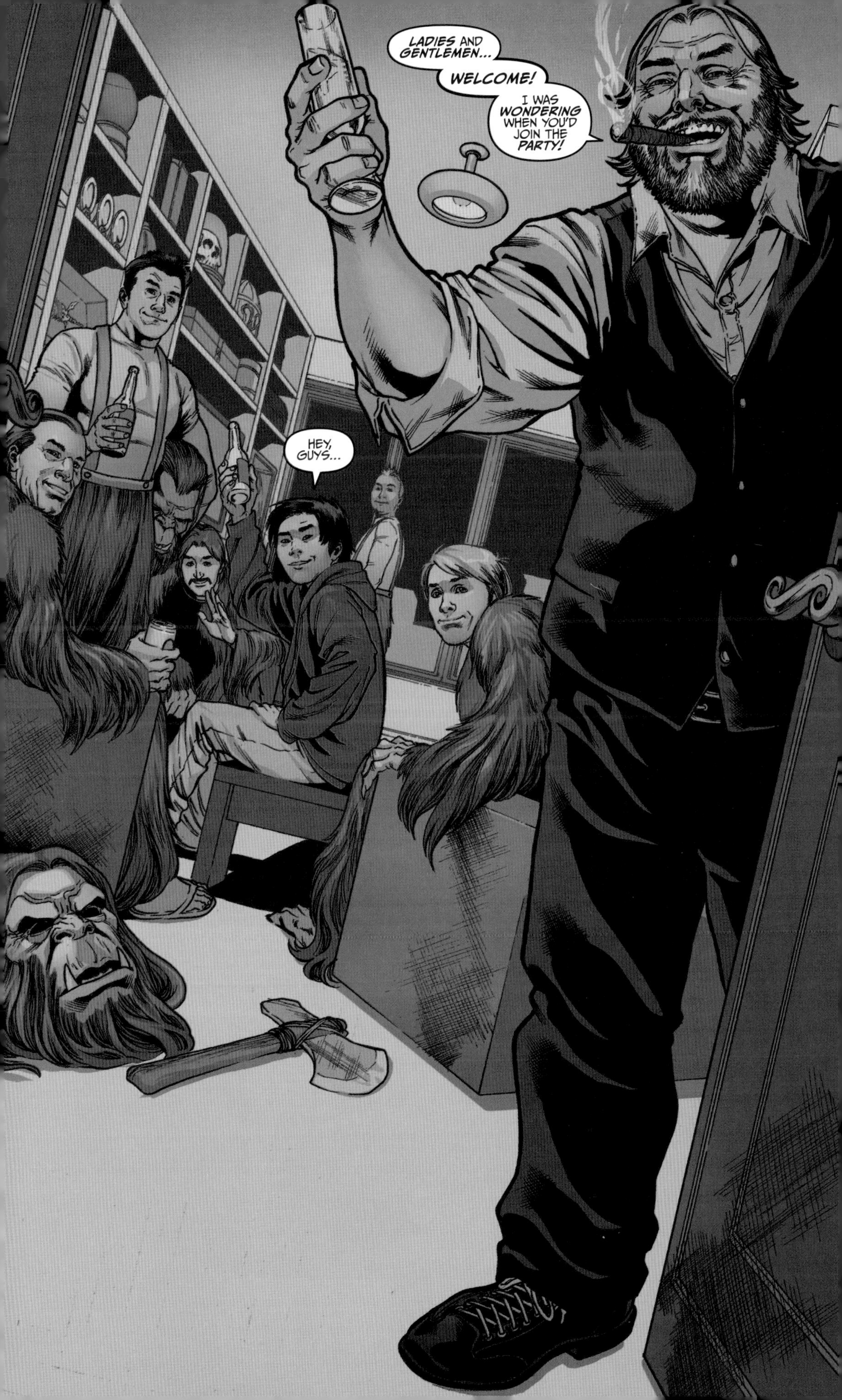

LADIES AND GENTLEMEN...
WELCOME!
I WAS WONDERING WHEN YOU'D JOIN THE PARTY!
HEY, GUYS...

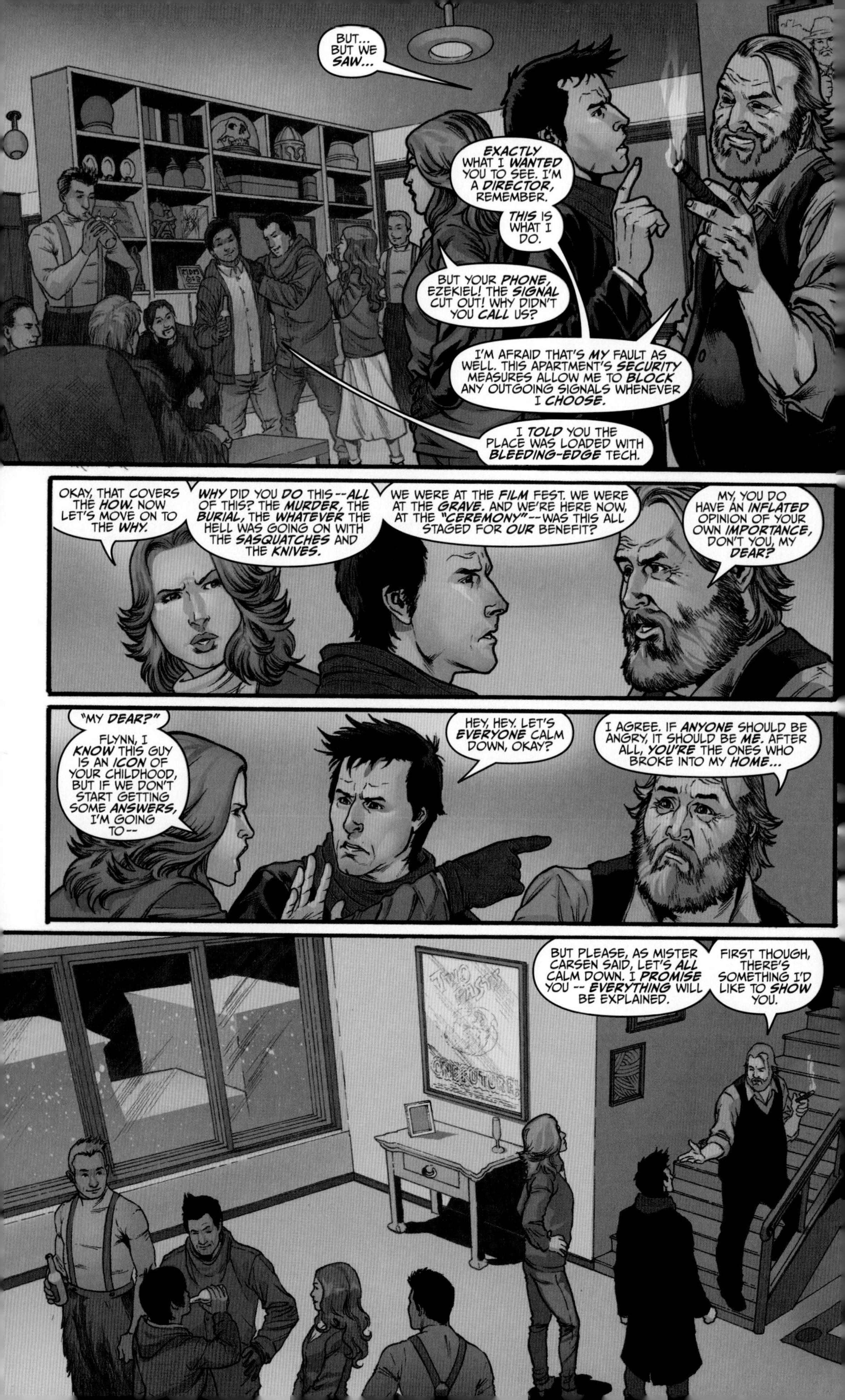
BUT... BUT WE SAW...
EXACTLY WHAT I WANTED YOU TO SEE. I'M A DIRECTOR, REMEMBER.
THIS IS WHAT I DO.
BUT YOUR PHONE, EZEKIEL! THE SIGNAL CUT OUT! WHY DIDN'T YOU CALL US?
I'M AFRAID THAT'S MY FAULT AS WELL. THIS APARTMENT'S SECURITY MEASURES ALLOW ME TO BLOCK ANY OUTGOING SIGNALS WHENEVER I CHOOSE.
I TOLD YOU THE PLACE WAS LOADED WITH BLEEDING-EDGE TECH.
OKAY, THAT COVERS THE HOW. NOW LET'S MOVE ON TO THE WHY.
WHY DID YOU DO THIS--ALL OF THIS? THE MURDER, THE BURIAL, THE WHATEVER THE HELL WAS GOING ON WITH THE SASQUATCHES AND THE KNIVES.
WE WERE AT THE FILM FEST. WE WERE AT THE GRAVE. AND WE'RE HERE NOW, AT THE "CEREMONY"--WAS THIS ALL STAGED FOR OUR BENEFIT?
MY, YOU DO HAVE AN INFLATED OPINION OF YOUR OWN IMPORTANCE, DON'T YOU, MY DEAR?
"MY DEAR?"
FLYNN, I KNOW THIS GUY IS AN ICON OF YOUR CHILDHOOD, BUT IF WE DON'T START GETTING SOME ANSWERS, I'M GOING TO--
HEY, HEY. LET'S EVERYONE CALM DOWN, OKAY?
I AGREE. IF ANYONE SHOULD BE ANGRY, IT SHOULD BE ME. AFTER ALL, YOU'RE THE ONES WHO BROKE INTO MY HOME...
BUT PLEASE, AS MISTER CARSEN SAID, LET'S ALL CALM DOWN. I PROMISE YOU -- EVERYTHING WILL BE EXPLAINED.
FIRST THOUGH, THERE'S SOMETHING I'D LIKE TO SHOW YOU.

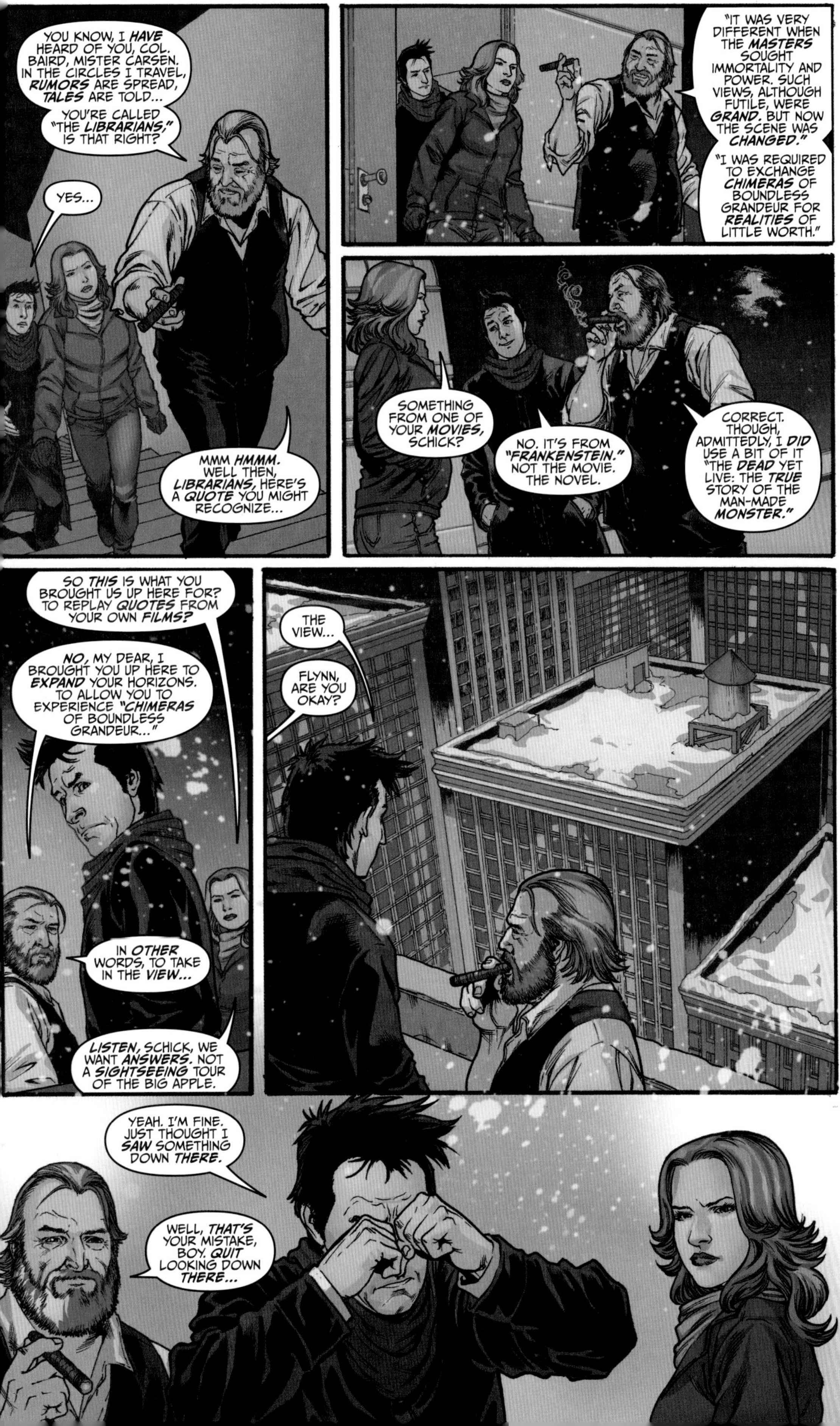
YOU KNOW, I HAVE HEARD OF YOU, COL. BAIRD, MISTER CARSEN. IN THE CIRCLES I TRAVEL, RUMORS ARE SPREAD, TALES ARE TOLD...
YOU'RE CALLED "THE LIBRARIANS," IS THAT RIGHT?
YES...
MMM HMMM. WELL THEN, LIBRARIANS, HERE'S A QUOTE YOU MIGHT RECOGNIZE...
"IT WAS VERY DIFFERENT WHEN THE MASTERS SOUGHT IMMORTALITY AND POWER. SUCH VIEWS, ALTHOUGH FUTILE, WERE GRAND. BUT NOW THE SCENE WAS CHANGED."
"I WAS REQUIRED TO EXCHANGE CHIMERAS OF BOUNDLESS GRANDEUR FOR REALITIES OF LITTLE WORTH."
SOMETHING FROM ONE OF YOUR MOVIES, SCHICK?
NO. IT'S FROM "FRANKENSTEIN." NOT THE MOVIE. THE NOVEL.
CORRECT. THOUGH, ADMITTEDLY, I DID USE A BIT OF IT "THE DEAD YET LIVE: THE TRUE STORY OF THE MAN-MADE MONSTER."
SO THIS IS WHAT YOU BROUGHT US UP HERE FOR? TO REPLAY QUOTES FROM YOUR OWN FILMS?
NO, MY DEAR, I BROUGHT YOU UP HERE TO EXPAND YOUR HORIZONS. TO ALLOW YOU TO EXPERIENCE "CHIMERAS OF BOUNDLESS GRANDEUR..."
IN OTHER WORDS, TO TAKE IN THE VIEW...
LISTEN, SCHICK, WE WANT ANSWERS. NOT A SIGHTSEEING TOUR OF THE BIG APPLE.
THE VIEW...
FLYNN, ARE YOU OKAY?
YEAH. I'M FINE. JUST THOUGHT I SAW SOMETHING DOWN THERE.
WELL, THAT'S YOUR MISTAKE, BOY. QUIT LOOKING DOWN THERE...

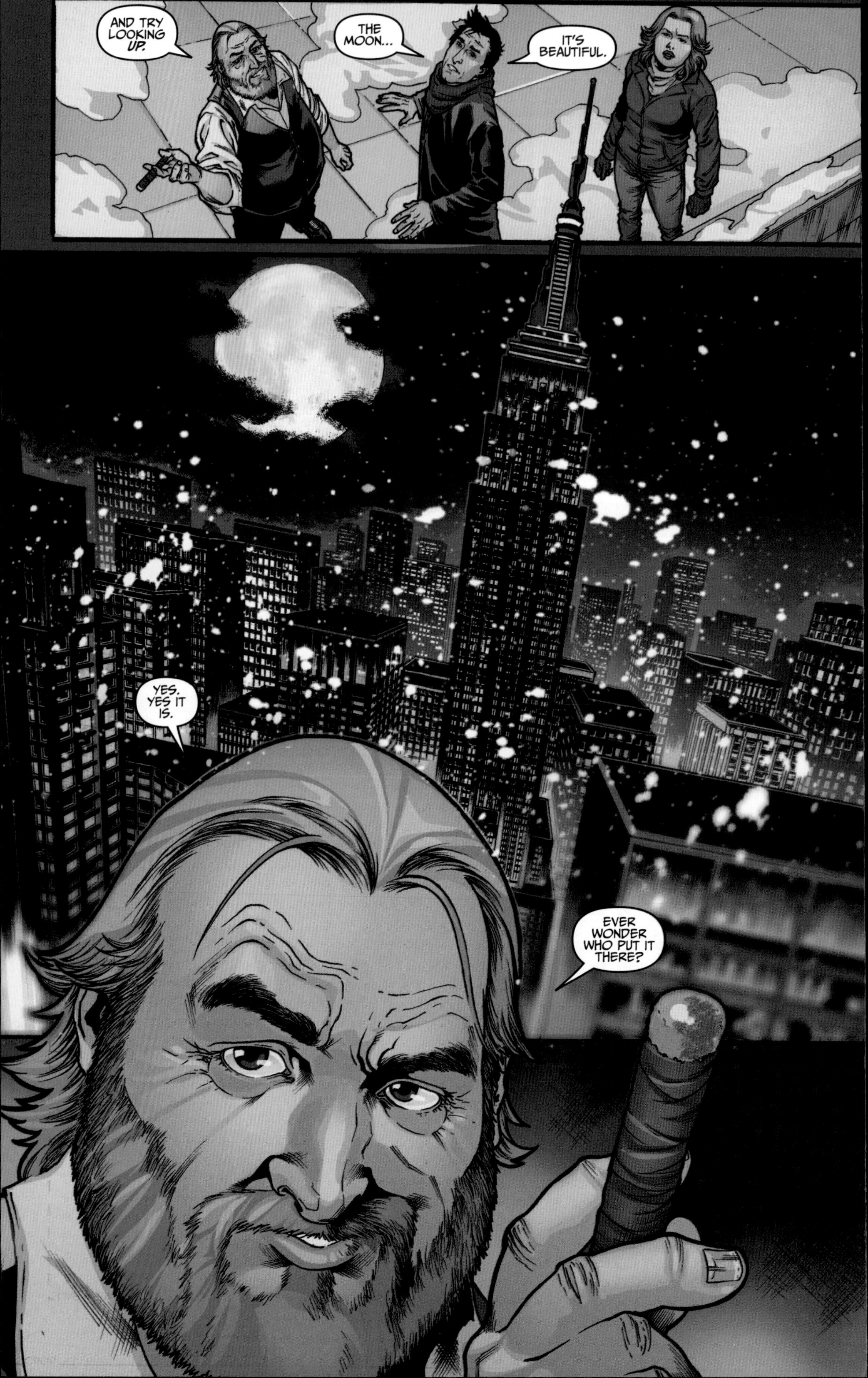
AND TRY LOOKING *UP.*
THE MOON...
IT'S BEAUTIFUL.
YES. YES IT IS.
EVER WONDER WHO PUT IT THERE?

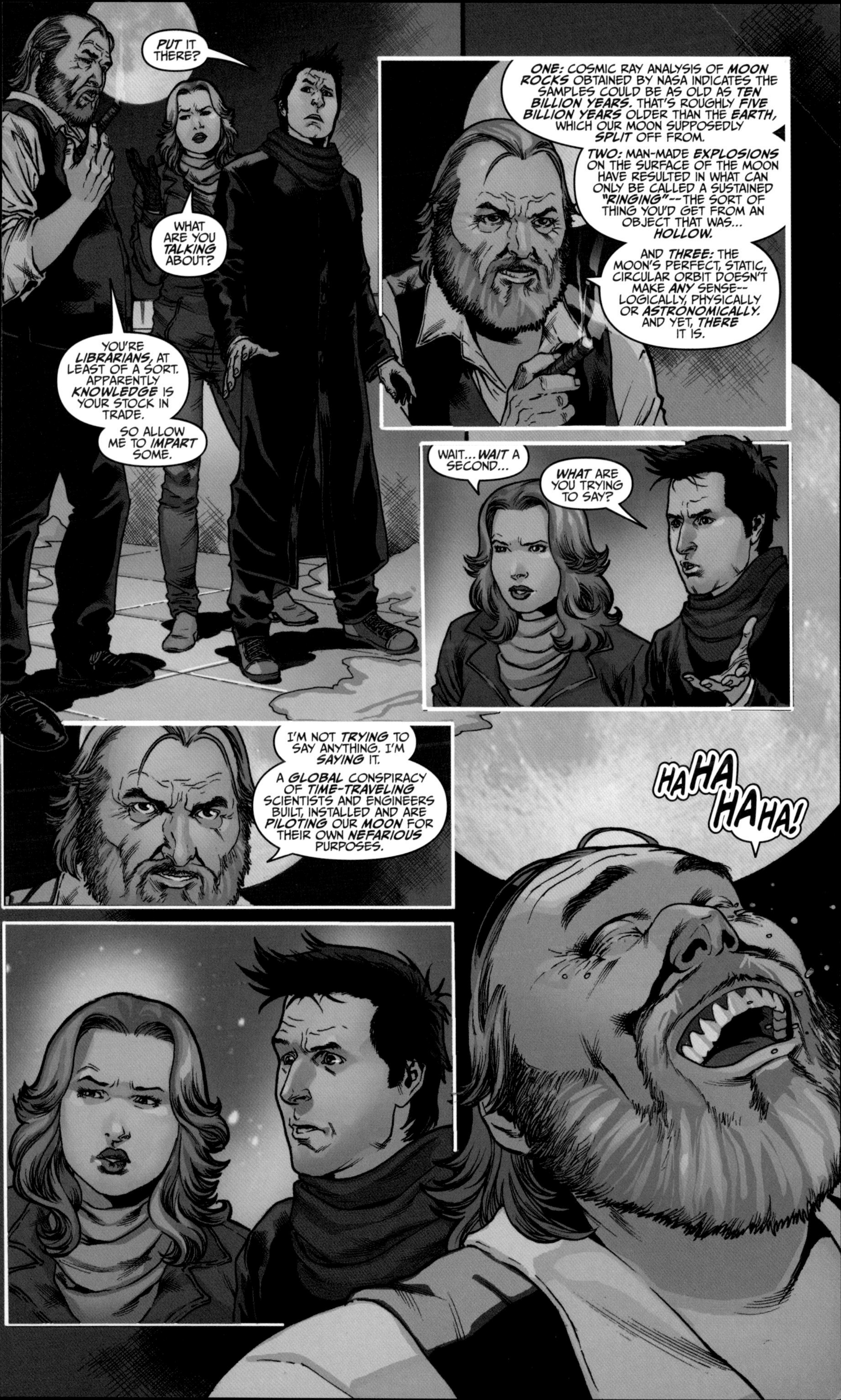

PUT IT THERE?
WHAT ARE YOU TALKING ABOUT?
YOU'RE LIBRARIANS, AT LEAST OF A SORT. APPARENTLY KNOWLEDGE IS YOUR STOCK IN TRADE.
SO ALLOW ME TO IMPART SOME.
ONE: COSMIC RAY ANALYSIS OF MOON ROCKS OBTAINED BY NASA INDICATES THE SAMPLES COULD BE AS OLD AS TEN BILLION YEARS. THAT'S ROUGHLY FIVE BILLION YEARS OLDER THAN THE EARTH, WHICH OUR MOON SUPPOSEDLY SPLIT OFF FROM.
TWO: MAN-MADE EXPLOSIONS ON THE SURFACE OF THE MOON HAVE RESULTED IN WHAT CAN ONLY BE CALLED A SUSTAINED "RINGING"--THE SORT OF THING YOU'D GET FROM AN OBJECT THAT WAS... HOLLOW.
AND THREE: THE MOON'S PERFECT, STATIC, CIRCULAR ORBIT DOESN'T MAKE ANY SENSE--LOGICALLY, PHYSICALLY OR ASTRONOMICALLY. AND YET, THERE IT IS.
WAIT... WAIT A SECOND...
WHAT ARE YOU TRYING TO SAY?
I'M NOT TRYING TO SAY ANYTHING. I'M SAYING IT.
A GLOBAL CONSPIRACY OF TIME-TRAVELING SCIENTISTS AND ENGINEERS BUILT, INSTALLED AND ARE PILOTING OUR MOON FOR THEIR OWN NEFARIOUS PURPOSES.
HAHA HAHA!

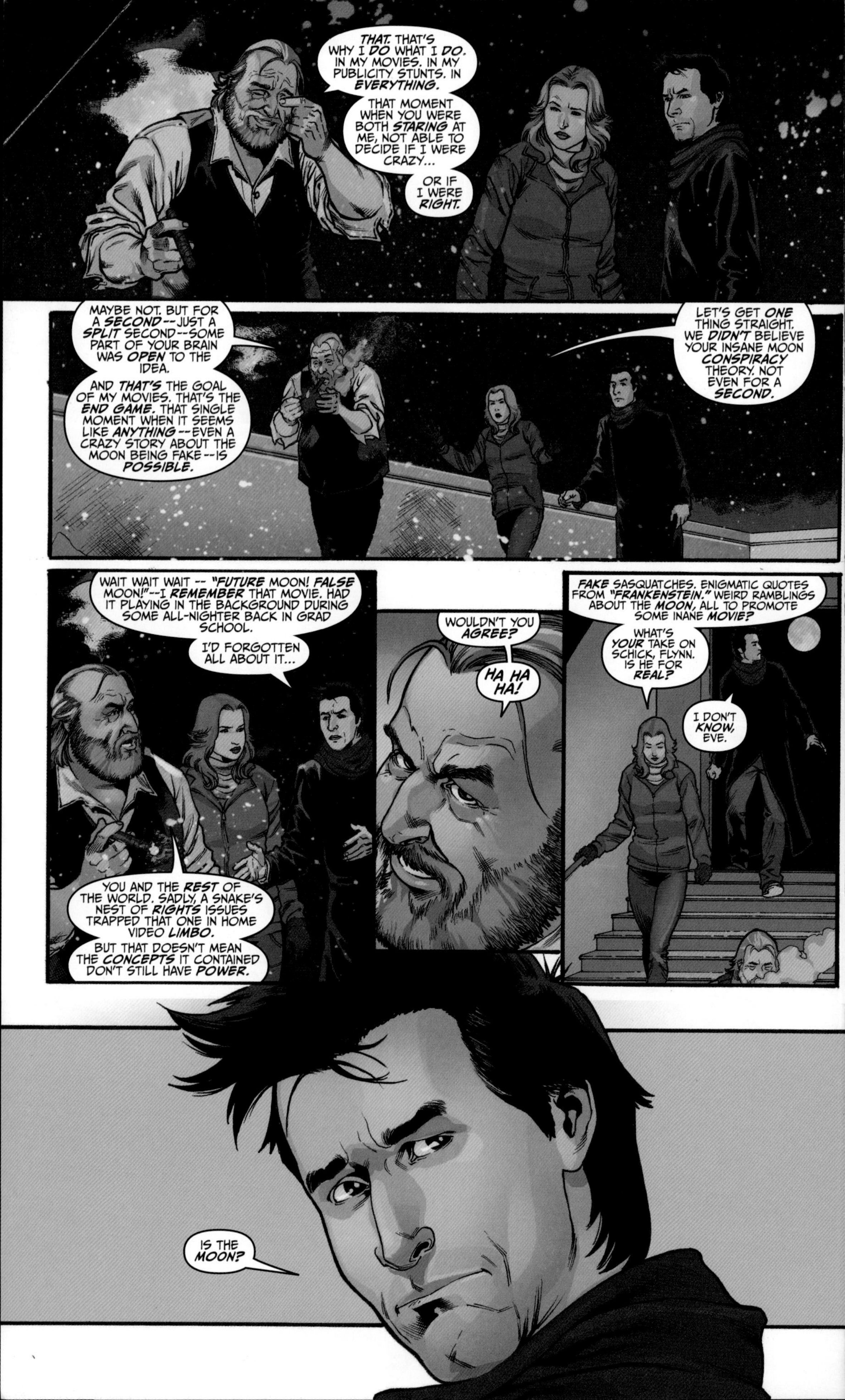
THAT. THAT'S WHY I DO WHAT I DO. IN MY MOVIES. IN MY PUBLICITY STUNTS. IN EVERYTHING.
THAT MOMENT WHEN YOU WERE BOTH STARING AT ME, NOT ABLE TO DECIDE IF I WERE CRAZY...
OR IF I WERE RIGHT.
LET'S GET ONE THING STRAIGHT. WE DIDN'T BELIEVE YOUR INSANE MOON CONSPIRACY THEORY. NOT EVEN FOR A SECOND.
MAYBE NOT. BUT FOR A SECOND--JUST A SPLIT SECOND--SOME PART OF YOUR BRAIN WAS OPEN TO THE IDEA.
AND THAT'S THE GOAL OF MY MOVIES. THAT'S THE END GAME. THAT SINGLE MOMENT WHEN IT SEEMS LIKE ANYTHING--EVEN A CRAZY STORY ABOUT THE MOON BEING FAKE--IS POSSIBLE.
WAIT WAIT WAIT -- "FUTURE MOON! FALSE MOON!"--I REMEMBER THAT MOVIE. HAD IT PLAYING IN THE BACKGROUND DURING SOME ALL-NIGHTER BACK IN GRAD SCHOOL.
I'D FORGOTTEN ALL ABOUT IT...
YOU AND THE REST OF THE WORLD. SADLY, A SNAKE'S NEST OF RIGHTS ISSUES TRAPPED THAT ONE IN HOME VIDEO LIMBO.
BUT THAT DOESN'T MEAN THE CONCEPTS IT CONTAINED DON'T STILL HAVE POWER.
WOULDN'T YOU AGREE?
HA HA HA!
FAKE SASQUATCHES. ENIGMATIC QUOTES FROM "FRANKENSTEIN." WEIRD RAMBLINGS ABOUT THE MOON, ALL TO PROMOTE SOME INANE MOVIE?
WHAT'S YOUR TAKE ON SCHICK, FLYNN. IS HE FOR REAL?
I DON'T KNOW, EVE.
IS THE MOON?

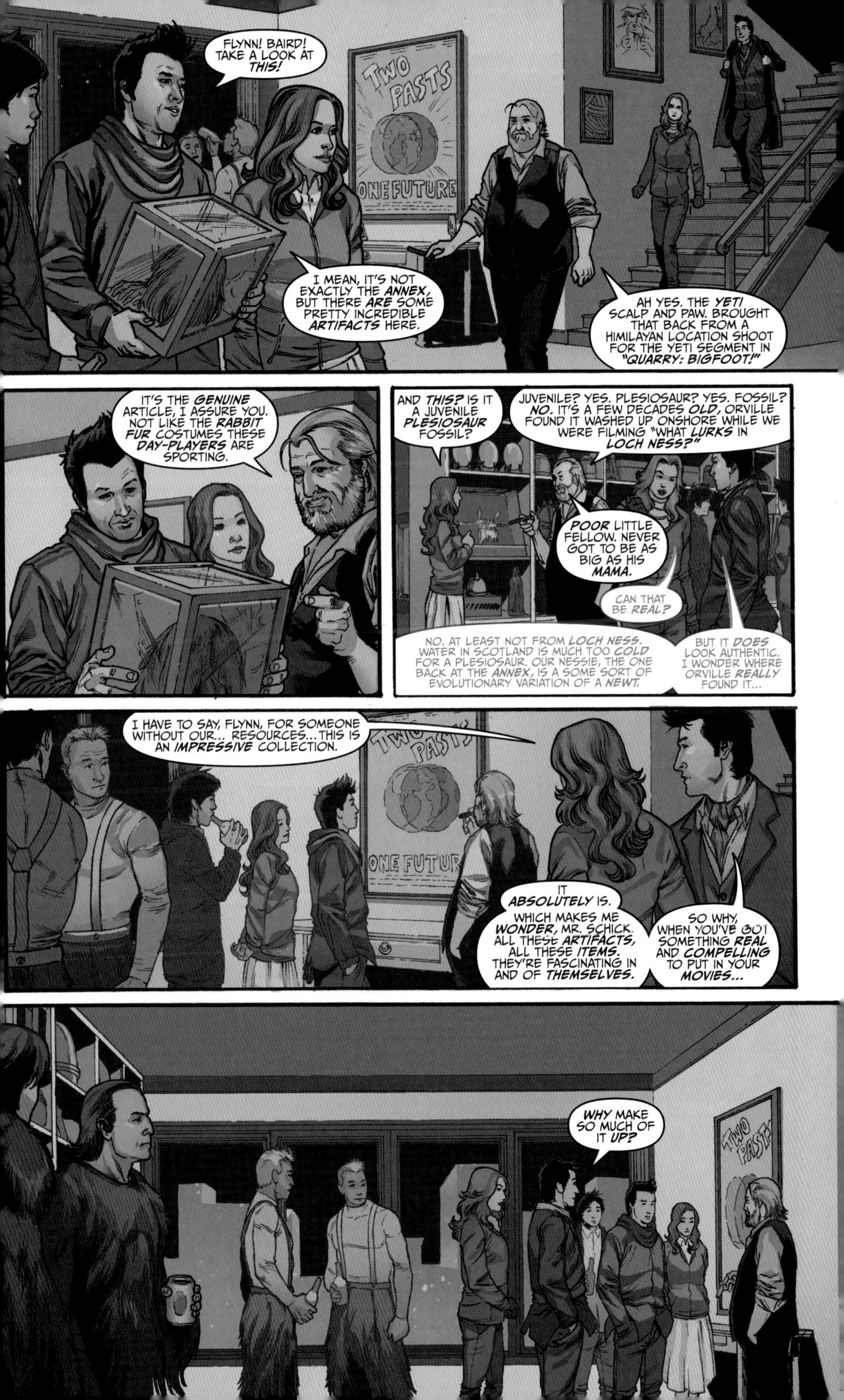
FLYNN! BAIRD! TAKE A LOOK AT THIS!
TWO PASTS ONE FUTURE
I MEAN, IT'S NOT EXACTLY THE ANNEX, BUT THERE ARE SOME PRETTY INCREDIBLE ARTIFACTS HERE.
AH YES. THE YETI SCALP AND PAW. BROUGHT THAT BACK FROM A HIMILAYAN LOCATION SHOOT FOR THE YETI SEGMENT IN "QUARRY: BIGFOOT!"
IT'S THE GENUINE ARTICLE, I ASSURE YOU. NOT LIKE THE RABBIT FUR COSTUMES THESE DAY-PLAYERS ARE SPORTING.
AND THIS? IS IT A JUVENILE PLESIOSAUR FOSSIL?
JUVENILE? YES. PLESIOSAUR? YES. FOSSIL? NO. IT'S A FEW DECADES OLD, ORVILLE FOUND IT WASHED UP ONSHORE WHILE WE WERE FILMING "WHAT LURKS IN LOCH NESS?"
POOR LITTLE FELLOW. NEVER GOT TO BE AS BIG AS HIS MAMA.
CAN THAT BE REAL?
NO. AT LEAST NOT FROM LOCH NESS. WATER IN SCOTLAND IS MUCH TOO COLD FOR A PLESIOSAUR. OUR NESSIE, THE ONE BACK AT THE ANNEX, IS A SOME SORT OF EVOLUTIONARY VARIATION OF A NEWT.
BUT IT DOES LOOK AUTHENTIC. I WONDER WHERE ORVILLE REALLY FOUND IT...
I HAVE TO SAY, FLYNN, FOR SOMEONE WITHOUT OUR... RESOURCES...THIS IS AN IMPRESSIVE COLLECTION.
IT ABSOLUTELY IS. WHICH MAKES ME WONDER, MR. SCHICK. ALL THESE ARTIFACTS, ALL THESE ITEMS. THEY'RE FASCINATING IN AND OF THEMSELVES.
SO WHY, WHEN YOU'VE GOT SOMETHING REAL AND COMPELLING TO PUT IN YOUR MOVIES...
WHY MAKE SO MUCH OF IT UP?

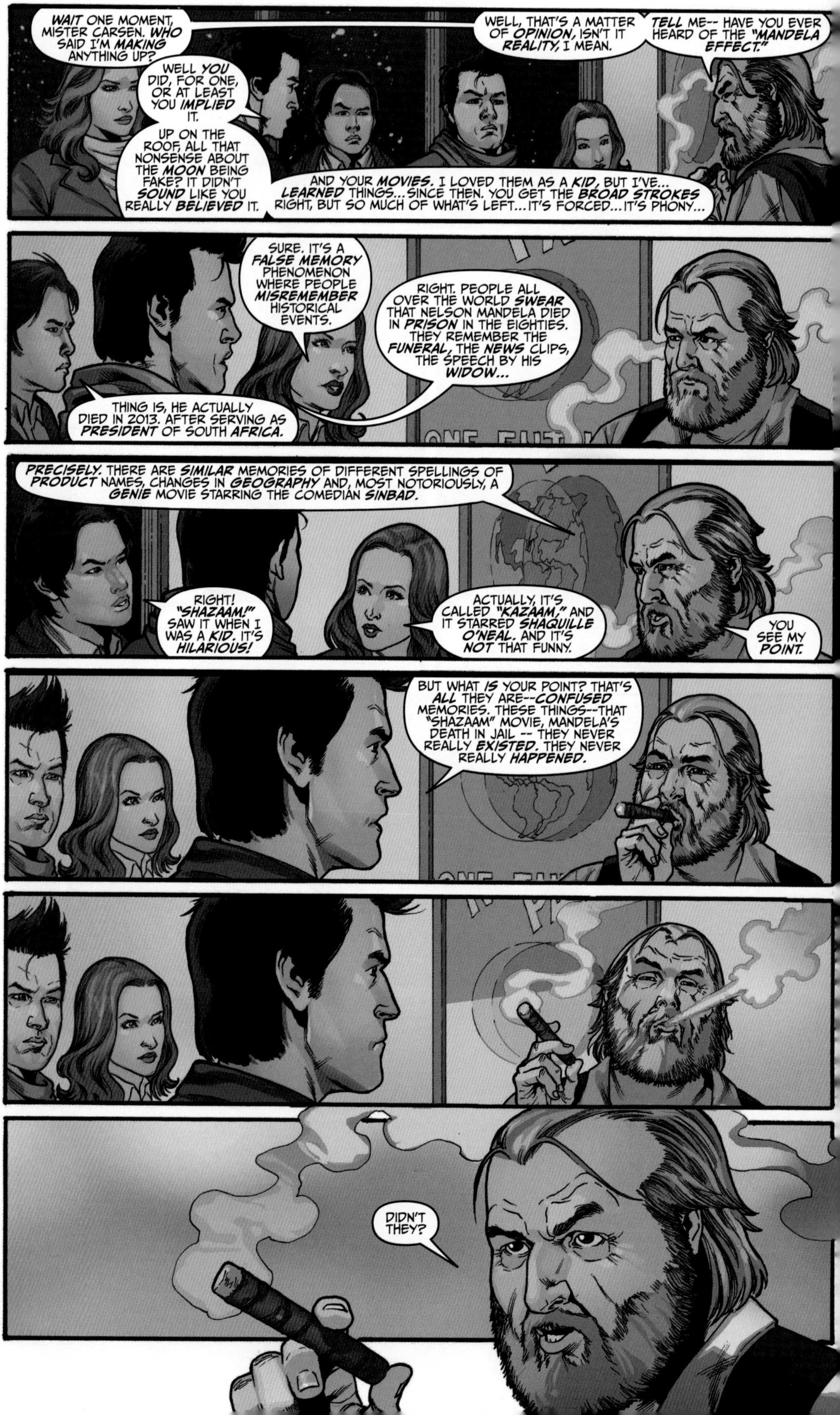
WAIT ONE MOMENT, MISTER CARSEN. WHO SAID I'M MAKING ANYTHING UP?
WELL YOU DID, FOR ONE, OR AT LEAST YOU IMPLIED IT.
UP ON THE ROOF, ALL THAT NONSENSE ABOUT THE MOON BEING FAKE? IT DIDN'T SOUND LIKE YOU REALLY BELIEVED IT.
AND YOUR MOVIES. I LOVED THEM AS A KID, BUT I'VE... LEARNED THINGS... SINCE THEN. YOU GET THE BROAD STROKES RIGHT, BUT SO MUCH OF WHAT'S LEFT... IT'S FORCED... IT'S PHONY...
WELL, THAT'S A MATTER OF OPINION, ISN'T IT REALITY, I MEAN.
TELL ME-- HAVE YOU EVER HEARD OF THE "MANDELA EFFECT."
SURE. IT'S A FALSE MEMORY PHENOMENON WHERE PEOPLE MISREMEMBER HISTORICAL EVENTS.
RIGHT. PEOPLE ALL OVER THE WORLD SWEAR THAT NELSON MANDELA DIED IN PRISON IN THE EIGHTIES. THEY REMEMBER THE FUNERAL, THE NEWS CLIPS, THE SPEECH BY HIS WIDOW...
THING IS, HE ACTUALLY DIED IN 2013. AFTER SERVING AS PRESIDENT OF SOUTH AFRICA.
PRECISELY. THERE ARE SIMILAR MEMORIES OF DIFFERENT SPELLINGS OF PRODUCT NAMES, CHANGES IN GEOGRAPHY AND, MOST NOTORIOUSLY, A GENIE MOVIE STARRING THE COMEDIAN SINBAD.
RIGHT! "SHAZAAM!" SAW IT WHEN I WAS A KID. IT'S HILARIOUS!
ACTUALLY, IT'S CALLED "KAZAAM," AND IT STARRED SHAQUILLE O'NEAL. AND IT'S NOT THAT FUNNY.
YOU SEE MY POINT.
BUT WHAT IS YOUR POINT? THAT'S ALL THEY ARE--CONFUSED MEMORIES. THESE THINGS--THAT "SHAZAAM" MOVIE, MANDELA'S DEATH IN JAIL -- THEY NEVER REALLY EXISTED. THEY NEVER REALLY HAPPENED.
DIDN'T THEY?

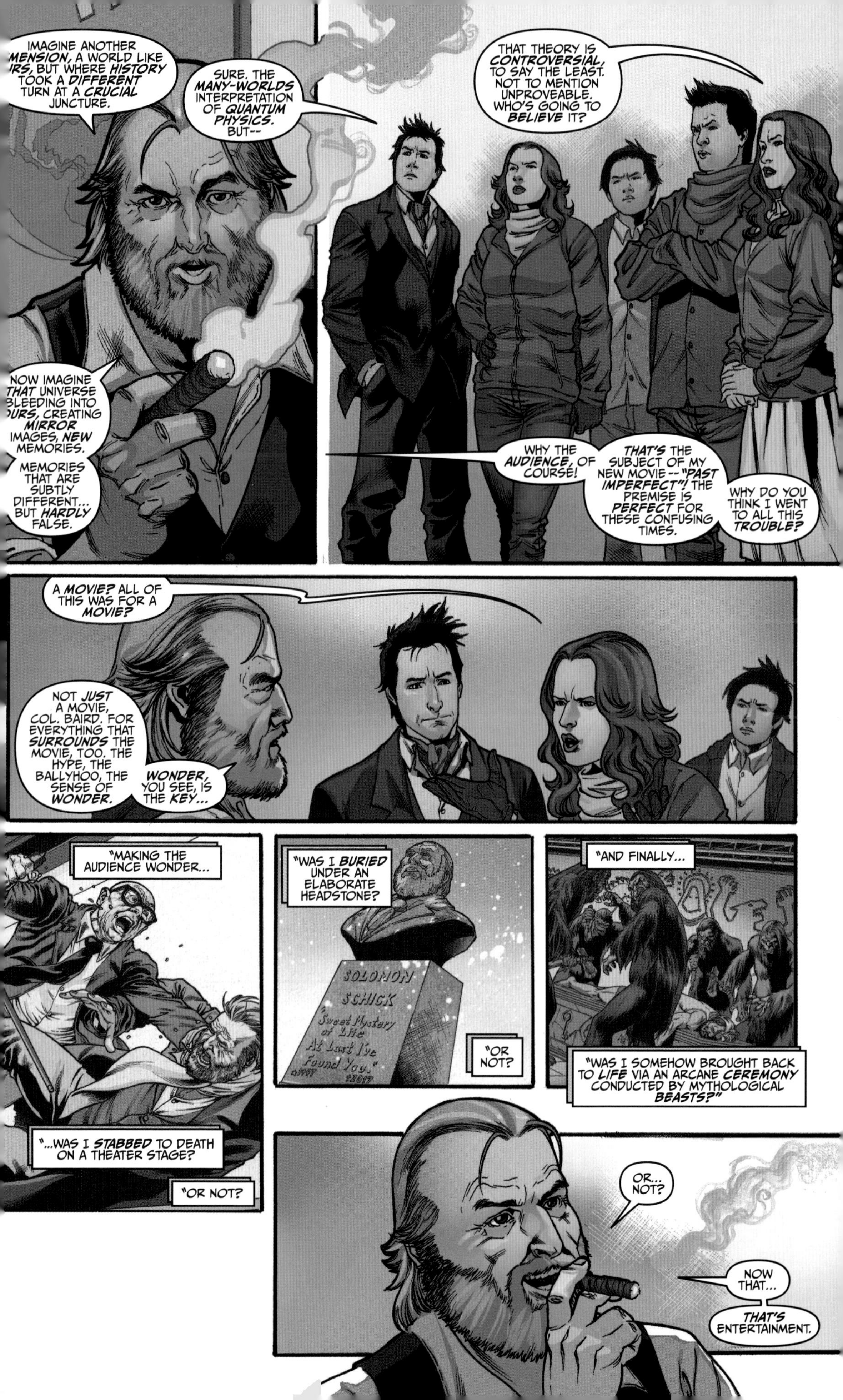
IMAGINE ANOTHER MENSION, A WORLD LIKE URS, BUT WHERE HISTORY TOOK A DIFFERENT TURN AT A CRUCIAL JUNCTURE.
SURE. THE MANY-WORLDS INTERPRETATION OF QUANTUM PHYSICS. BUT--
NOW IMAGINE THAT UNIVERSE BLEEDING INTO URS, CREATING MIRROR IMAGES, NEW MEMORIES.
MEMORIES THAT ARE SUBTLY DIFFERENT... BUT HARDLY FALSE.
THAT THEORY IS CONTROVERSIAL, TO SAY THE LEAST. NOT TO MENTION UNPROVEABLE. WHO'S GOING TO BELIEVE IT?
WHY THE AUDIENCE, OF COURSE!
THAT'S THE SUBJECT OF MY NEW MOVIE -- "PAST IMPERFECT"! THE PREMISE IS PERFECT FOR THESE CONFUSING TIMES.
WHY DO YOU THINK I WENT TO ALL THIS TROUBLE?
A MOVIE? ALL OF THIS WAS FOR A MOVIE?
NOT JUST A MOVIE, COL. BAIRD. FOR EVERYTHING THAT SURROUNDS THE MOVIE, TOO. THE HYPE, THE BALLYHOO, THE SENSE OF WONDER.
WONDER, YOU SEE, IS THE KEY...
"MAKING THE AUDIENCE WONDER...
"...WAS I STABBED TO DEATH ON A THEATER STAGE?
"OR NOT?
"WAS I BURIED UNDER AN ELABORATE HEADSTONE?
SOLOMON SCHICK
"Sweet Mystery of Life At Last I've Found You."
"OR NOT?
"AND FINALLY...
"WAS I SOMEHOW BROUGHT BACK TO LIFE VIA AN ARCANE CEREMONY CONDUCTED BY MYTHOLOGICAL BEASTS?"
OR... NOT?
NOW THAT...
THAT'S ENTERTAINMENT.

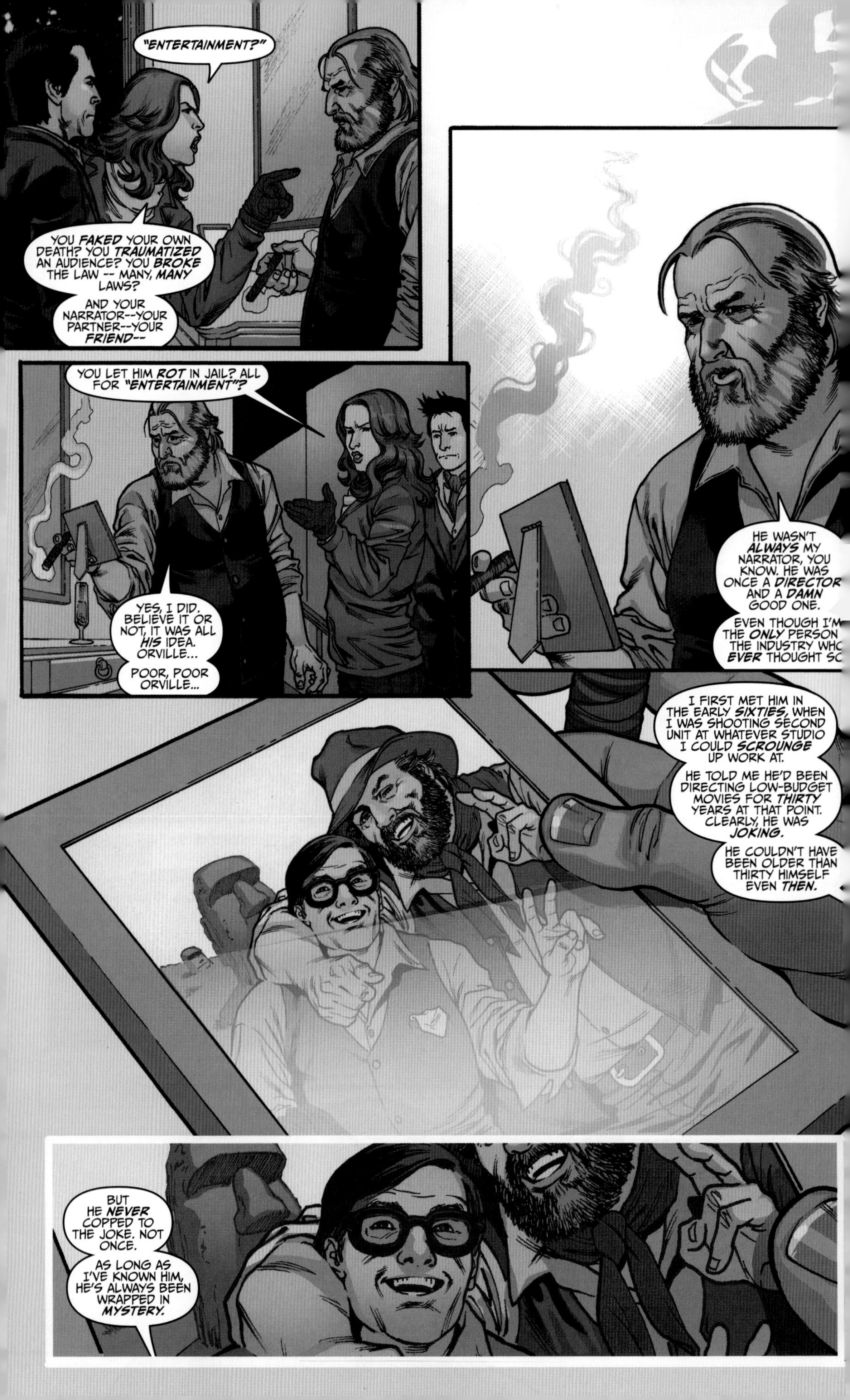
"ENTERTAINMENT?"
YOU FAKED YOUR OWN DEATH? YOU TRAUMATIZED AN AUDIENCE? YOU BROKE THE LAW -- MANY, MANY LAWS?
AND YOUR NARRATOR--YOUR PARTNER--YOUR FRIEND--
YOU LET HIM ROT IN JAIL? ALL FOR "ENTERTAINMENT"?
YES, I DID. BELIEVE IT OR NOT, IT WAS ALL HIS IDEA. ORVILLE...
POOR, POOR ORVILLE...
HE WASN'T ALWAYS MY NARRATOR, YOU KNOW. HE WAS ONCE A DIRECTOR AND A DAMN GOOD ONE.
EVEN THOUGH I'M THE ONLY PERSON THE INDUSTRY WHO EVER THOUGHT SC
I FIRST MET HIM IN THE EARLY SIXTIES, WHEN I WAS SHOOTING SECOND UNIT AT WHATEVER STUDIO I COULD SCROUNGE UP WORK AT.
HE TOLD ME HE'D BEEN DIRECTING LOW-BUDGET MOVIES FOR THIRTY YEARS AT THAT POINT. CLEARLY, HE WAS JOKING.
HE COULDN'T HAVE BEEN OLDER THAN THIRTY HIMSELF EVEN THEN.
BUT HE NEVER COPPED TO THE JOKE. NOT ONCE.
AS LONG AS I'VE KNOWN HIM, HE'S ALWAYS BEEN WRAPPED IN MYSTERY.

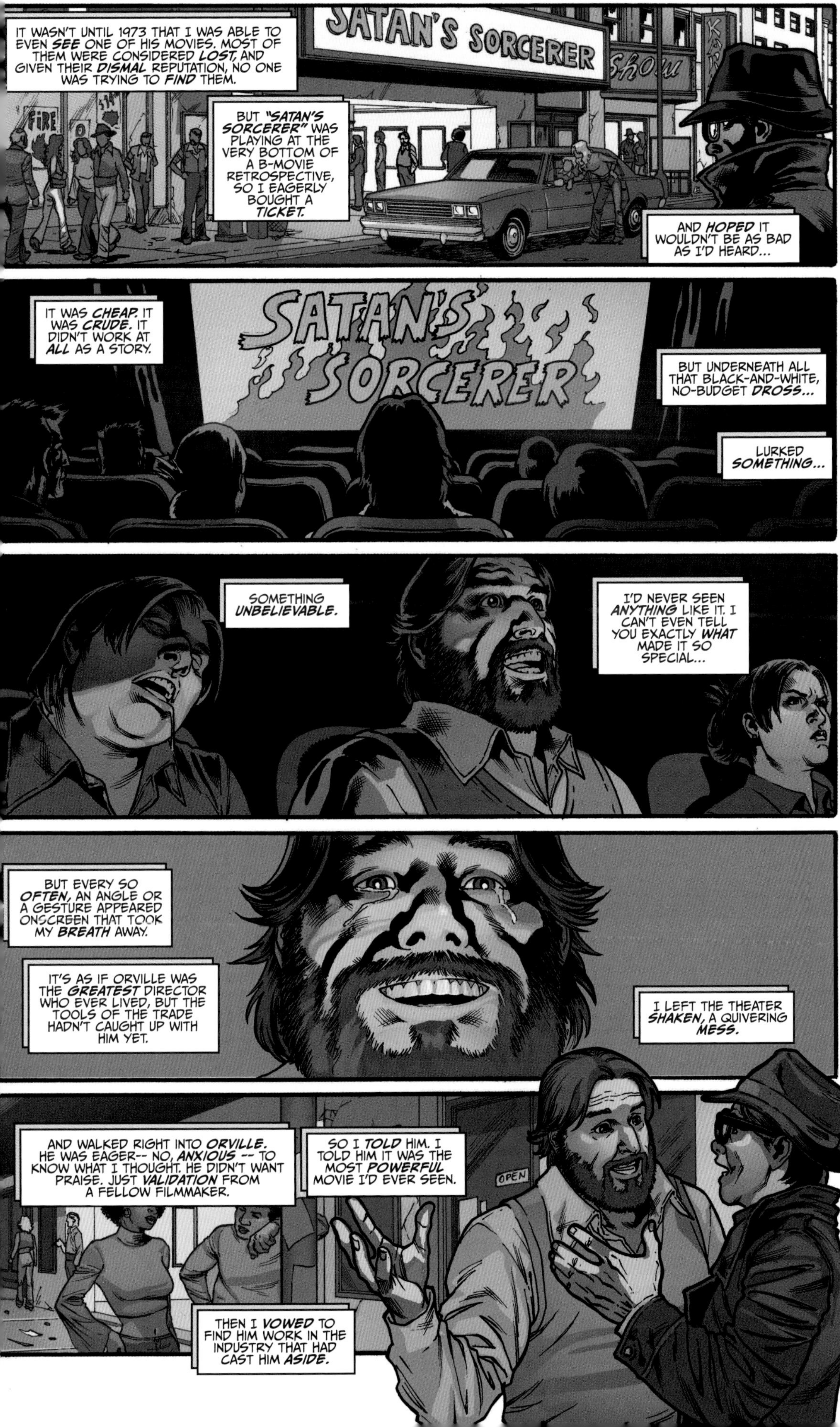
IT WASN'T UNTIL 1973 THAT I WAS ABLE TO EVEN SEE ONE OF HIS MOVIES. MOST OF THEM WERE CONSIDERED LOST, AND GIVEN THEIR DISMAL REPUTATION, NO ONE WAS TRYING TO FIND THEM.
SATAN'S SORCERER
BUT "SATAN'S SORCERER" WAS PLAYING AT THE VERY BOTTOM OF A B-MOVIE RETROSPECTIVE, SO I EAGERLY BOUGHT A TICKET.
AND HOPED IT WOULDN'T BE AS BAD AS I'D HEARD...
IT WAS CHEAP. IT WAS CRUDE. IT DIDN'T WORK AT ALL AS A STORY.
SATAN'S SORCERER
BUT UNDERNEATH ALL THAT BLACK-AND-WHITE, NO-BUDGET DROSS...
LURKED SOMETHING...
SOMETHING UNBELIEVABLE.
I'D NEVER SEEN ANYTHING LIKE IT. I CAN'T EVEN TELL YOU EXACTLY WHAT MADE IT SO SPECIAL...
BUT EVERY SO OFTEN, AN ANGLE OR A GESTURE APPEARED ONSCREEN THAT TOOK MY BREATH AWAY.
IT'S AS IF ORVILLE WAS THE GREATEST DIRECTOR WHO EVER LIVED, BUT THE TOOLS OF THE TRADE HADN'T CAUGHT UP WITH HIM YET.
I LEFT THE THEATER SHAKEN, A QUIVERING MESS.
AND WALKED RIGHT INTO ORVILLE. HE WAS EAGER-- NO, ANXIOUS -- TO KNOW WHAT I THOUGHT. HE DIDN'T WANT PRAISE. JUST VALIDATION FROM A FELLOW FILMMAKER.
SO I TOLD HIM. I TOLD HIM IT WAS THE MOST POWERFUL MOVIE I'D EVER SEEN.
OPEN
THEN I VOWED TO FIND HIM WORK IN THE INDUSTRY THAT HAD CAST HIM ASIDE.

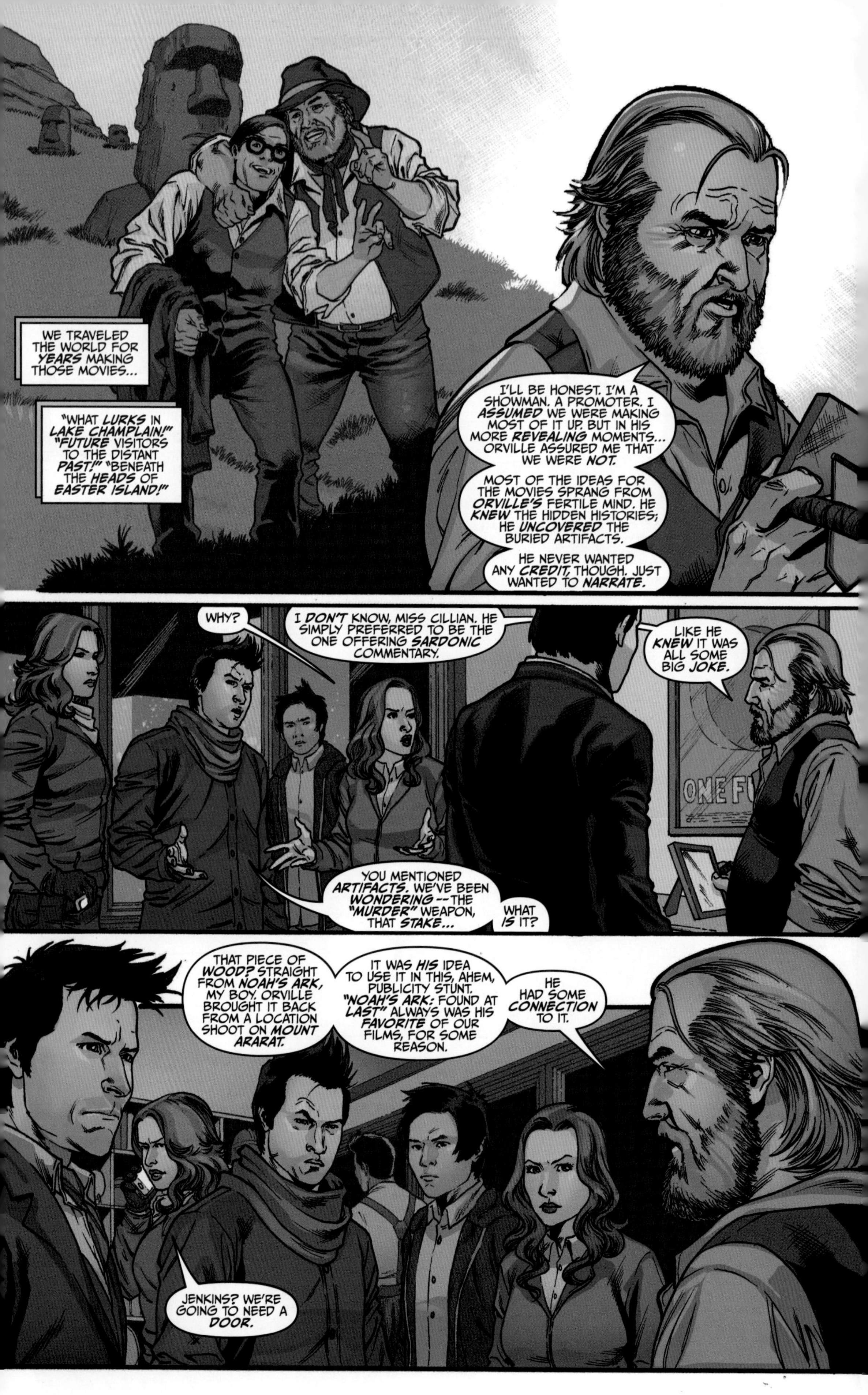
WE TRAVELED THE WORLD FOR YEARS MAKING THOSE MOVIES...
"WHAT LURKS IN LAKE CHAMPLAIN!" "FUTURE VISITORS TO THE DISTANT PAST!" "BENEATH THE HEADS OF EASTER ISLAND!"
I'LL BE HONEST. I'M A SHOWMAN. A PROMOTER. I ASSUMED WE WERE MAKING MOST OF IT UP. BUT IN HIS MORE REVEALING MOMENTS... ORVILLE ASSURED ME THAT WE WERE NOT.
MOST OF THE IDEAS FOR THE MOVIES SPRANG FROM ORVILLE'S FERTILE MIND. HE KNEW THE HIDDEN HISTORIES; HE UNCOVERED THE BURIED ARTIFACTS.
HE NEVER WANTED ANY CREDIT, THOUGH. JUST WANTED TO NARRATE.
WHY?
I DON'T KNOW, MISS CILLIAN. HE SIMPLY PREFERRED TO BE THE ONE OFFERING SARDONIC COMMENTARY.
LIKE HE KNEW IT WAS ALL SOME BIG JOKE.
ONE FU
YOU MENTIONED ARTIFACTS. WE'VE BEEN WONDERING -- THE "MURDER" WEAPON, THAT STAKE...
WHAT IS IT?
THAT PIECE OF WOOD? STRAIGHT FROM NOAH'S ARK, MY BOY. ORVILLE BROUGHT IT BACK FROM A LOCATION SHOOT ON MOUNT ARARAT.
IT WAS HIS IDEA TO USE IT IN THIS, AHEM, PUBLICITY STUNT. "NOAH'S ARK: FOUND AT LAST" ALWAYS WAS HIS FAVORITE OF OUR FILMS, FOR SOME REASON.
HE HAD SOME CONNECTION TO IT.
JENKINS? WE'RE GOING TO NEED A DOOR.

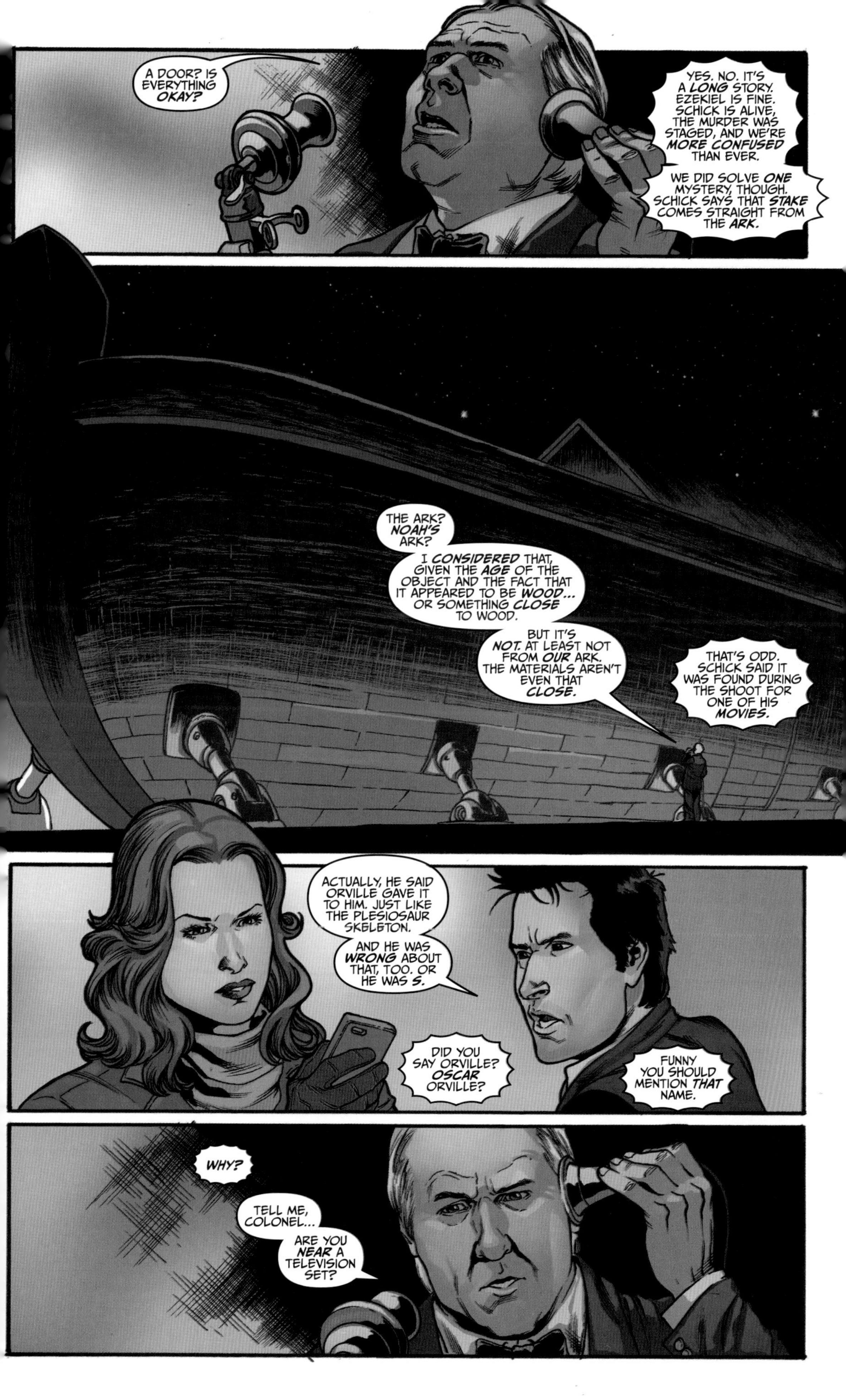
A DOOR? IS EVERYTHING OKAY?
YES. NO. IT'S A LONG STORY. EZEKIEL IS FINE. SCHICK IS ALIVE, THE MURDER WAS STAGED, AND WE'RE MORE CONFUSED THAN EVER.
WE DID SOLVE ONE MYSTERY, THOUGH. SCHICK SAYS THAT STAKE COMES STRAIGHT FROM THE ARK.
THE ARK? NOAH'S ARK?
I CONSIDERED THAT, GIVEN THE AGE OF THE OBJECT AND THE FACT THAT IT APPEARED TO BE WOOD... OR SOMETHING CLOSE TO WOOD.
BUT IT'S NOT. AT LEAST NOT FROM OUR ARK. THE MATERIALS AREN'T EVEN THAT CLOSE.
THAT'S ODD. SCHICK SAID IT WAS FOUND DURING THE SHOOT FOR ONE OF HIS MOVIES.
ACTUALLY, HE SAID ORVILLE GAVE IT TO HIM. JUST LIKE THE PLESIOSAUR SKELETON.
AND HE WAS WRONG ABOUT THAT, TOO. OR HE WAS S.
DID YOU SAY ORVILLE? OSCAR ORVILLE?
FUNNY YOU SHOULD MENTION THAT NAME.
WHY?
TELL ME, COLONEL...
ARE YOU NEAR A TELEVISION SET?

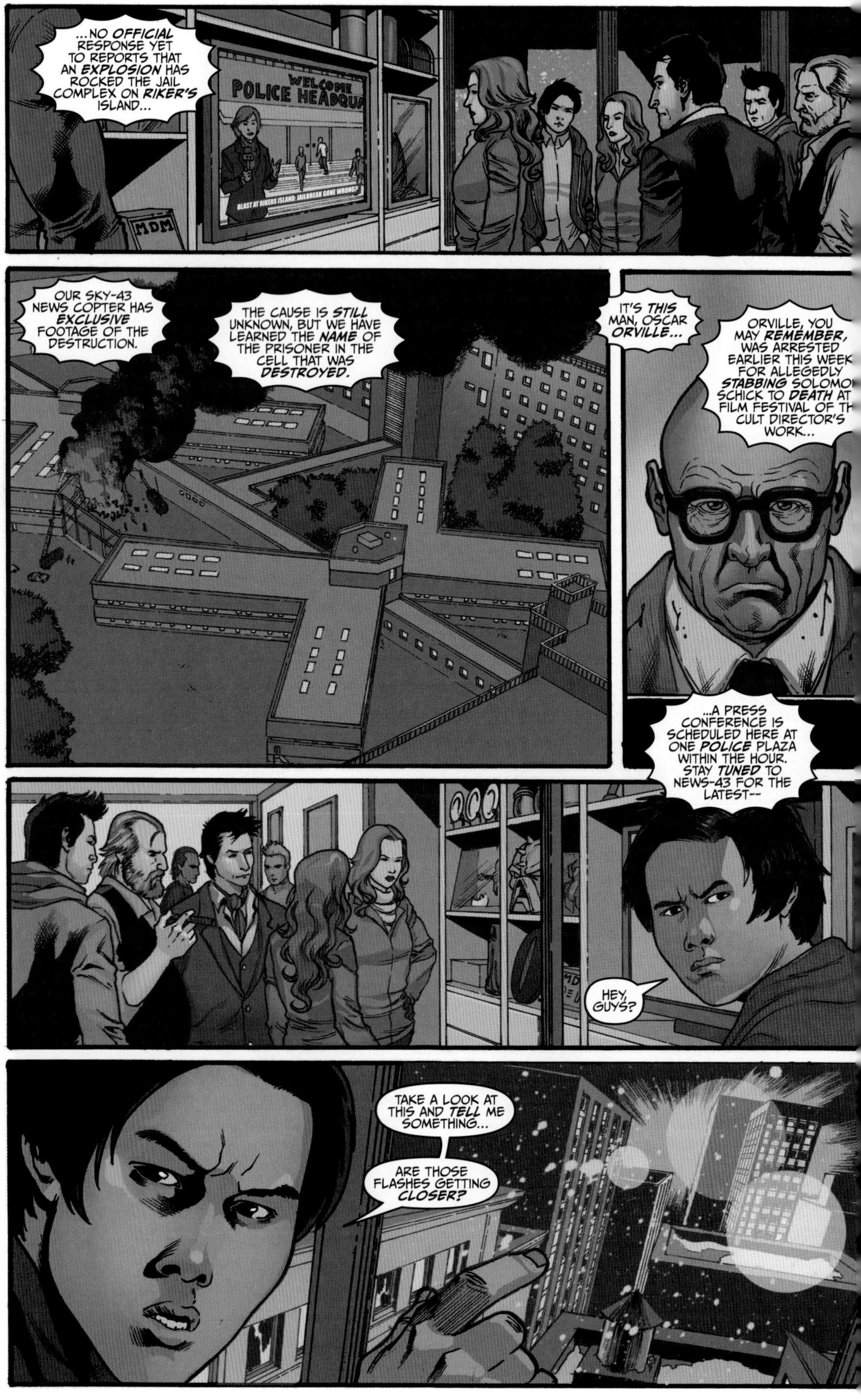

...NO OFFICIAL RESPONSE YET TO REPORTS THAT AN EXPLOSION HAS ROCKED THE JAIL COMPLEX ON RIKER'S ISLAND...
WELCOME
POLICE HEADQUA
BLAST AT RIKERS ISLAND: JAILBREAK GONE WRONG?
MDM
OUR SKY-43 NEWS COPTER HAS EXCLUSIVE FOOTAGE OF THE DESTRUCTION.
THE CAUSE IS STILL UNKNOWN, BUT WE HAVE LEARNED THE NAME OF THE PRISONER IN THE CELL THAT WAS DESTROYED.
IT'S THIS MAN, OSCAR ORVILLE...
ORVILLE, YOU MAY REMEMBER, WAS ARRESTED EARLIER THIS WEEK FOR ALLEGEDLY STABBING SOLOMO SCHICK TO DEATH AT FILM FESTIVAL OF TH CULT DIRECTOR'S WORK...
...A PRESS CONFERENCE IS SCHEDULED HERE AT ONE POLICE PLAZA WITHIN THE HOUR. STAY TUNED TO NEWS-43 FOR THE LATEST--
HEY, GUYS?
TAKE A LOOK AT THIS AND TELL ME SOMETHING...
ARE THOSE FLASHES GETTING CLOSER?

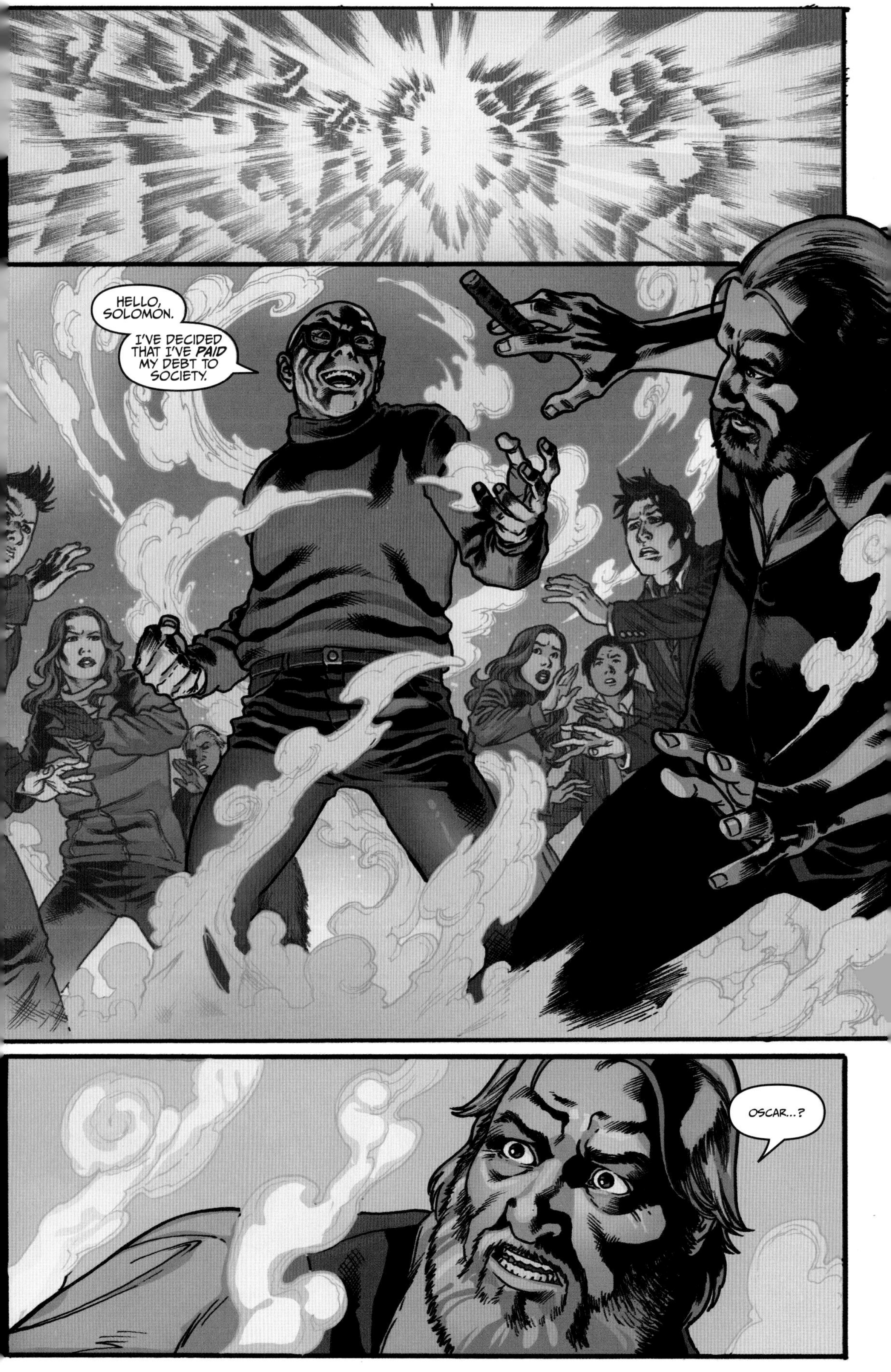
HELLO, SOLOMON.
I'VE DECIDED THAT I'VE *PAID* MY DEBT TO SOCIETY.
OSCAR...?

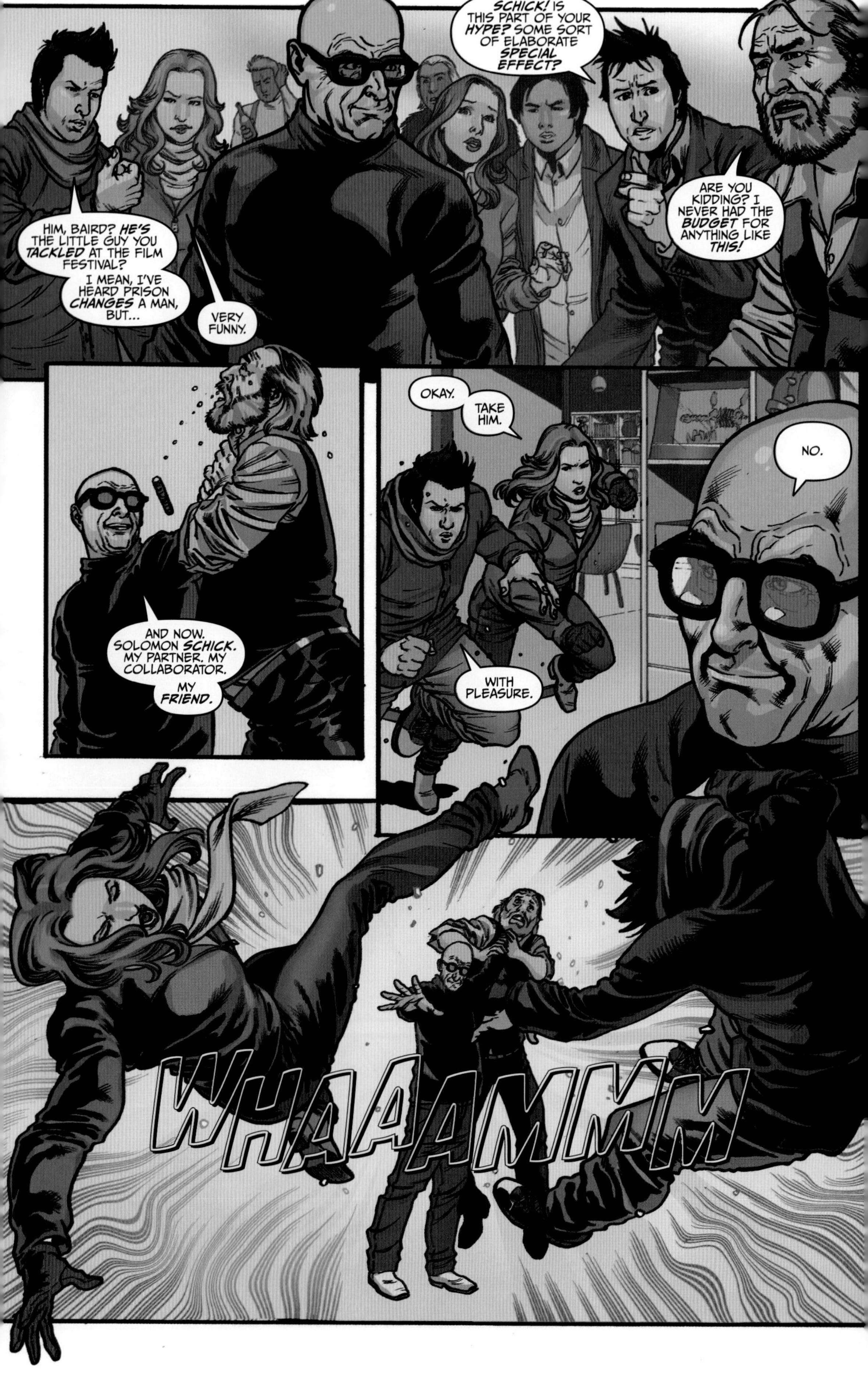
SCHICK! IS THIS PART OF YOUR HYPE? SOME SORT OF ELABORATE SPECIAL EFFECT?
ARE YOU KIDDING? I NEVER HAD THE BUDGET FOR ANYTHING LIKE THIS!
HIM, BAIRD? HE'S THE LITTLE GUY YOU TACKLED AT THE FILM FESTIVAL?
I MEAN, I'VE HEARD PRISON CHANGES A MAN, BUT...
VERY FUNNY.
AND NOW. SOLOMON SCHICK. MY PARTNER. MY COLLABORATOR.
MY FRIEND.
OKAY.
TAKE HIM.
WITH PLEASURE.
NO.
WHAAAMMM

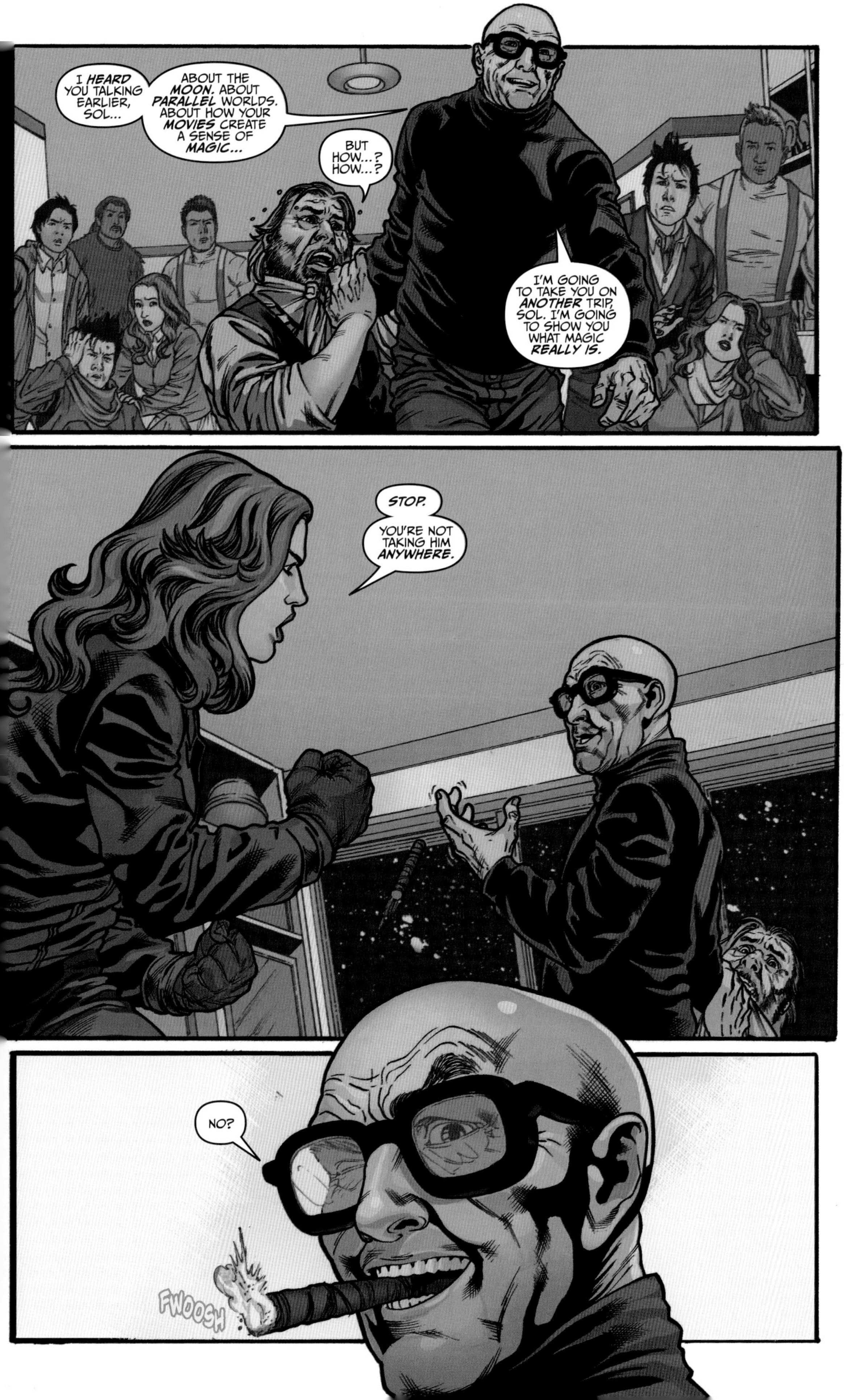
I HEARD YOU TALKING EARLIER, SOL...
ABOUT THE MOON. ABOUT PARALLEL WORLDS. ABOUT HOW YOUR MOVIES CREATE A SENSE OF MAGIC...
BUT HOW...? HOW...?
I'M GOING TO TAKE YOU ON ANOTHER TRIP, SOL. I'M GOING TO SHOW YOU WHAT MAGIC REALLY IS.
STOP.
YOU'RE NOT TAKING HIM ANYWHERE.
NO?
FWOOSH

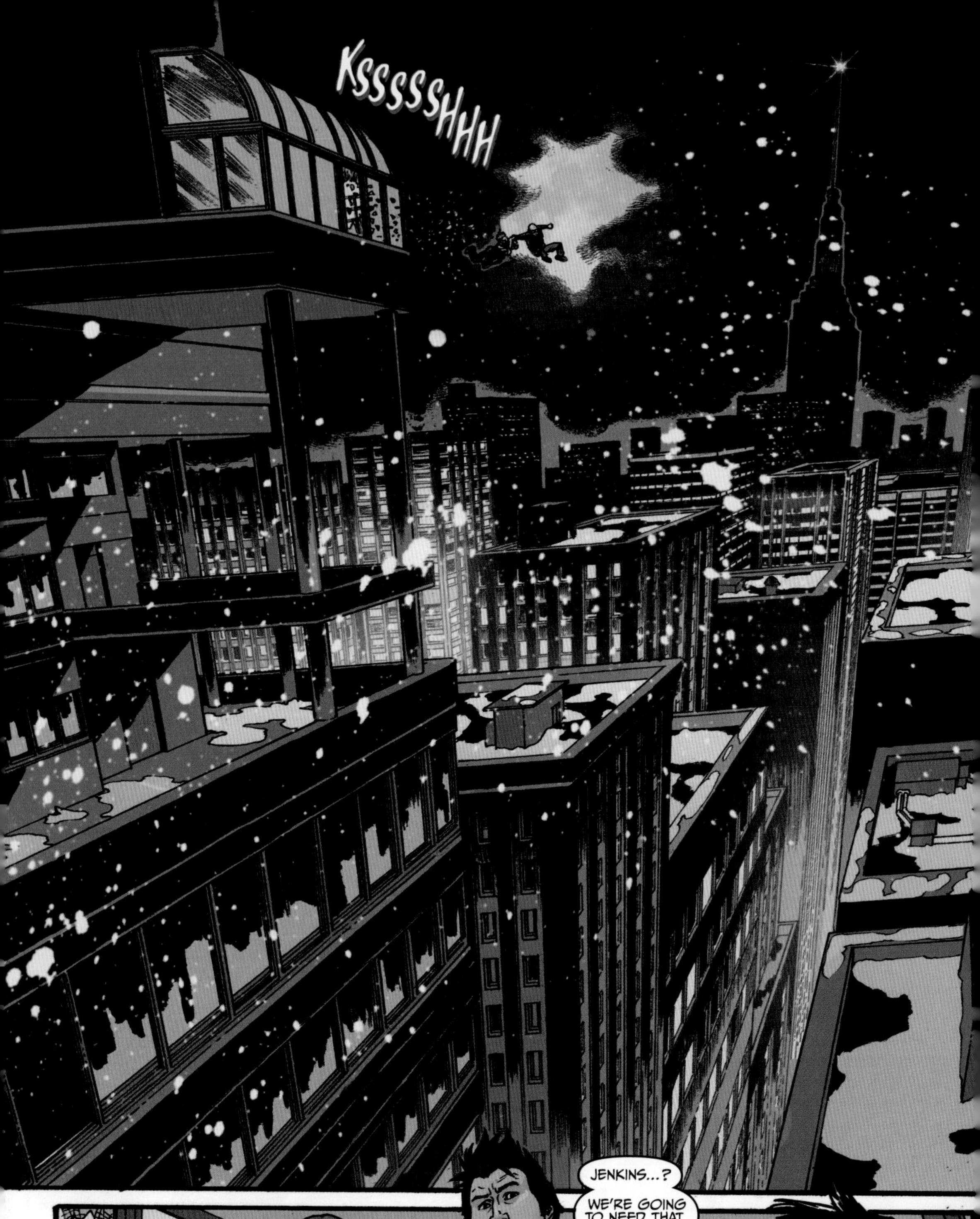
KSSSSSHHH

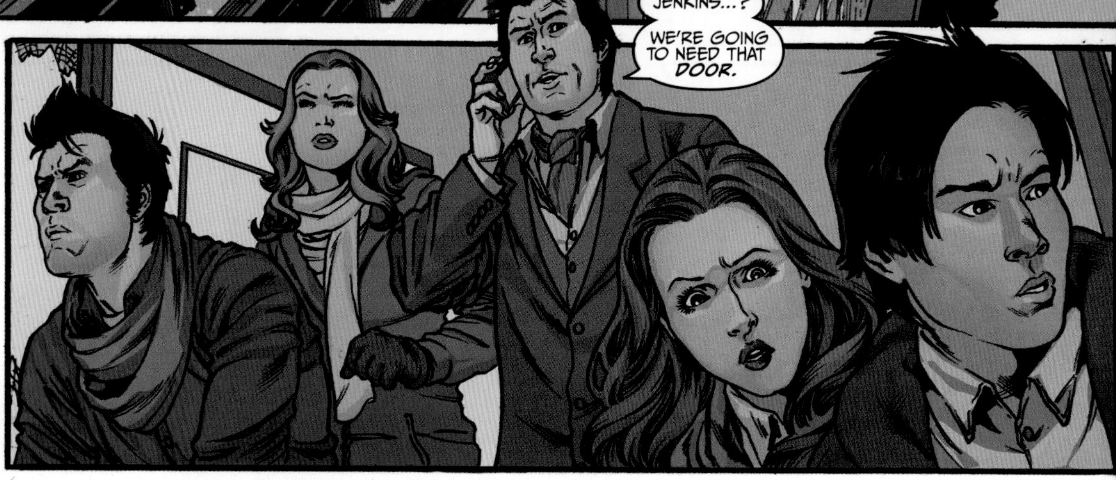
JENKINS...?
WE'RE GOING TO NEED THAT DOOR.

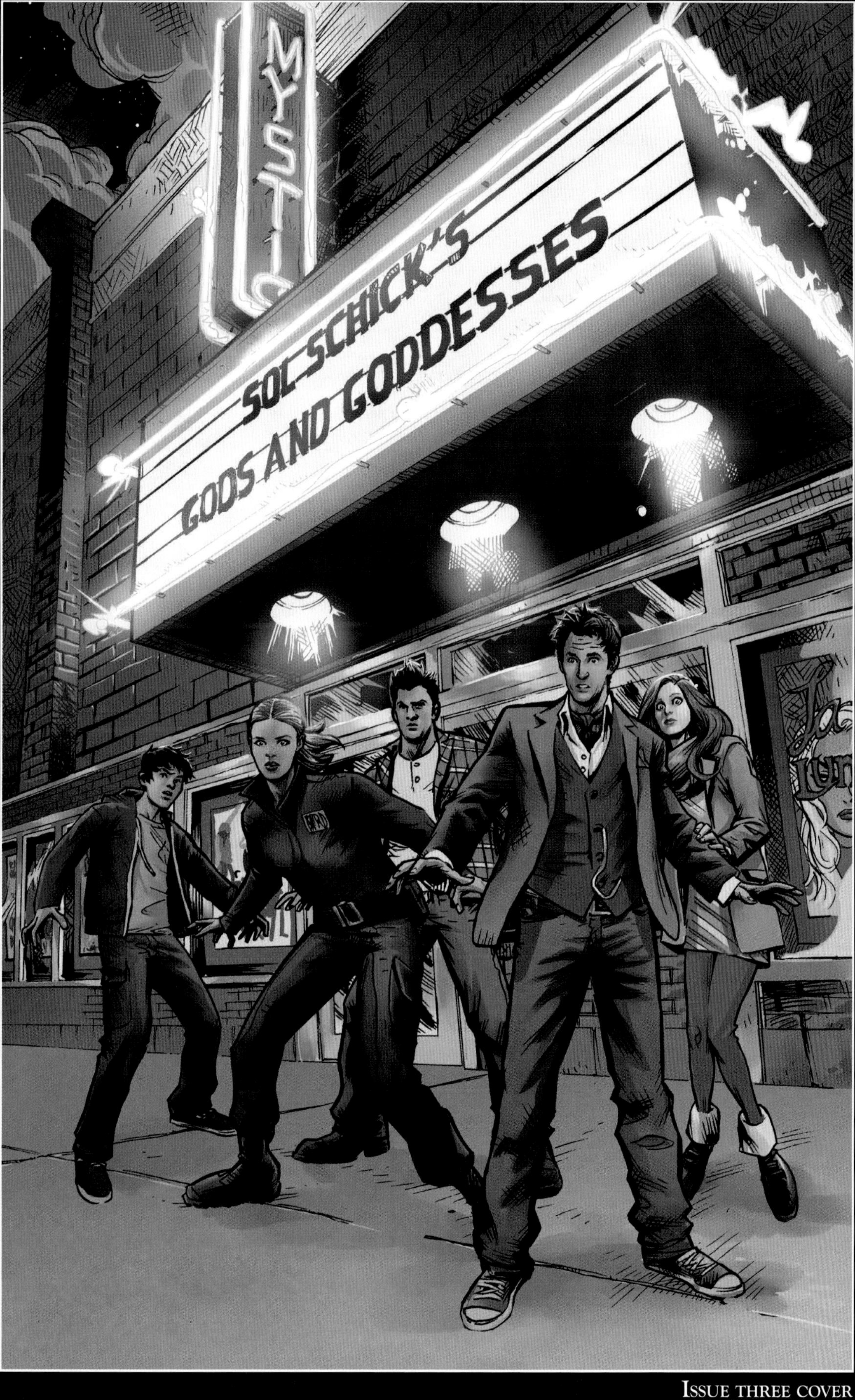
SOL SCHICK'S
GODS AND GODDESSES

Issue three cover
art by Karl Moline

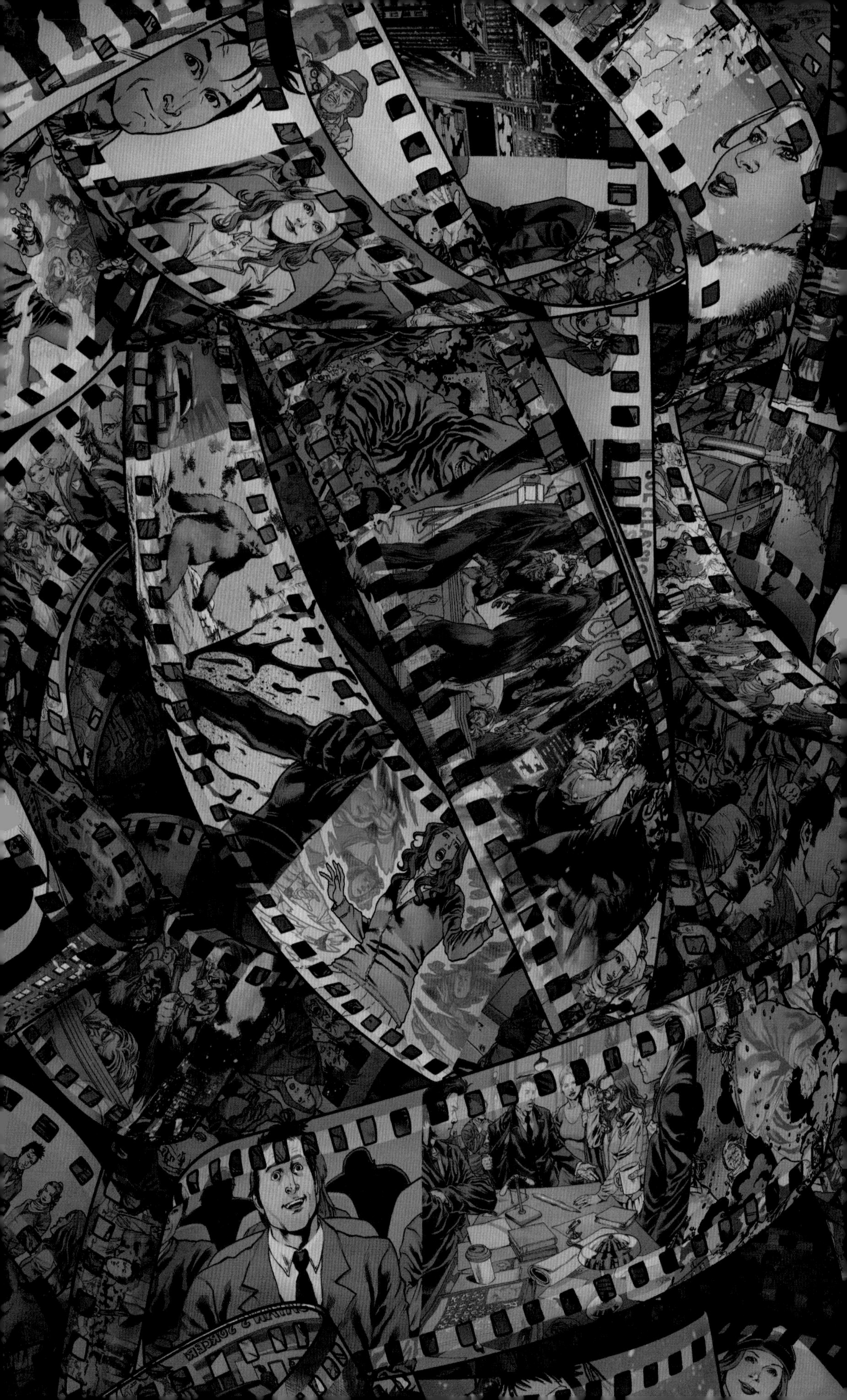

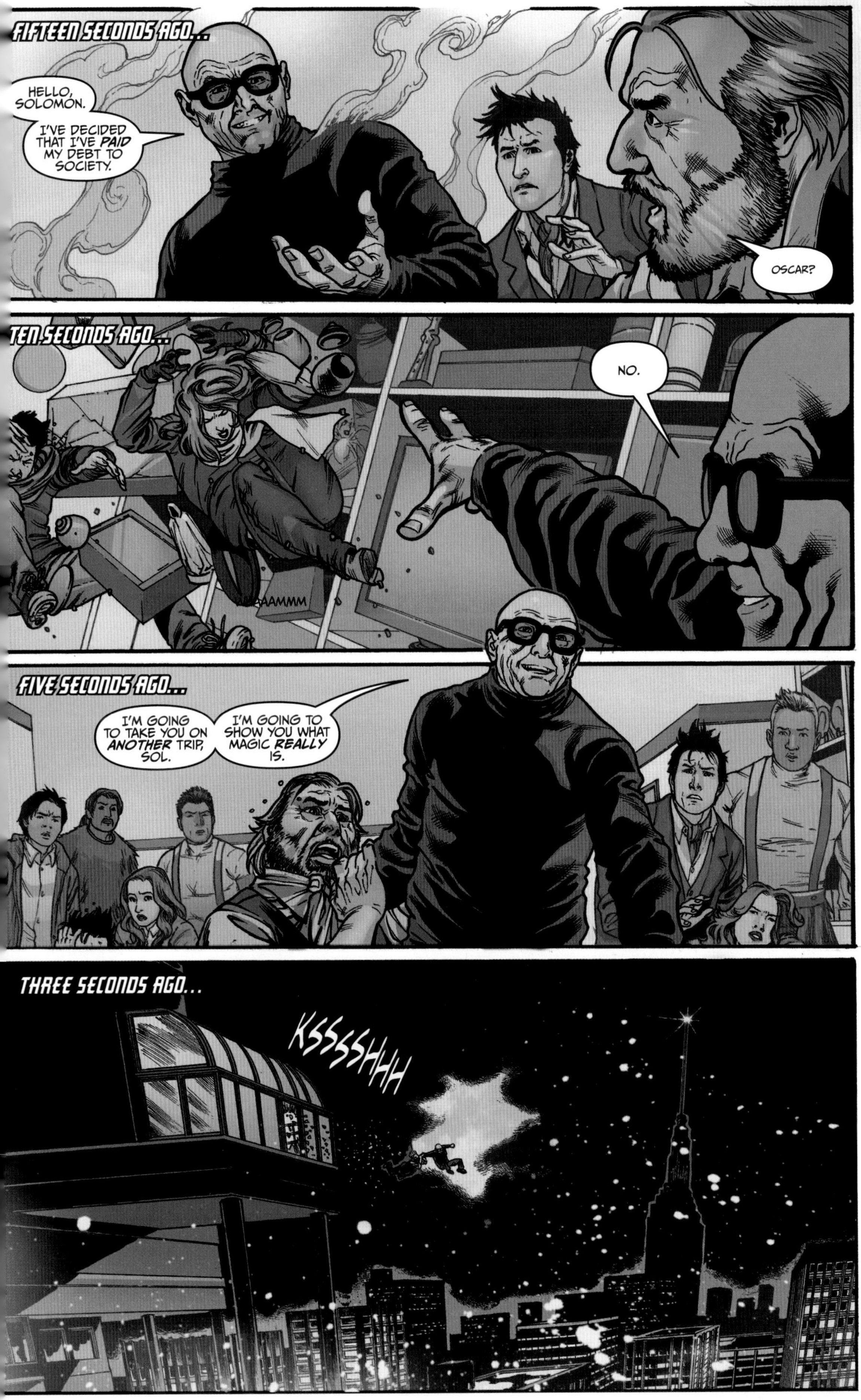
FIFTEEN SECONDS AGO...
HELLO, SOLOMON.
I'VE DECIDED THAT I'VE PAID MY DEBT TO SOCIETY.
OSCAR?
TEN SECONDS AGO...
NO.
AAMMM
FIVE SECONDS AGO...
I'M GOING TO TAKE YOU ON ANOTHER TRIP, SOL.
I'M GOING TO SHOW YOU WHAT MAGIC REALLY IS.
THREE SECONDS AGO...
KSSSSHHH

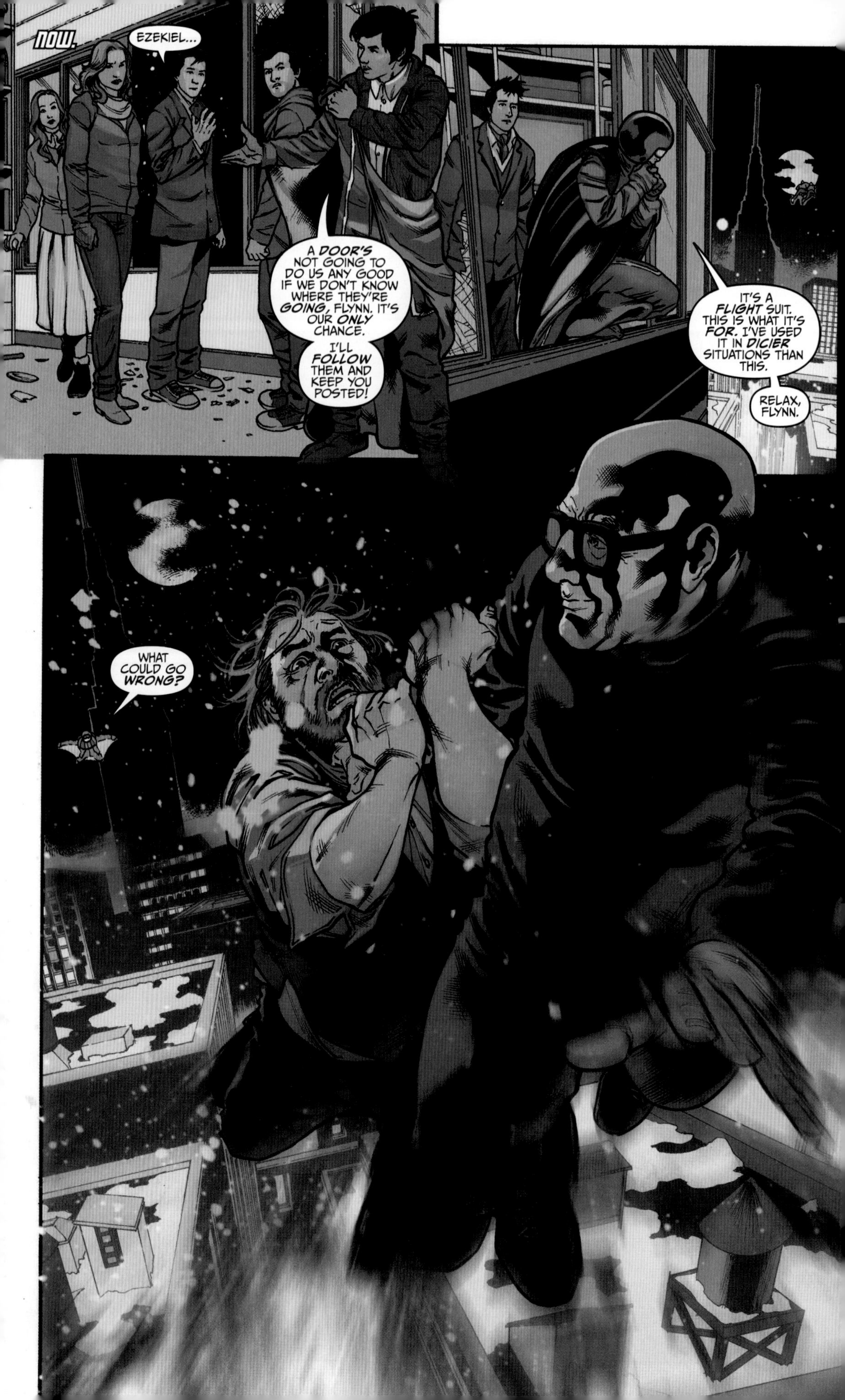
NOW.
EZEKIEL...
A DOOR'S NOT GOING TO DO US ANY GOOD IF WE DON'T KNOW WHERE THEY'RE GOING, FLYNN. IT'S OUR ONLY CHANCE.
I'LL FOLLOW THEM AND KEEP YOU POSTED!
IT'S A FLIGHT SUIT. THIS IS WHAT IT'S FOR. I'VE USED IT IN DICIER SITUATIONS THAN THIS.
RELAX, FLYNN.
WHAT COULD GO WRONG?

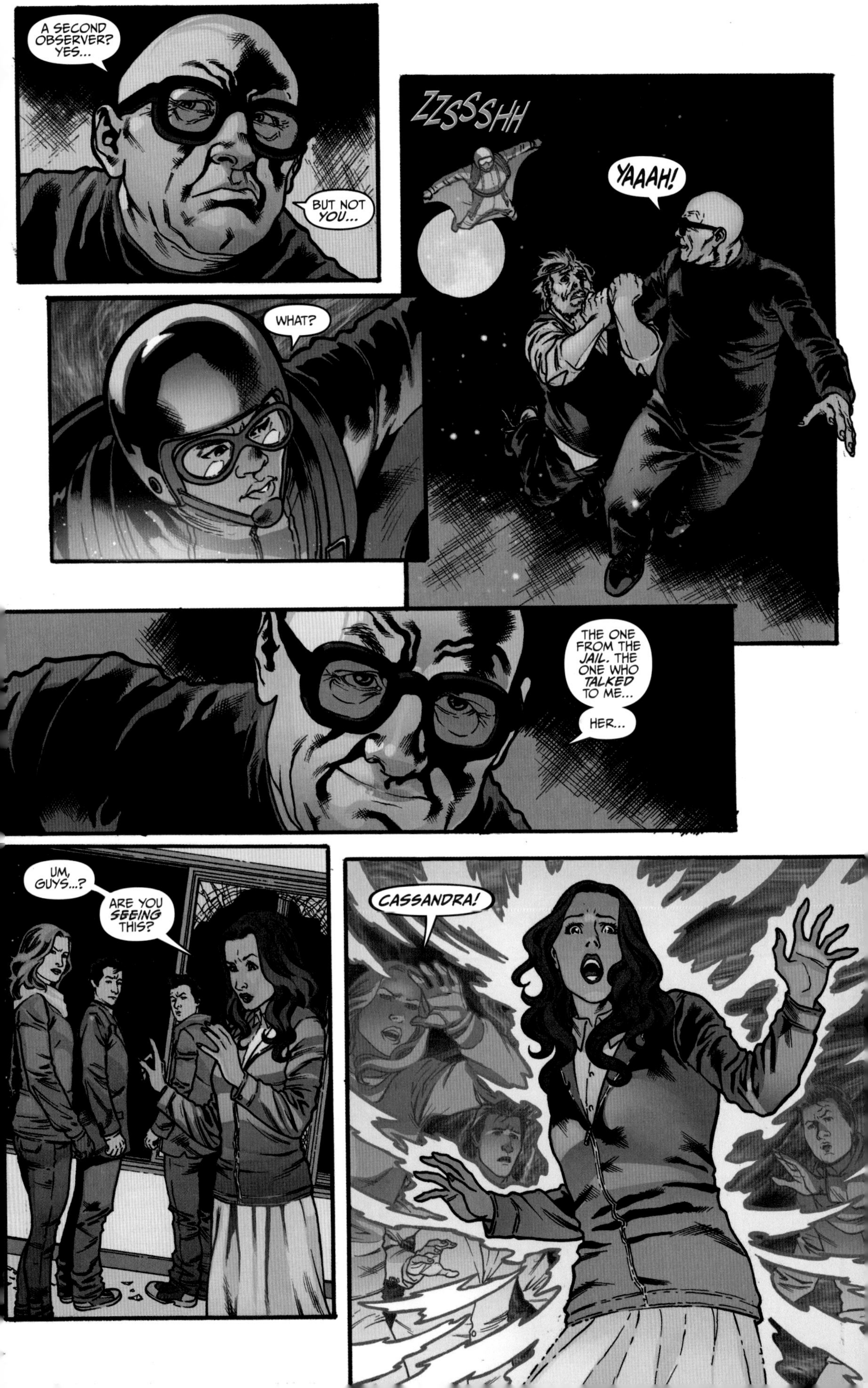
A SECOND OBSERVER? YES...
BUT NOT YOU...
ZZSSSHH
YAAAH!
WHAT?
THE ONE FROM THE JAIL. THE ONE WHO TALKED TO ME...
HER...
UM, GUYS...?
ARE YOU SEEING THIS?
CASSANDRA!

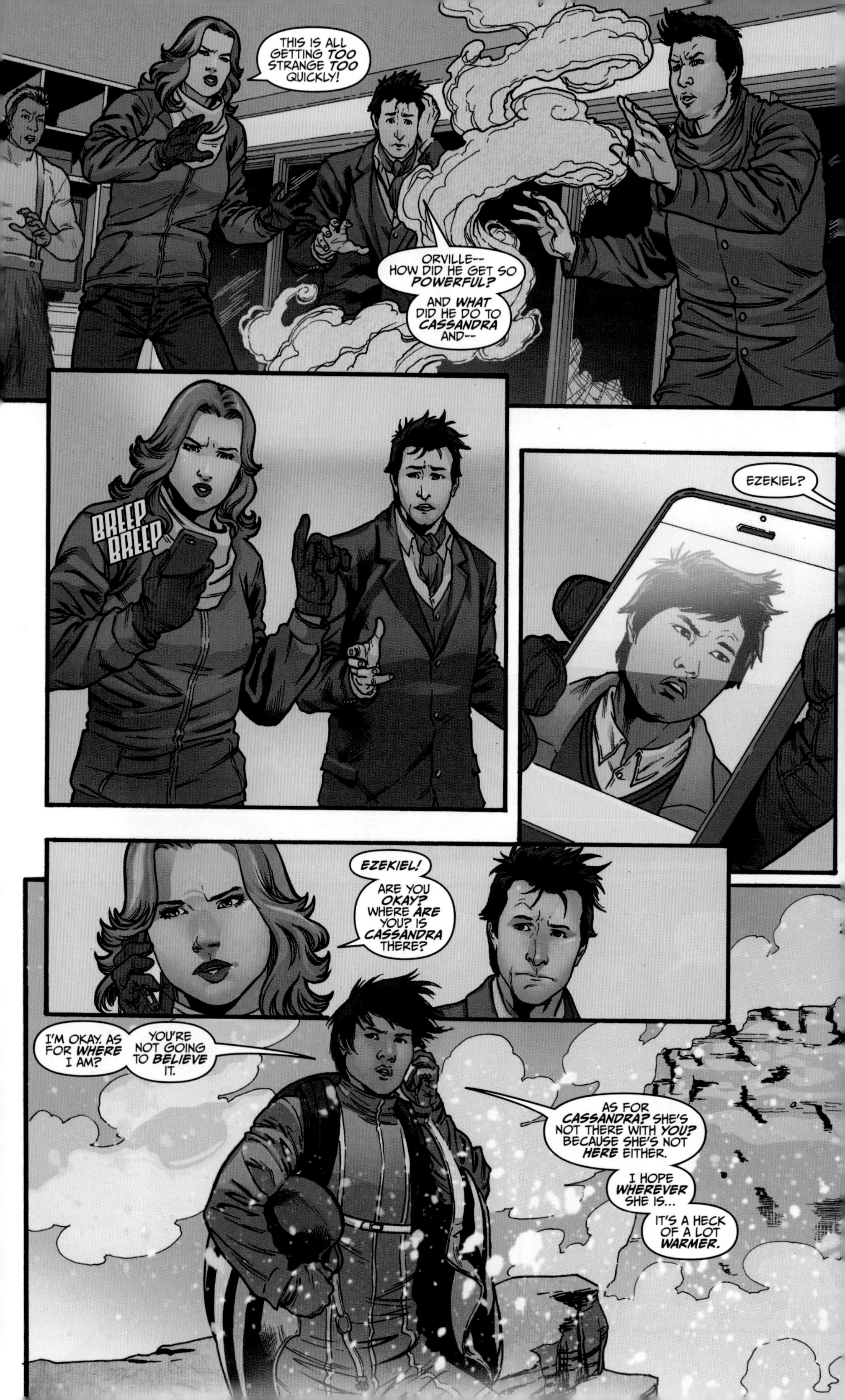
THIS IS ALL GETTING TOO STRANGE TOO QUICKLY!
ORVILLE-- HOW DID HE GET SO POWERFUL?
AND WHAT DID HE DO TO CASSANDRA AND--
BREEP BREEP
EZEKIEL?
EZEKIEL!
ARE YOU OKAY? WHERE ARE YOU? IS CASSANDRA THERE?
I'M OKAY. AS FOR WHERE I AM?
YOU'RE NOT GOING TO BELIEVE IT.
AS FOR CASSANDRA? SHE'S NOT THERE WITH YOU? BECAUSE SHE'S NOT HERE EITHER.
I HOPE WHEREVER SHE IS...
IT'S A HECK OF A LOT WARMER.

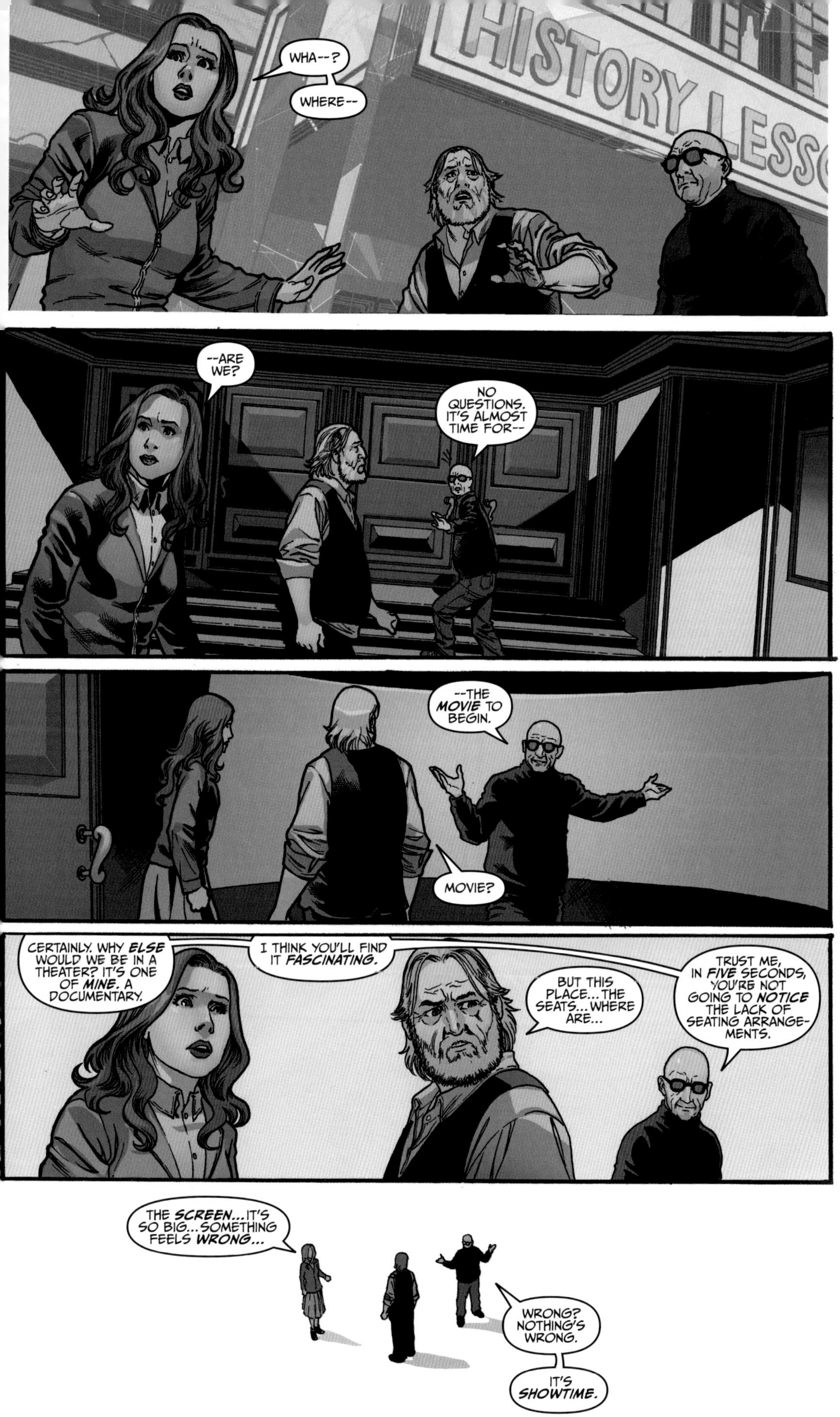
HISTORY LESS
WHA--?
WHERE--
--ARE WE?
NO QUESTIONS. IT'S ALMOST TIME FOR--
--THE MOVIE TO BEGIN.
MOVIE?
CERTAINLY. WHY ELSE WOULD WE BE IN A THEATER? IT'S ONE OF MINE. A DOCUMENTARY.
I THINK YOU'LL FIND IT FASCINATING.
BUT THIS PLACE... THE SEATS... WHERE ARE...
TRUST ME, IN FIVE SECONDS, YOU'RE NOT GOING TO NOTICE THE LACK OF SEATING ARRANGE-MENTS.
THE SCREEN... IT'S SO BIG... SOMETHING FEELS WRONG...
WRONG? NOTHING'S WRONG.
IT'S SHOWTIME.

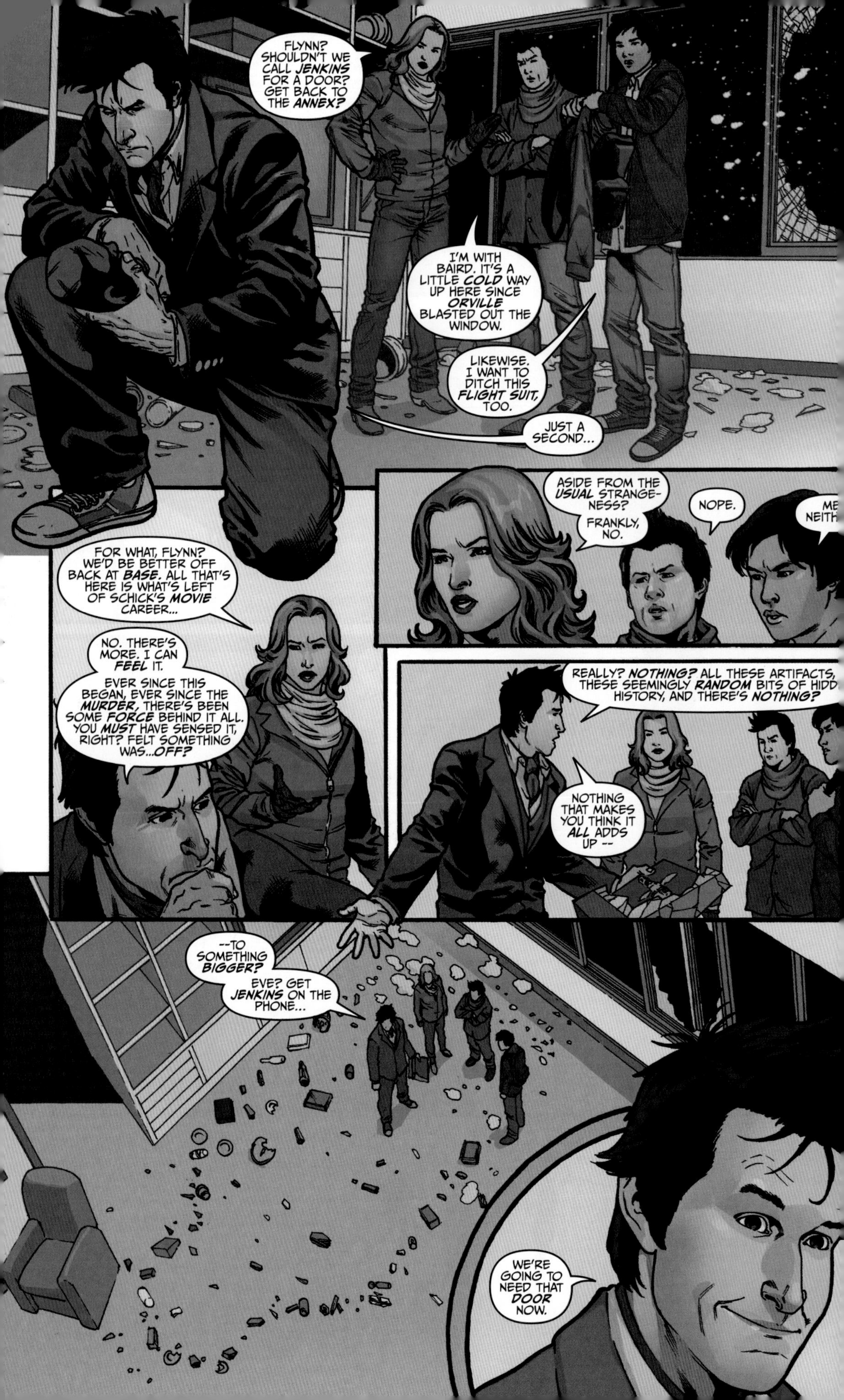
FLYNN? SHOULDN'T WE CALL JENKINS FOR A DOOR? GET BACK TO THE ANNEX?
I'M WITH BAIRD. IT'S A LITTLE COLD WAY UP HERE SINCE ORVILLE BLASTED OUT THE WINDOW.
LIKEWISE. I WANT TO DITCH THIS FLIGHT SUIT, TOO.
JUST A SECOND...
FOR WHAT, FLYNN? WE'D BE BETTER OFF BACK AT BASE. ALL THAT'S HERE IS WHAT'S LEFT OF SCHICK'S MOVIE CAREER...
NO. THERE'S MORE. I CAN FEEL IT.
EVER SINCE THIS BEGAN, EVER SINCE THE MURDER, THERE'S BEEN SOME FORCE BEHIND IT ALL. YOU MUST HAVE SENSED IT, RIGHT? FELT SOMETHING WAS...OFF?
ASIDE FROM THE USUAL STRANGE-NESS?
FRANKLY, NO.
NOPE.
ME NEITH
REALLY? NOTHING? ALL THESE ARTIFACTS, THESE SEEMINGLY RANDOM BITS OF HIDD HISTORY, AND THERE'S NOTHING?
NOTHING THAT MAKES YOU THINK IT ALL ADDS UP --
--TO SOMETHING BIGGER?
EVE? GET JENKINS ON THE PHONE...
WE'RE GOING TO NEED THAT DOOR NOW.

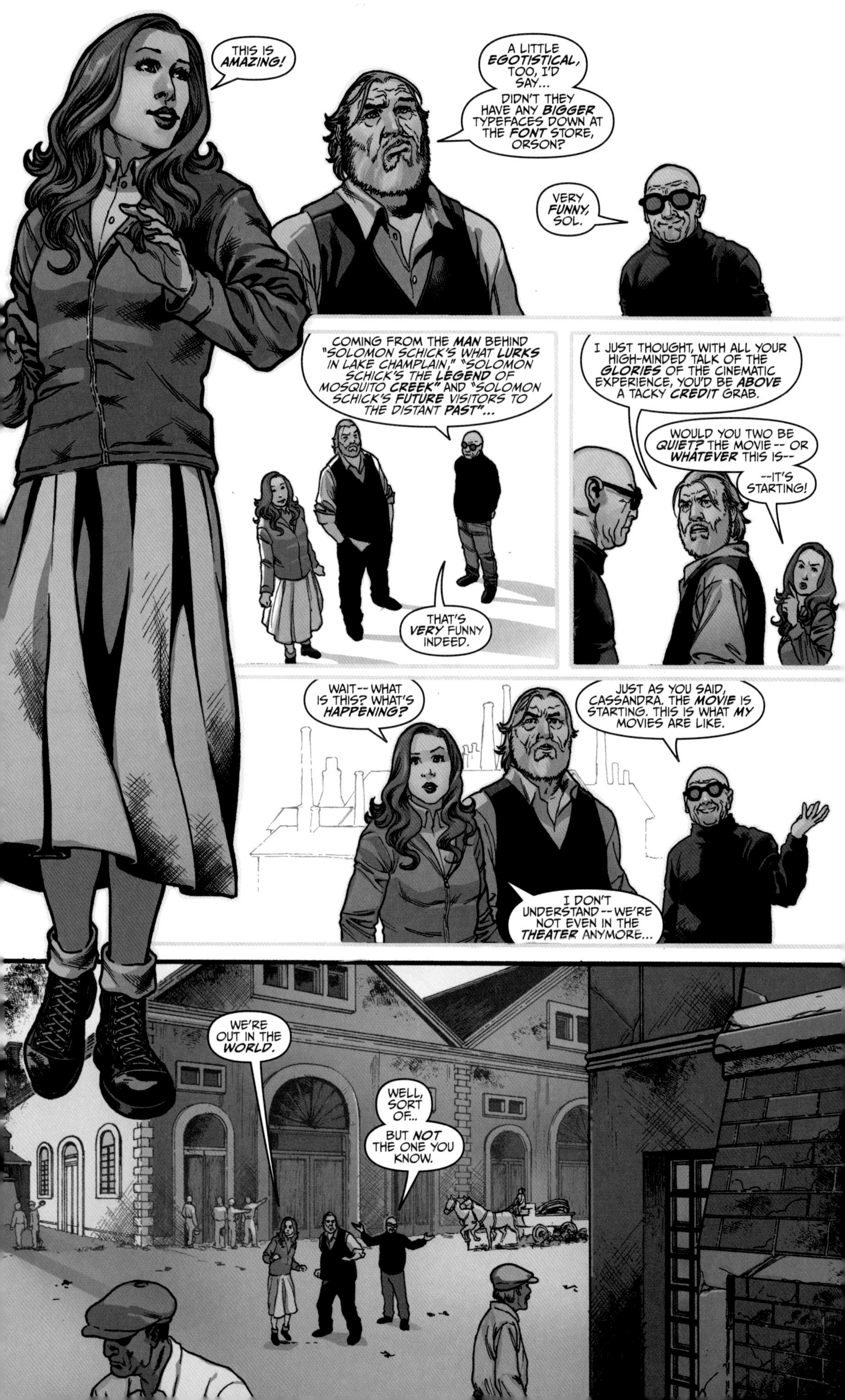
THIS IS AMAZING!
A LITTLE EGOTISTICAL, TOO, I'D SAY...
DIDN'T THEY HAVE ANY BIGGER TYPEFACES DOWN AT THE FONT STORE, ORSON?
VERY FUNNY, SOL.
COMING FROM THE MAN BEHIND "SOLOMON SCHICK'S WHAT LURKS IN LAKE CHAMPLAIN," "SOLOMON SCHICK'S THE LEGEND OF MOSQUITO CREEK" AND "SOLOMON SCHICK'S FUTURE VISITORS TO THE DISTANT PAST"...
THAT'S VERY FUNNY INDEED.
I JUST THOUGHT, WITH ALL YOUR HIGH-MINDED TALK OF THE GLORIES OF THE CINEMATIC EXPERIENCE, YOU'D BE ABOVE A TACKY CREDIT GRAB.
WOULD YOU TWO BE QUIET? THE MOVIE -- OR WHATEVER THIS IS--
--IT'S STARTING!
WAIT-- WHAT IS THIS? WHAT'S HAPPENING?
JUST AS YOU SAID, CASSANDRA. THE MOVIE IS STARTING. THIS IS WHAT MY MOVIES ARE LIKE.
I DON'T UNDERSTAND -- WE'RE NOT EVEN IN THE THEATER ANYMORE...
WE'RE OUT IN THE WORLD.
WELL, SORT OF...
BUT NOT THE ONE YOU KNOW.

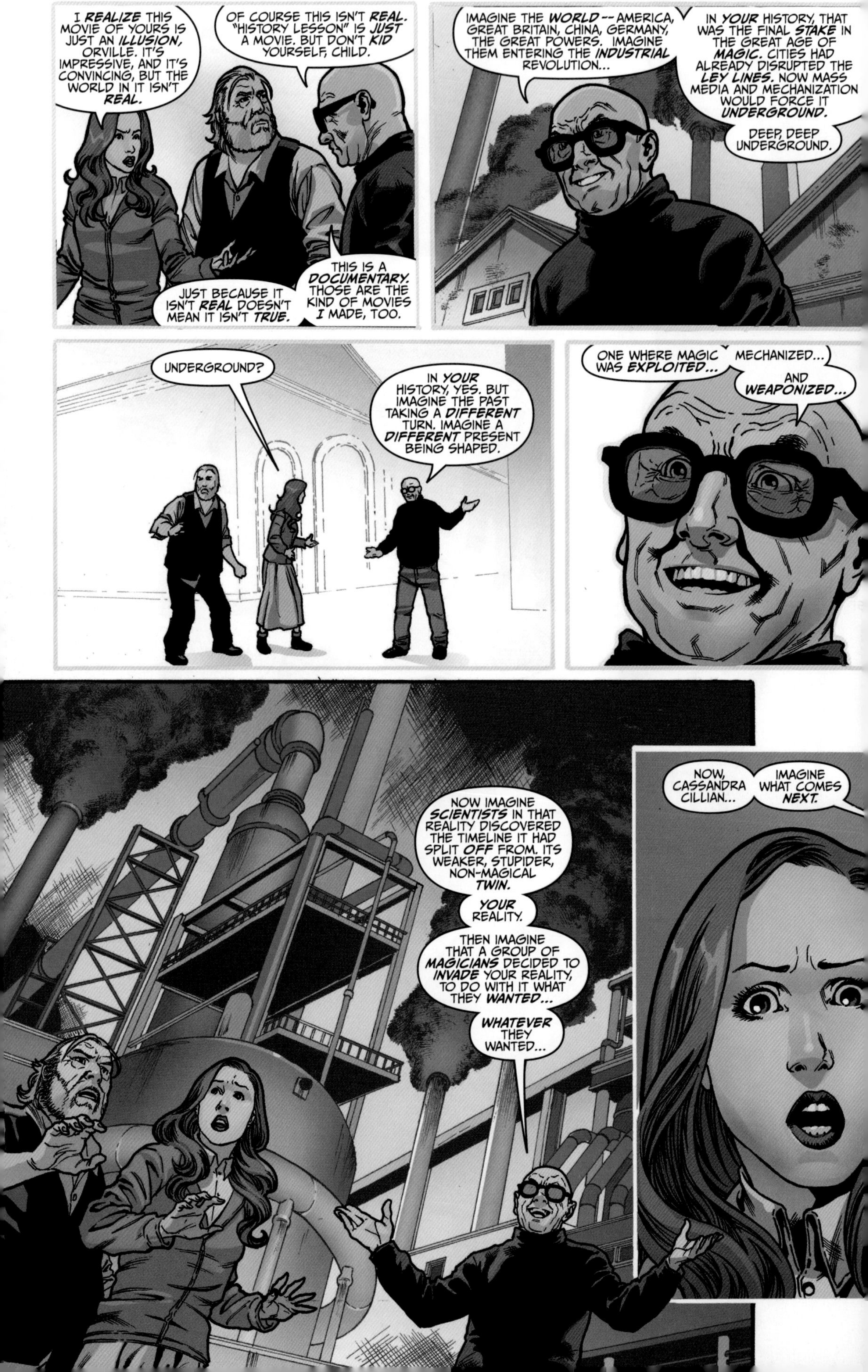
I REALIZE THIS MOVIE OF YOURS IS JUST AN ILLUSION, ORVILLE. IT'S IMPRESSIVE, AND IT'S CONVINCING, BUT THE WORLD IN IT ISN'T REAL.
OF COURSE THIS ISN'T REAL. "HISTORY LESSON" IS JUST A MOVIE. BUT DON'T KID YOURSELF, CHILD.
JUST BECAUSE IT ISN'T REAL DOESN'T MEAN IT ISN'T TRUE.
THIS IS A DOCUMENTARY. THOSE ARE THE KIND OF MOVIES I MADE, TOO.
IMAGINE THE WORLD -- AMERICA, GREAT BRITAIN, CHINA, GERMANY, THE GREAT POWERS. IMAGINE THEM ENTERING THE INDUSTRIAL REVOLUTION...
IN YOUR HISTORY, THAT WAS THE FINAL STAKE IN THE GREAT AGE OF MAGIC. CITIES HAD ALREADY DISRUPTED THE LEY LINES. NOW MASS MEDIA AND MECHANIZATION WOULD FORCE IT UNDERGROUND.
DEEP, DEEP UNDERGROUND.
UNDERGROUND?
IN YOUR HISTORY, YES. BUT IMAGINE THE PAST TAKING A DIFFERENT TURN. IMAGINE A DIFFERENT PRESENT BEING SHAPED.
ONE WHERE MAGIC WAS EXPLOITED...
MECHANIZED...
AND WEAPONIZED...
NOW IMAGINE SCIENTISTS IN THAT REALITY DISCOVERED THE TIMELINE IT HAD SPLIT OFF FROM. ITS WEAKER, STUPIDER, NON-MAGICAL TWIN.
YOUR REALITY.
THEN IMAGINE THAT A GROUP OF MAGICIANS DECIDED TO INVADE YOUR REALITY, TO DO WITH IT WHAT THEY WANTED...
WHATEVER THEY WANTED...
NOW, CASSANDRA CILLIAN...
IMAGINE WHAT COMES NEXT.

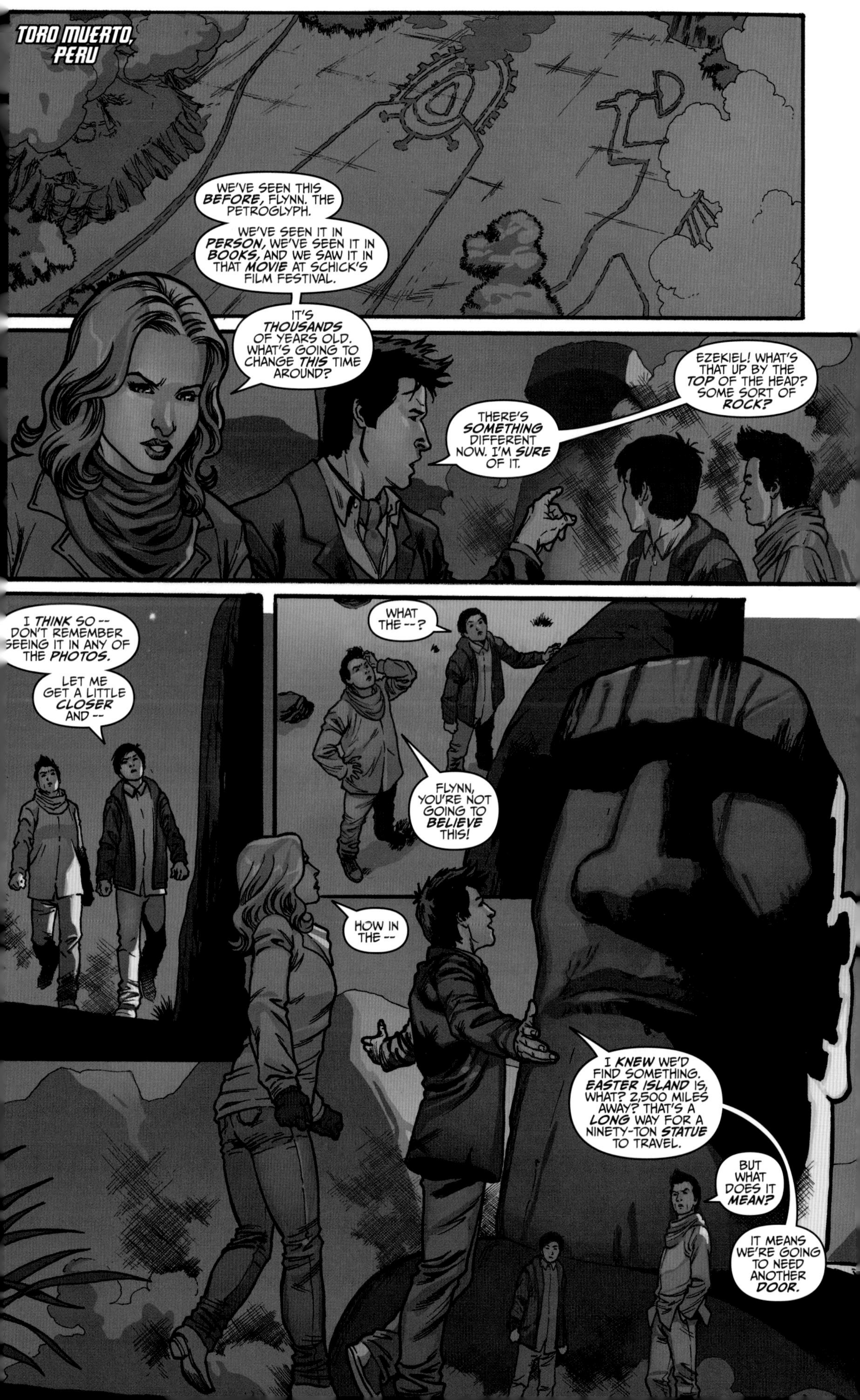
TORO MUERTO, PERU
WE'VE SEEN THIS BEFORE, FLYNN. THE PETROGLYPH.
WE'VE SEEN IT IN PERSON, WE'VE SEEN IT IN BOOKS, AND WE SAW IT IN THAT MOVIE AT SCHICK'S FILM FESTIVAL.
IT'S THOUSANDS OF YEARS OLD. WHAT'S GOING TO CHANGE THIS TIME AROUND?
THERE'S SOMETHING DIFFERENT NOW. I'M SURE OF IT.
EZEKIEL! WHAT'S THAT UP BY THE TOP OF THE HEAD? SOME SORT OF ROCK?
I THINK SO -- DON'T REMEMBER SEEING IT IN ANY OF THE PHOTOS.
LET ME GET A LITTLE CLOSER AND --
WHAT THE --?
FLYNN, YOU'RE NOT GOING TO BELIEVE THIS!
HOW IN THE --
I KNEW WE'D FIND SOMETHING. EASTER ISLAND IS, WHAT? 2,500 MILES AWAY? THAT'S A LONG WAY FOR A NINETY-TON STATUE TO TRAVEL.
BUT WHAT DOES IT MEAN?
IT MEANS WE'RE GOING TO NEED ANOTHER DOOR.

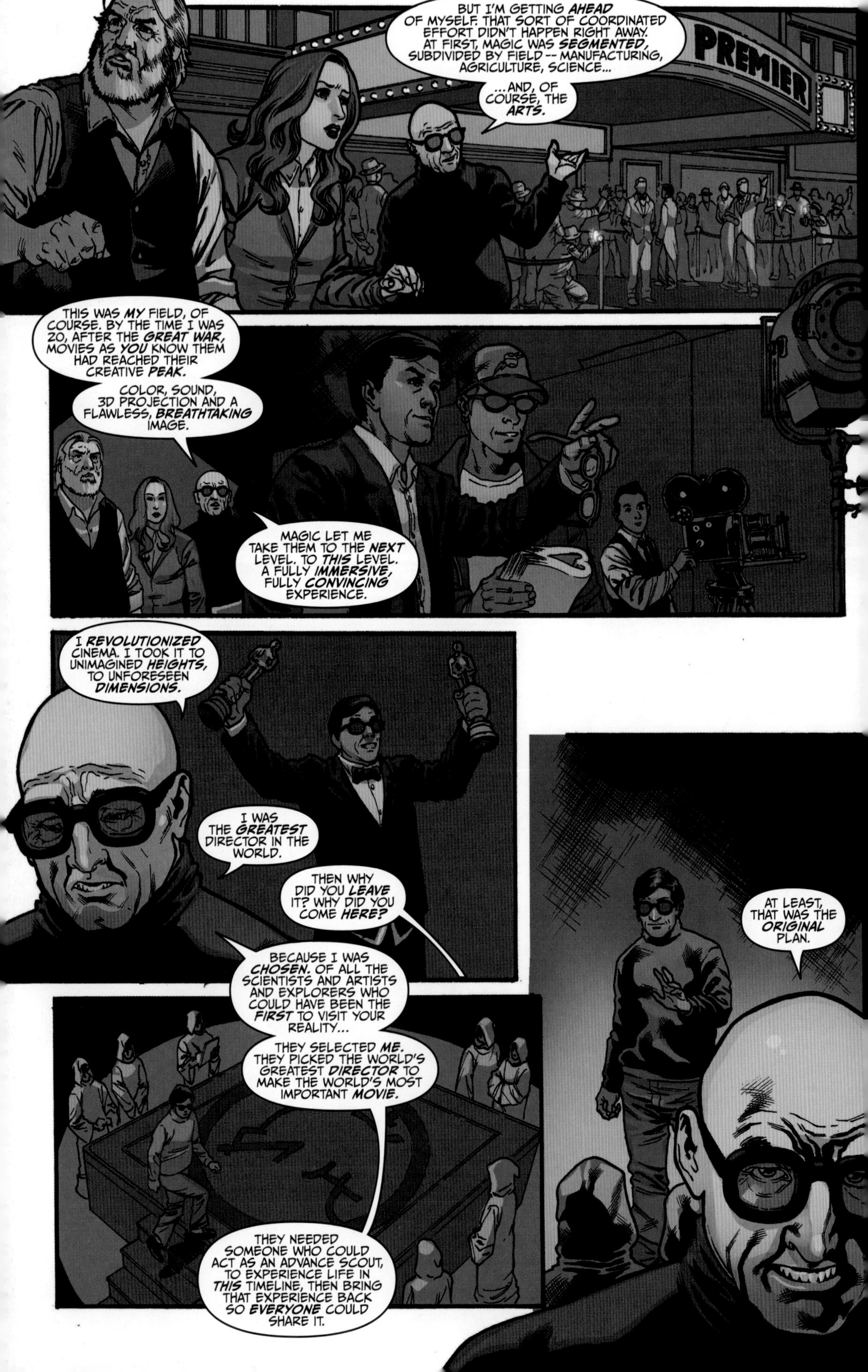
BUT I'M GETTING AHEAD OF MYSELF. THAT SORT OF COORDINATED EFFORT DIDN'T HAPPEN RIGHT AWAY. AT FIRST, MAGIC WAS SEGMENTED, SUBDIVIDED BY FIELD -- MANUFACTURING, AGRICULTURE, SCIENCE...
...AND, OF COURSE, THE ARTS.
PREMIER
THIS WAS MY FIELD, OF COURSE. BY THE TIME I WAS 20, AFTER THE GREAT WAR, MOVIES AS YOU KNOW THEM HAD REACHED THEIR CREATIVE PEAK.
COLOR, SOUND, 3D PROJECTION AND A FLAWLESS, BREATHTAKING IMAGE.
MAGIC LET ME TAKE THEM TO THE NEXT LEVEL. TO THIS LEVEL. A FULLY IMMERSIVE, FULLY CONVINCING EXPERIENCE.
I REVOLUTIONIZED CINEMA. I TOOK IT TO UNIMAGINED HEIGHTS, TO UNFORESEEN DIMENSIONS.
I WAS THE GREATEST DIRECTOR IN THE WORLD.
THEN WHY DID YOU LEAVE IT? WHY DID YOU COME HERE?
BECAUSE I WAS CHOSEN. OF ALL THE SCIENTISTS AND ARTISTS AND EXPLORERS WHO COULD HAVE BEEN THE FIRST TO VISIT YOUR REALITY...
THEY SELECTED ME. THEY PICKED THE WORLD'S GREATEST DIRECTOR TO MAKE THE WORLD'S MOST IMPORTANT MOVIE.
THEY NEEDED SOMEONE WHO COULD ACT AS AN ADVANCE SCOUT, TO EXPERIENCE LIFE IN THIS TIMELINE, THEN BRING THAT EXPERIENCE BACK SO EVERYONE COULD SHARE IT.
AT LEAST, THAT WAS THE ORIGINAL PLAN.

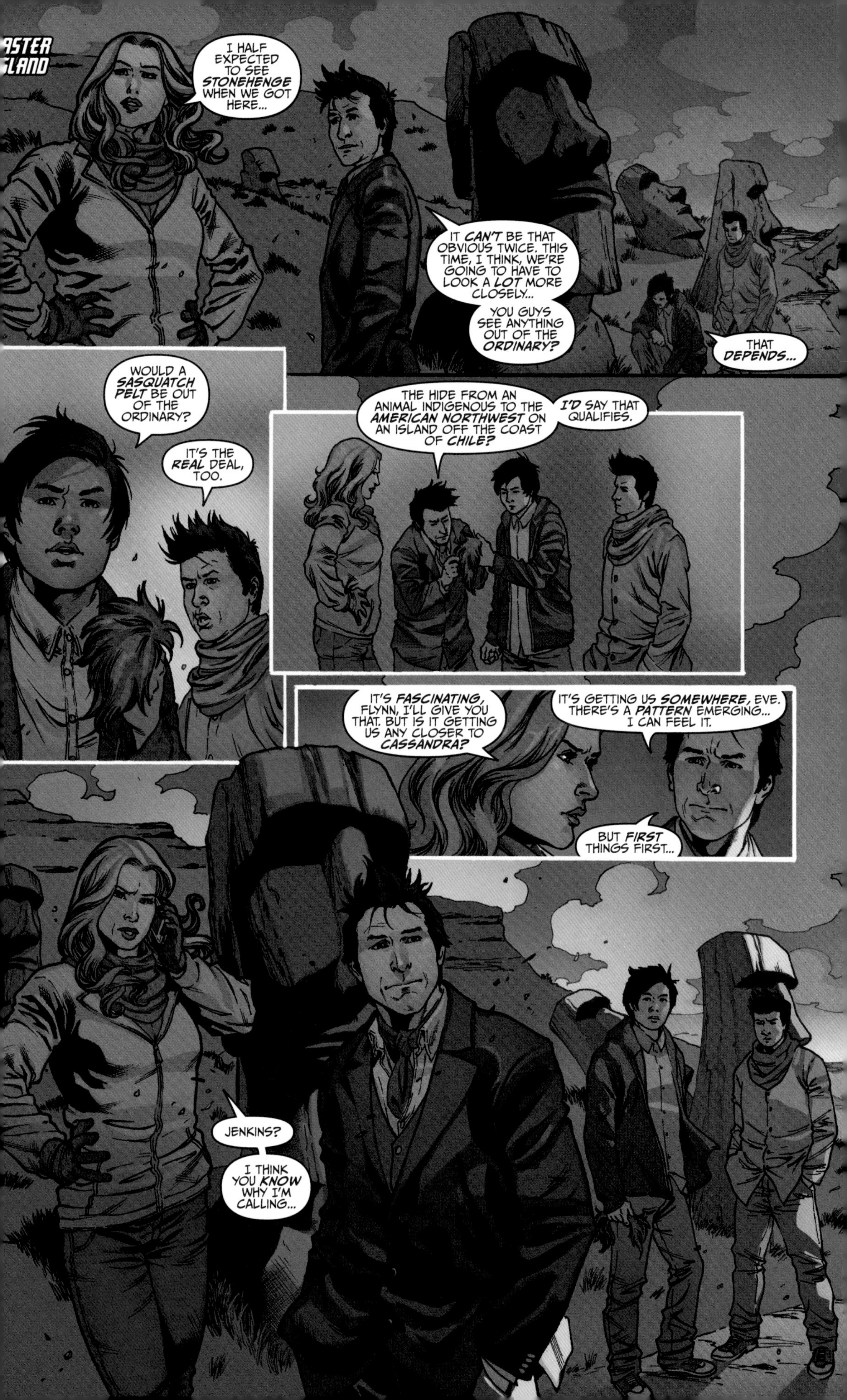
ASTER
ILAND
I HALF EXPECTED TO SEE STONEHENGE WHEN WE GOT HERE...
IT CAN'T BE THAT OBVIOUS TWICE. THIS TIME, I THINK, WE'RE GOING TO HAVE TO LOOK A LOT MORE CLOSELY...
YOU GUYS SEE ANYTHING OUT OF THE ORDINARY?
THAT DEPENDS...
WOULD A SASQUATCH PELT BE OUT OF THE ORDINARY?
IT'S THE REAL DEAL, TOO.
THE HIDE FROM AN ANIMAL INDIGENOUS TO THE AMERICAN NORTHWEST ON AN ISLAND OFF THE COAST OF CHILE?
I'D SAY THAT QUALIFIES.
IT'S FASCINATING, FLYNN, I'LL GIVE YOU THAT. BUT IS IT GETTING US ANY CLOSER TO CASSANDRA?
IT'S GETTING US SOMEWHERE, EVE. THERE'S A PATTERN EMERGING... I CAN FEEL IT.
BUT FIRST THINGS FIRST...
JENKINS?
I THINK YOU KNOW WHY I'M CALLING...

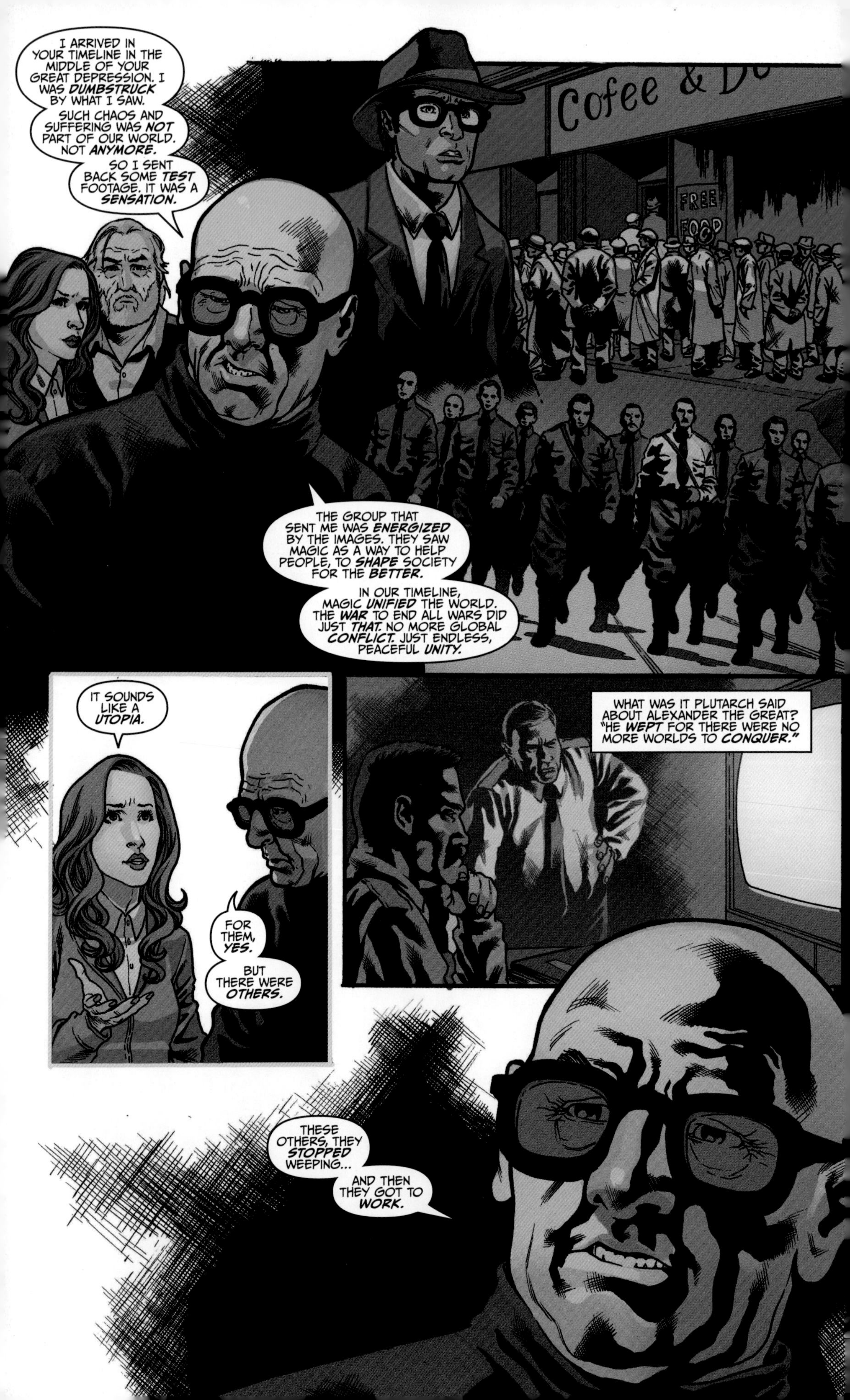

I ARRIVED IN YOUR TIMELINE IN THE MIDDLE OF YOUR GREAT DEPRESSION. I WAS DUMBSTRUCK BY WHAT I SAW.
SUCH CHAOS AND SUFFERING WAS NOT PART OF OUR WORLD. NOT ANYMORE.
SO I SENT BACK SOME TEST FOOTAGE. IT WAS A SENSATION.
Cofee & Do
FREE FOOD
THE GROUP THAT SENT ME WAS ENERGIZED BY THE IMAGES. THEY SAW MAGIC AS A WAY TO HELP PEOPLE, TO SHAPE SOCIETY FOR THE BETTER.
IN OUR TIMELINE, MAGIC UNIFIED THE WORLD. THE WAR TO END ALL WARS DID JUST THAT. NO MORE GLOBAL CONFLICT. JUST ENDLESS, PEACEFUL UNITY.
IT SOUNDS LIKE A UTOPIA.
FOR THEM, YES.
BUT THERE WERE OTHERS.
WHAT WAS IT PLUTARCH SAID ABOUT ALEXANDER THE GREAT? "HE WEPT FOR THERE WERE NO MORE WORLDS TO CONQUER."
THESE OTHERS, THEY STOPPED WEEPING...
AND THEN THEY GOT TO WORK.

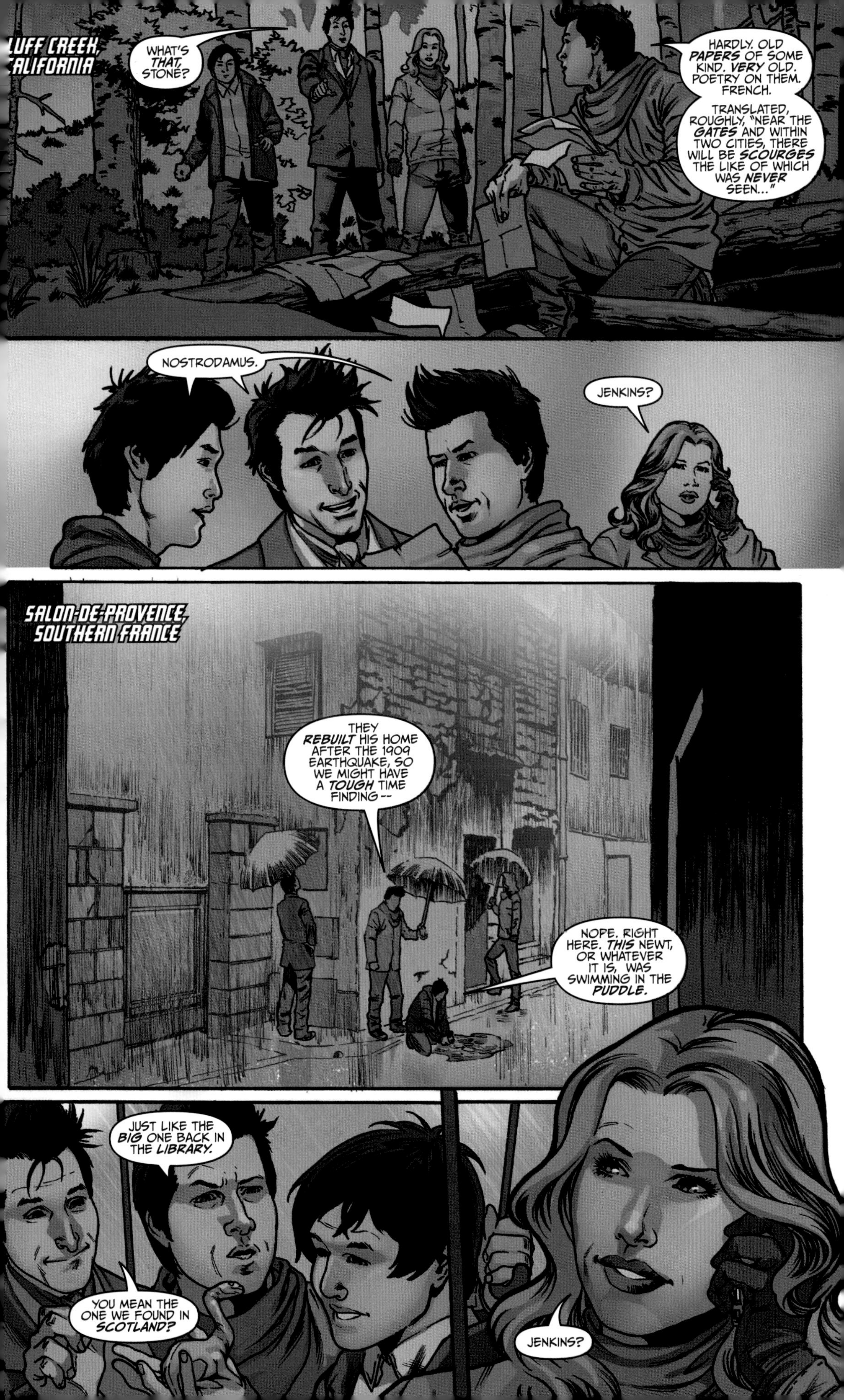
LUFF CREEK, CALIFORNIA
WHAT'S THAT, STONE?
HARDLY. OLD PAPERS OF SOME KIND. VERY OLD. POETRY ON THEM. FRENCH.
TRANSLATED, ROUGHLY, "NEAR THE GATES AND WITHIN TWO CITIES, THERE WILL BE SCOURGES THE LIKE OF WHICH WAS NEVER SEEN..."
NOSTRODAMUS.
JENKINS?
SALON-DE-PROVENCE, SOUTHERN FRANCE
THEY REBUILT HIS HOME AFTER THE 1909 EARTHQUAKE, SO WE MIGHT HAVE A TOUGH TIME FINDING--
NOPE. RIGHT HERE. THIS NEWT, OR WHATEVER IT IS, WAS SWIMMING IN THE PUDDLE.
JUST LIKE THE BIG ONE BACK IN THE LIBRARY.
YOU MEAN THE ONE WE FOUND IN SCOTLAND?
JENKINS?

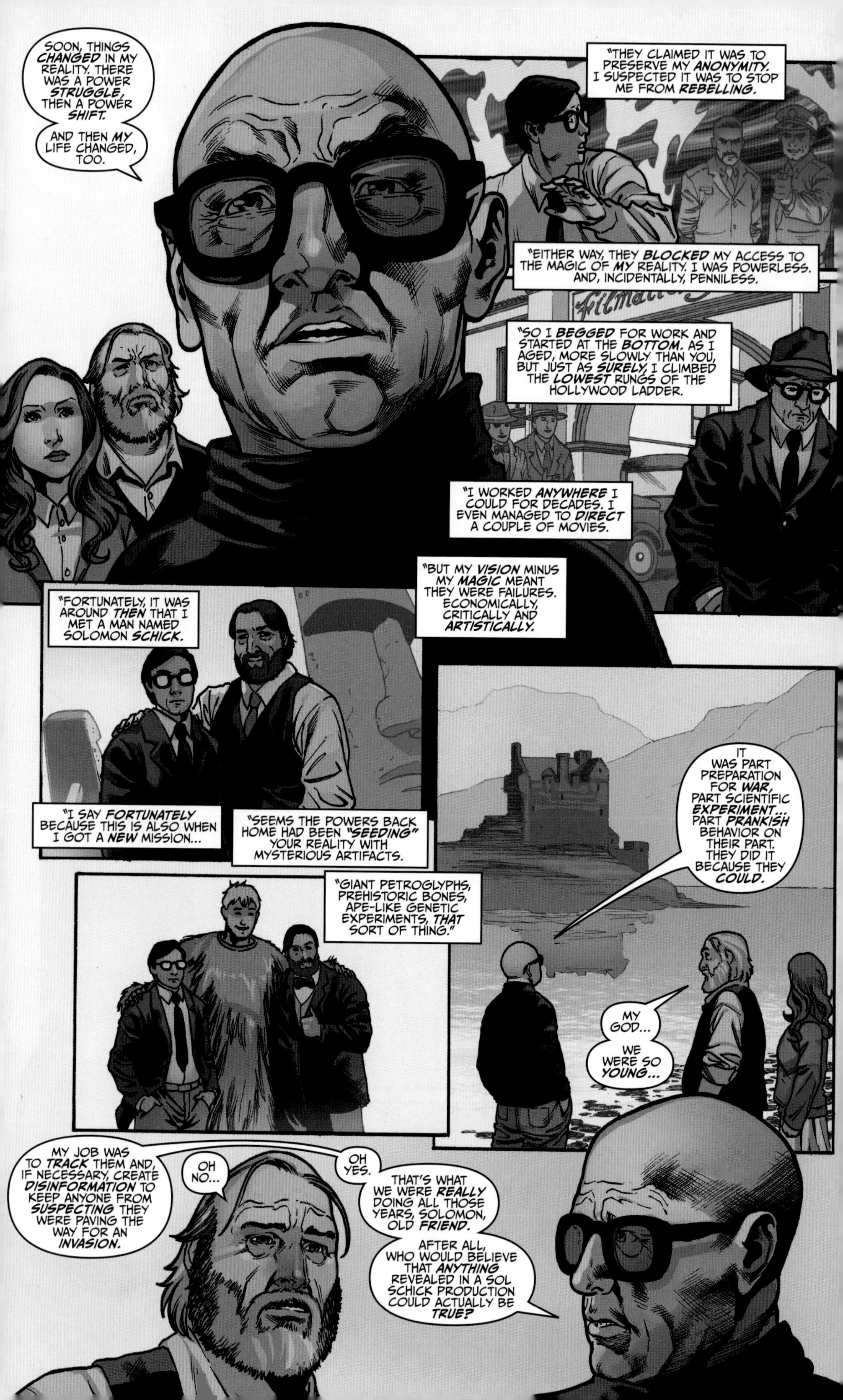

SOON, THINGS CHANGED IN MY REALITY. THERE WAS A POWER STRUGGLE, THEN A POWER SHIFT.
AND THEN MY LIFE CHANGED, TOO.
"THEY CLAIMED IT WAS TO PRESERVE MY ANONYMITY. I SUSPECTED IT WAS TO STOP ME FROM REBELLING.
"EITHER WAY, THEY BLOCKED MY ACCESS TO THE MAGIC OF MY REALITY. I WAS POWERLESS. AND, INCIDENTALLY, PENNILESS.
"SO I BEGGED FOR WORK AND STARTED AT THE BOTTOM. AS I AGED, MORE SLOWLY THAN YOU, BUT JUST AS SURELY, I CLIMBED THE LOWEST RUNGS OF THE HOLLYWOOD LADDER.
"I WORKED ANYWHERE I COULD FOR DECADES. I EVEN MANAGED TO DIRECT A COUPLE OF MOVIES.
"BUT MY VISION MINUS MY MAGIC MEANT THEY WERE FAILURES. ECONOMICALLY, CRITICALLY AND ARTISTICALLY.
"FORTUNATELY, IT WAS AROUND THEN THAT I MET A MAN NAMED SOLOMON SCHICK.
"I SAY FORTUNATELY BECAUSE THIS IS ALSO WHEN I GOT A NEW MISSION...
"SEEMS THE POWERS BACK HOME HAD BEEN "SEEDING" YOUR REALITY WITH MYSTERIOUS ARTIFACTS.
"GIANT PETROGLYPHS, PREHISTORIC BONES, APE-LIKE GENETIC EXPERIMENTS, THAT SORT OF THING."
IT WAS PART PREPARATION FOR WAR, PART SCIENTIFIC EXPERIMENT... PART PRANKISH BEHAVIOR ON THEIR PART. THEY DID IT BECAUSE THEY COULD.
MY GOD...
WE WERE SO YOUNG...
MY JOB WAS TO TRACK THEM AND, IF NECESSARY, CREATE DISINFORMATION TO KEEP ANYONE FROM SUSPECTING THEY WERE PAVING THE WAY FOR AN INVASION.
OH NO...
OH YES.
THAT'S WHAT WE WERE REALLY DOING ALL THOSE YEARS, SOLOMON, OLD FRIEND.
AFTER ALL, WHO WOULD BELIEVE THAT ANYTHING REVEALED IN A SOL SCHICK PRODUCTION COULD ACTUALLY BE TRUE?

...AND THEN, AFTER CADES OF *WAITING*... SPOUTING THAT INANE VEL IN YOUR MOVIES... OF ENDURING A LIFE WITHOUT *MAGIC*...

I *FINALLY* GOT THE WORD.

"THE *RESISTANCE* BACK HOME -- THE ONES WHO *SENT* ME ORIGINALLY -- HAD BEEN DEFEATED AND *IMPRISONED*.

"*IMPRISONED* IN *YOUR* REALITY, IN FACT, WHERE THEY COULD *NO LONGER* STAND IN OUR *WAY*."

...MISTER *SOLOMON SCHICK!*

IMPRISONED? *WHERE?*

NICE TRY. THE POINT IS, THE *LAST* OBSTACLE HAD BEEN *REMOVED*.

I GOT THE *NEWS* JUST AS WE WERE TO FAKE YOUR *DEATH*...

THE *INVASION* COULD BEGIN.

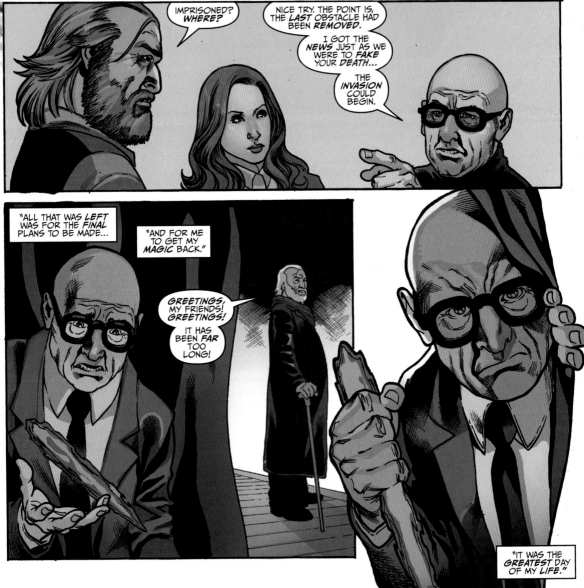

"ALL THAT WAS *LEFT* WAS FOR THE *FINAL* PLANS TO BE MADE...

"AND FOR ME TO GET MY *MAGIC* BACK."

GREETINGS, MY FRIENDS! *GREETINGS!* IT HAS BEEN *FAR* TOO *LONG!*

"IT WAS THE *GREATEST* DAY OF MY *LIFE*."

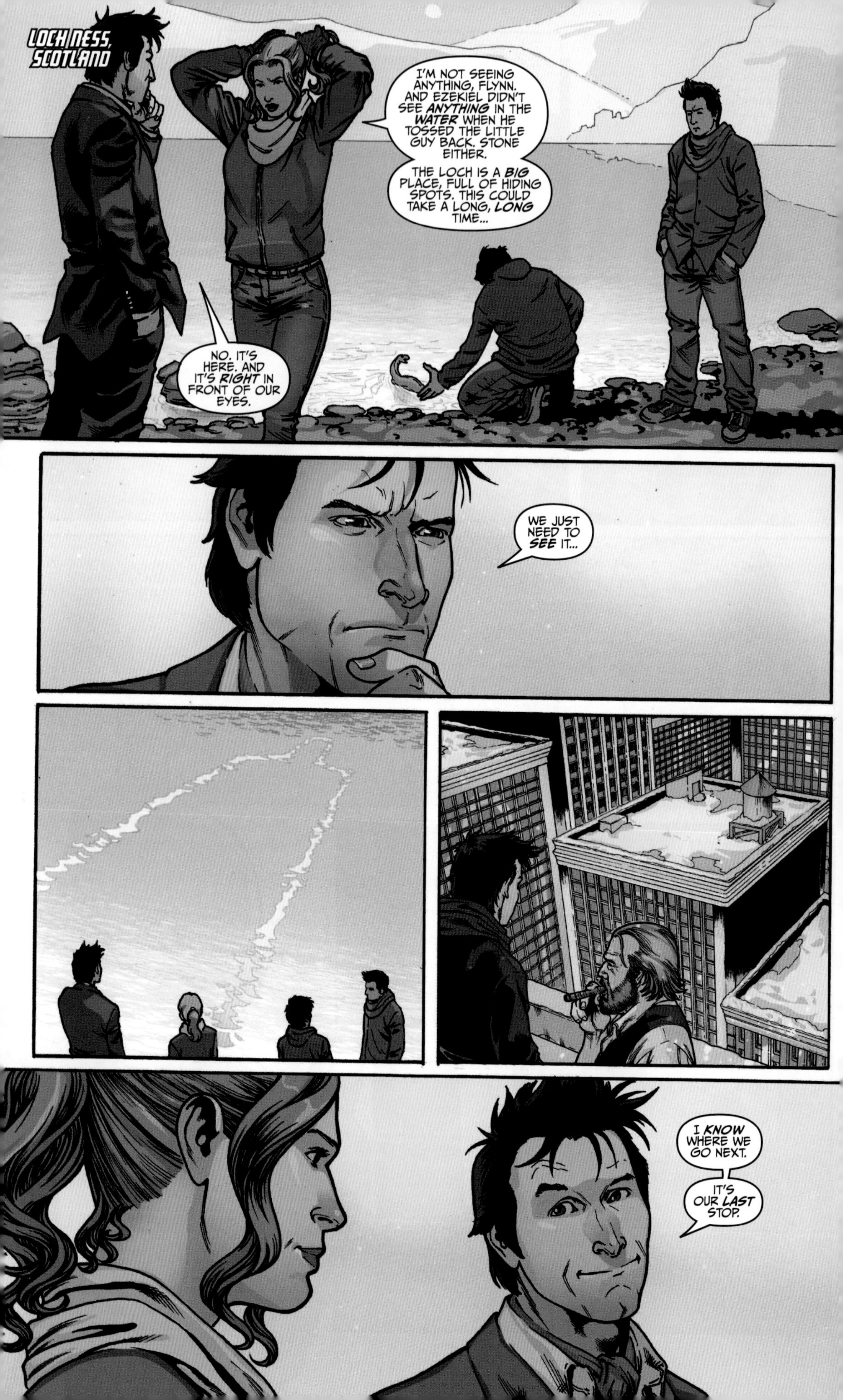
LOCH NESS, SCOTLAND
I'M NOT SEEING ANYTHING, FLYNN. AND EZEKIEL DIDN'T SEE ANYTHING IN THE WATER WHEN HE TOSSED THE LITTLE GUY BACK. STONE EITHER.
THE LOCH IS A BIG PLACE, FULL OF HIDING SPOTS. THIS COULD TAKE A LONG, LONG TIME...
NO. IT'S HERE. AND IT'S RIGHT IN FRONT OF OUR EYES.
WE JUST NEED TO SEE IT...
I KNOW WHERE WE GO NEXT.
IT'S OUR LAST STOP.

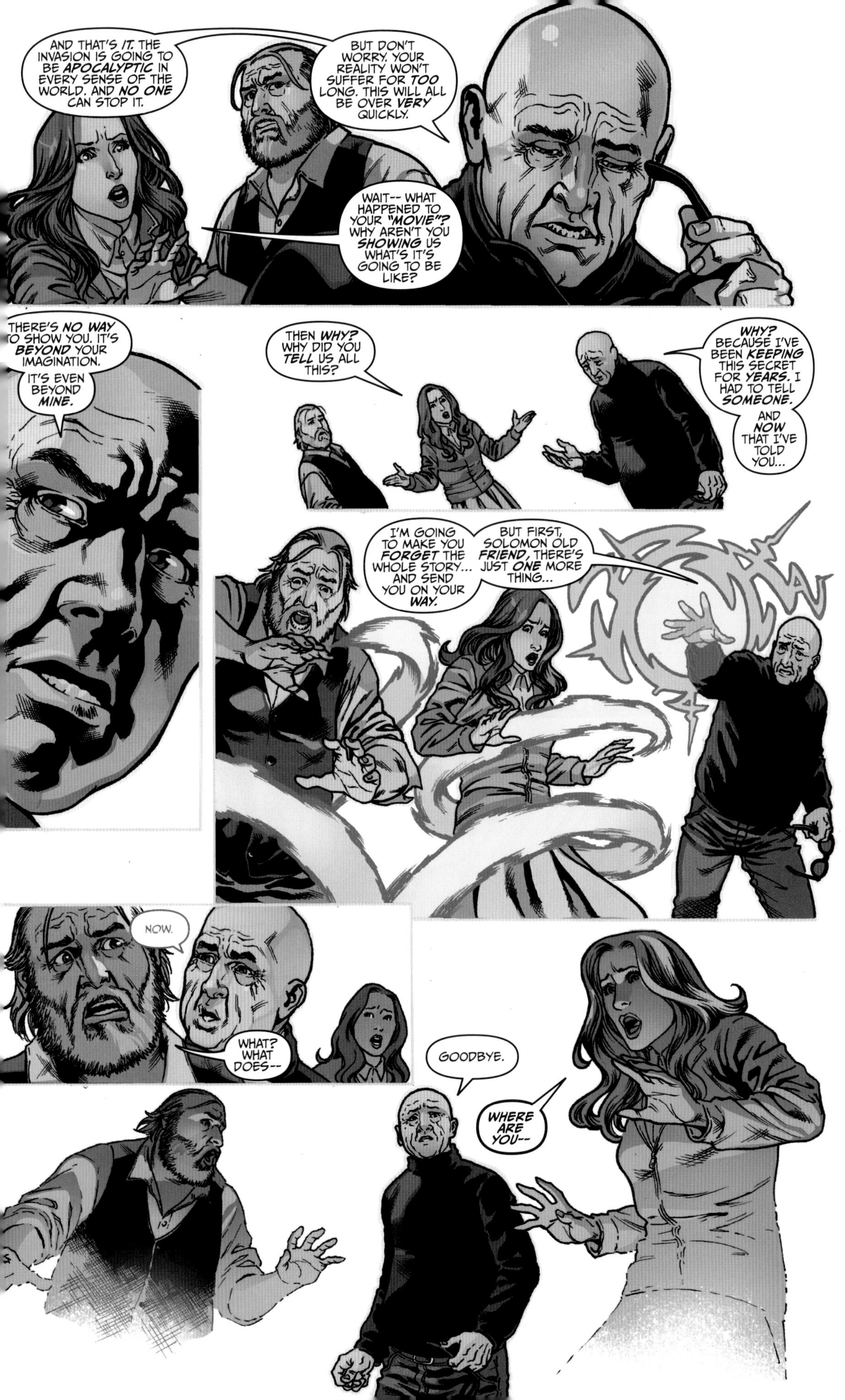
AND THAT'S IT. THE INVASION IS GOING TO BE APOCALYPTIC IN EVERY SENSE OF THE WORLD. AND NO ONE CAN STOP IT.
BUT DON'T WORRY. YOUR REALITY WON'T SUFFER FOR TOO LONG. THIS WILL ALL BE OVER VERY QUICKLY.
WAIT-- WHAT HAPPENED TO YOUR "MOVIE"? WHY AREN'T YOU SHOWING US WHAT'S IT'S GOING TO BE LIKE?
THERE'S NO WAY TO SHOW YOU. IT'S BEYOND YOUR IMAGINATION.
IT'S EVEN BEYOND MINE.
THEN WHY? WHY DID YOU TELL US ALL THIS?
WHY? BECAUSE I'VE BEEN KEEPING THIS SECRET FOR YEARS. I HAD TO TELL SOMEONE.
AND NOW THAT I'VE TOLD YOU...
I'M GOING TO MAKE YOU FORGET THE WHOLE STORY... AND SEND YOU ON YOUR WAY.
BUT FIRST, SOLOMON OLD FRIEND, THERE'S JUST ONE MORE THING...
NOW.
WHAT? WHAT DOES--
GOODBYE.
WHERE ARE YOU--

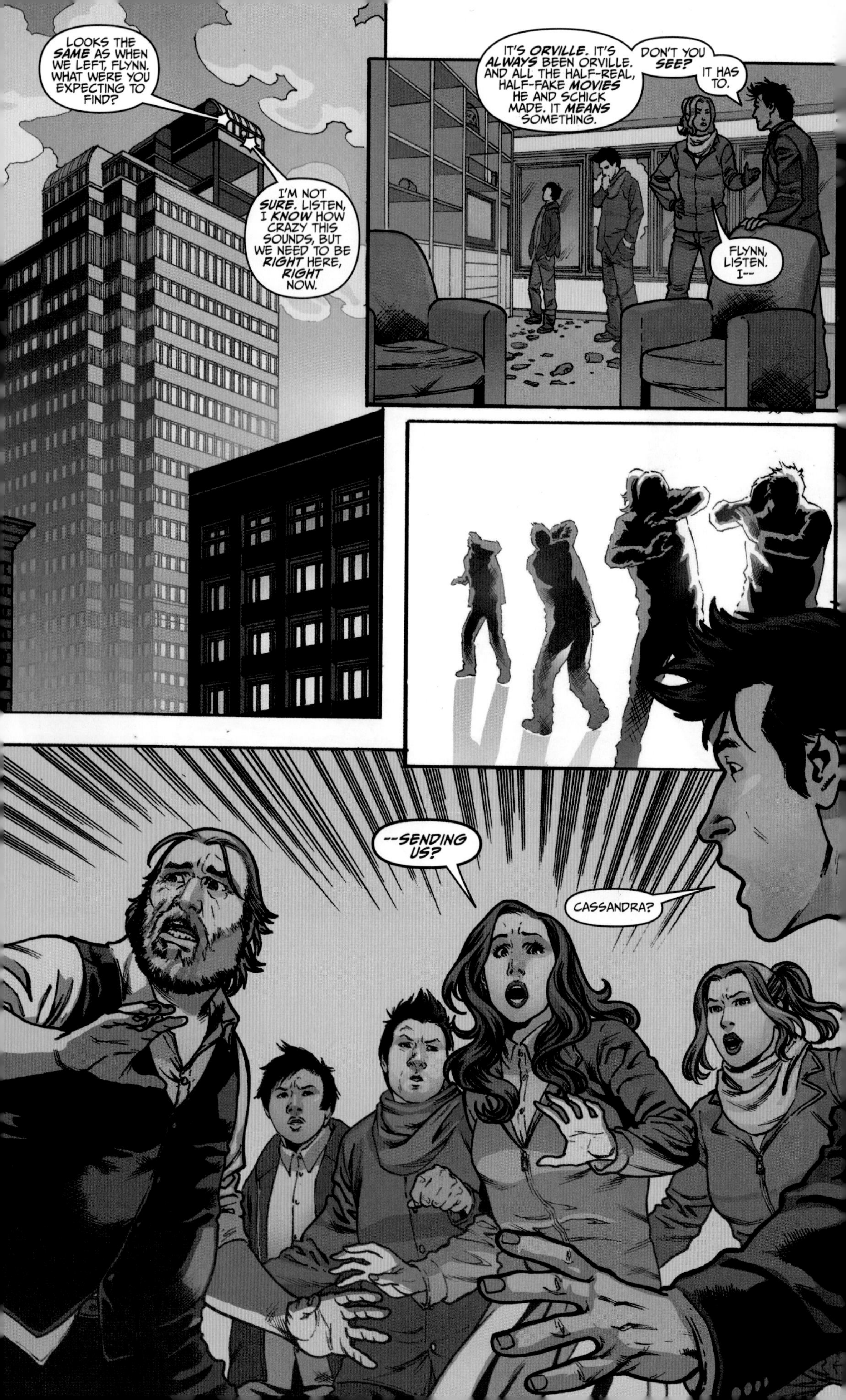
LOOKS THE SAME AS WHEN WE LEFT, FLYNN. WHAT WERE YOU EXPECTING TO FIND?
I'M NOT SURE. LISTEN, I KNOW HOW CRAZY THIS SOUNDS, BUT WE NEED TO BE RIGHT HERE, RIGHT NOW.
IT'S ORVILLE. IT'S ALWAYS BEEN ORVILLE. AND ALL THE HALF-REAL, HALF-FAKE MOVIES HE AND SCHICK MADE. IT MEANS SOMETHING.
DON'T YOU SEE?
IT HAS TO.
FLYNN, LISTEN. I--
--SENDING US?
CASSANDRA?

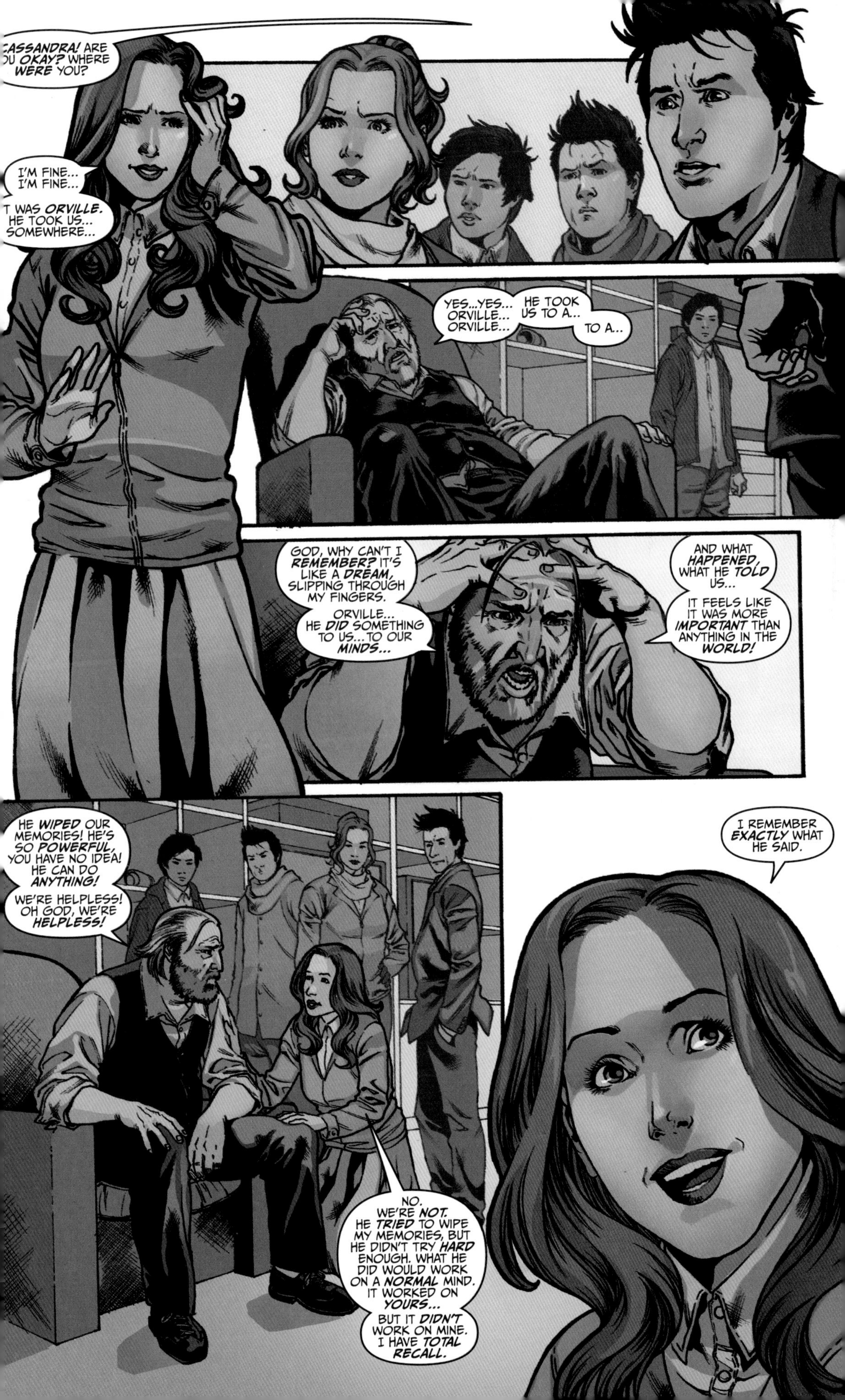

CASSANDRA! ARE OU OKAY? WHERE WERE YOU?
I'M FINE... I'M FINE...
T WAS ORVILLE. HE TOOK US... SOMEWHERE...
YES...YES... ORVILLE... ORVILLE...
HE TOOK US TO A...
TO A...
GOD, WHY CAN'T I REMEMBER? IT'S LIKE A DREAM, SLIPPING THROUGH MY FINGERS.
ORVILLE... HE DID SOMETHING TO US...TO OUR MINDS...
AND WHAT HAPPENED, WHAT HE TOLD US...
IT FEELS LIKE IT WAS MORE IMPORTANT THAN ANYTHING IN THE WORLD!
HE WIPED OUR MEMORIES! HE'S SO POWERFUL, YOU HAVE NO IDEA! HE CAN DO ANYTHING!
WE'RE HELPLESS! OH GOD, WE'RE HELPLESS!
NO. WE'RE NOT. HE TRIED TO WIPE MY MEMORIES, BUT HE DIDN'T TRY HARD ENOUGH. WHAT HE DID WOULD WORK ON A NORMAL MIND. IT WORKED ON YOURS...
BUT IT DIDN'T WORK ON MINE. I HAVE TOTAL RECALL.
I REMEMBER EXACTLY WHAT HE SAID.

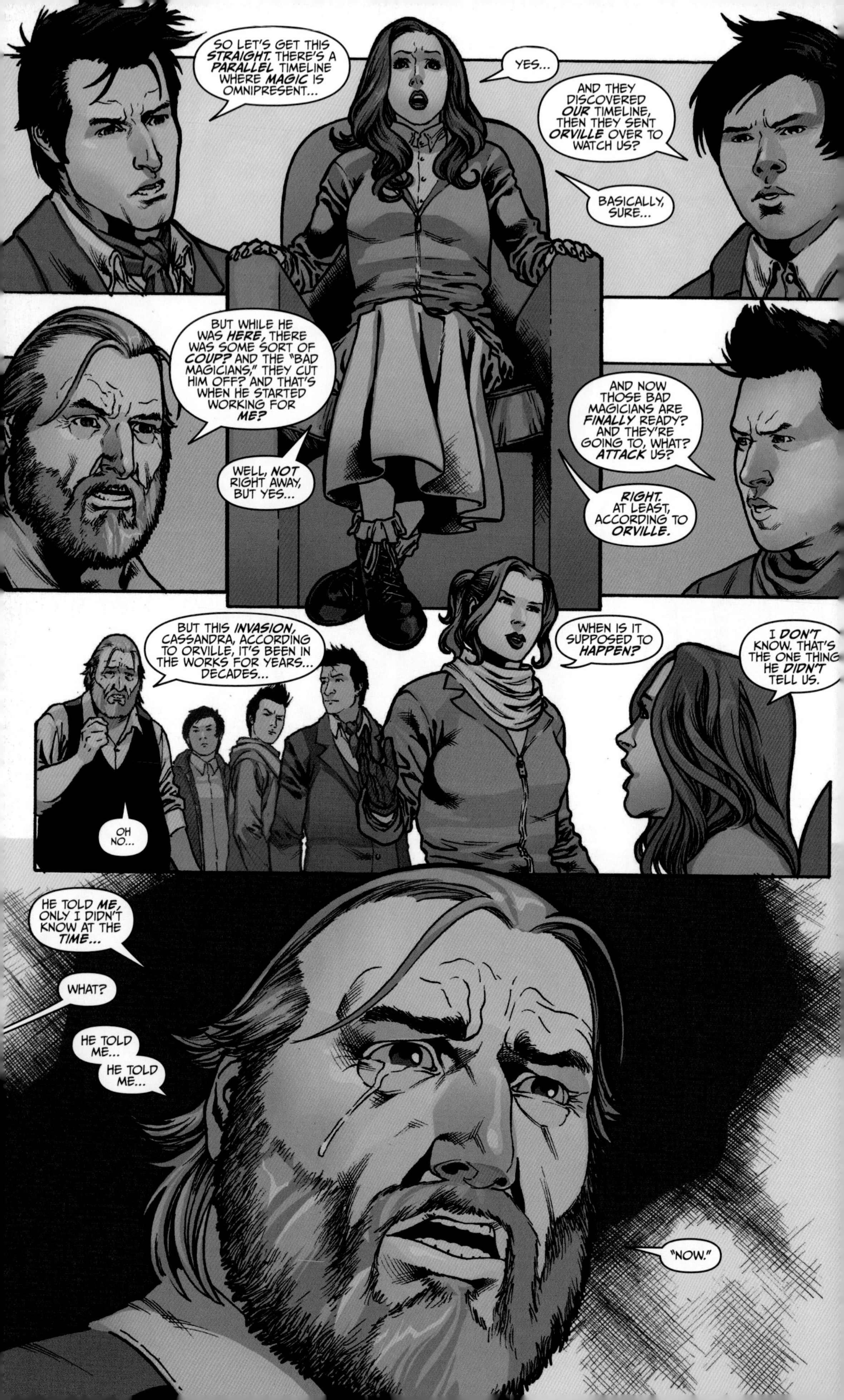
SO LET'S GET THIS STRAIGHT. THERE'S A PARALLEL TIMELINE WHERE MAGIC IS OMNIPRESENT...
YES...
AND THEY DISCOVERED OUR TIMELINE, THEN THEY SENT ORVILLE OVER TO WATCH US?
BASICALLY, SURE...
BUT WHILE HE WAS HERE, THERE WAS SOME SORT OF COUP? AND THE "BAD MAGICIANS," THEY CUT HIM OFF? AND THAT'S WHEN HE STARTED WORKING FOR ME?
WELL, NOT RIGHT AWAY, BUT YES...
AND NOW THOSE BAD MAGICIANS ARE FINALLY READY? AND THEY'RE GOING TO, WHAT? ATTACK US?
RIGHT. AT LEAST, ACCORDING TO ORVILLE.
BUT THIS INVASION, CASSANDRA, ACCORDING TO ORVILLE, IT'S BEEN IN THE WORKS FOR YEARS... DECADES...
WHEN IS IT SUPPOSED TO HAPPEN?
I DON'T KNOW. THAT'S THE ONE THING HE DIDN'T TELL US.
OH NO...
HE TOLD ME, ONLY I DIDN'T KNOW AT THE TIME...
WHAT?
HE TOLD ME...
HE TOLD ME...
"NOW."

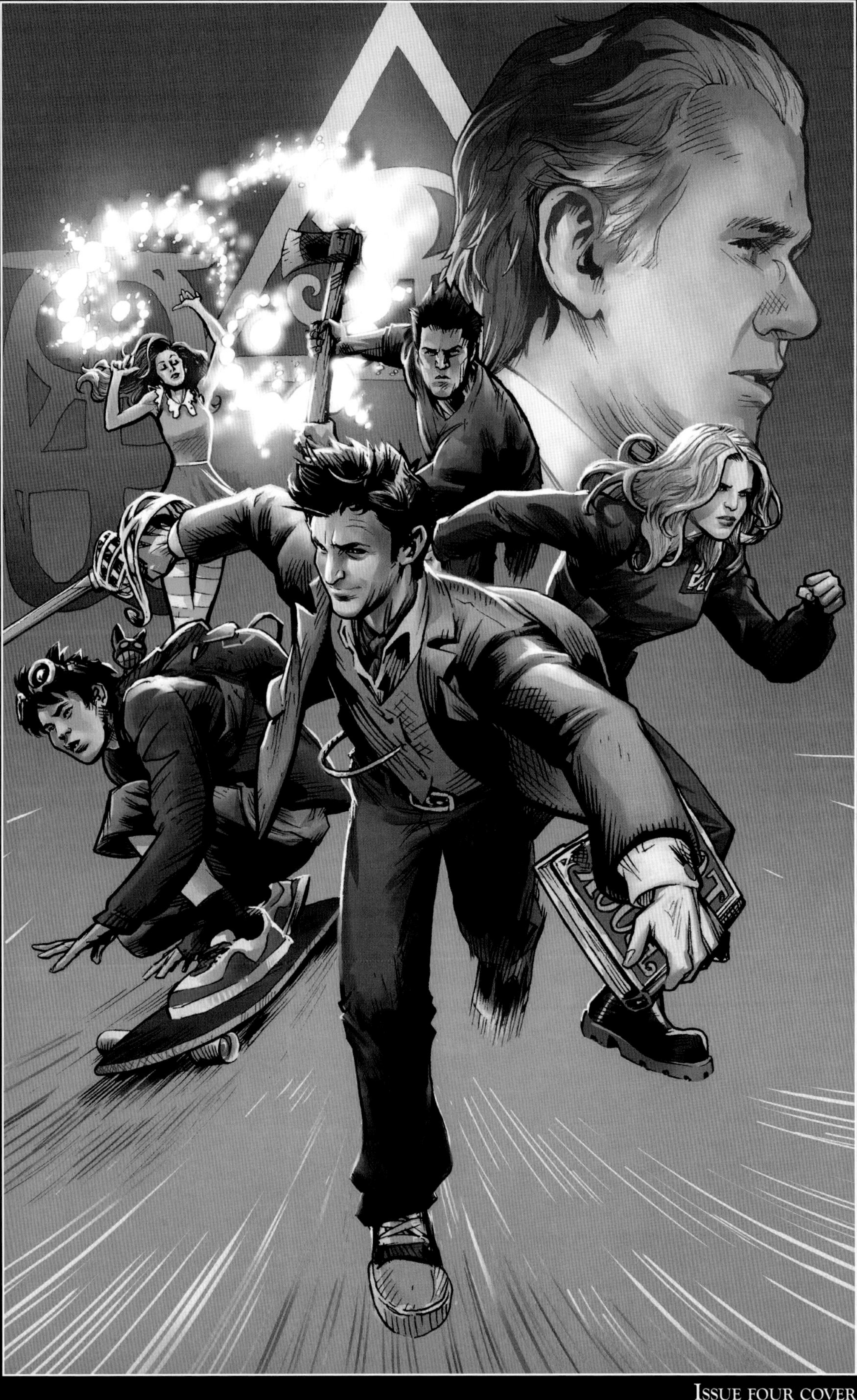

Issue four cover
art by KARL MOLINE

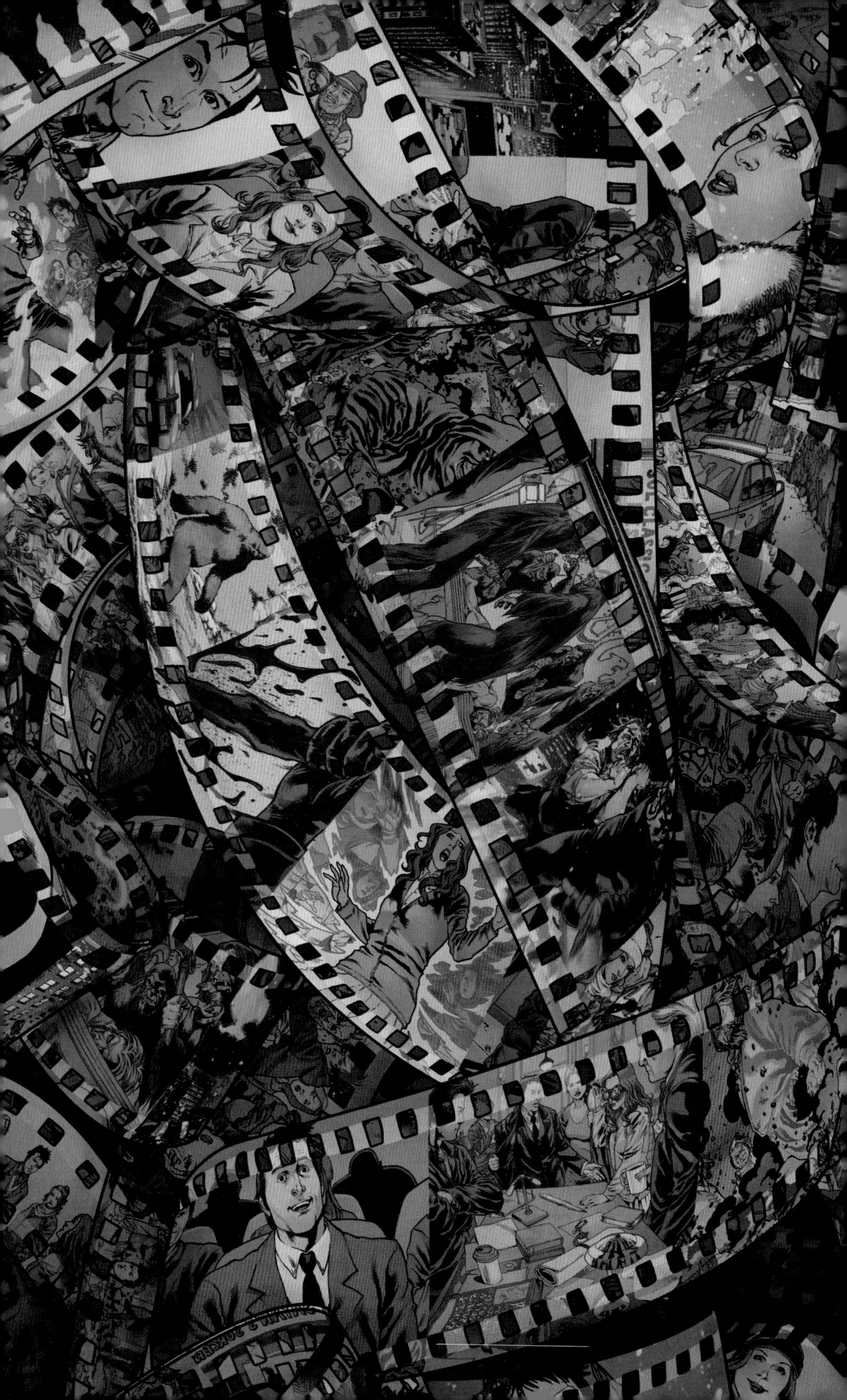

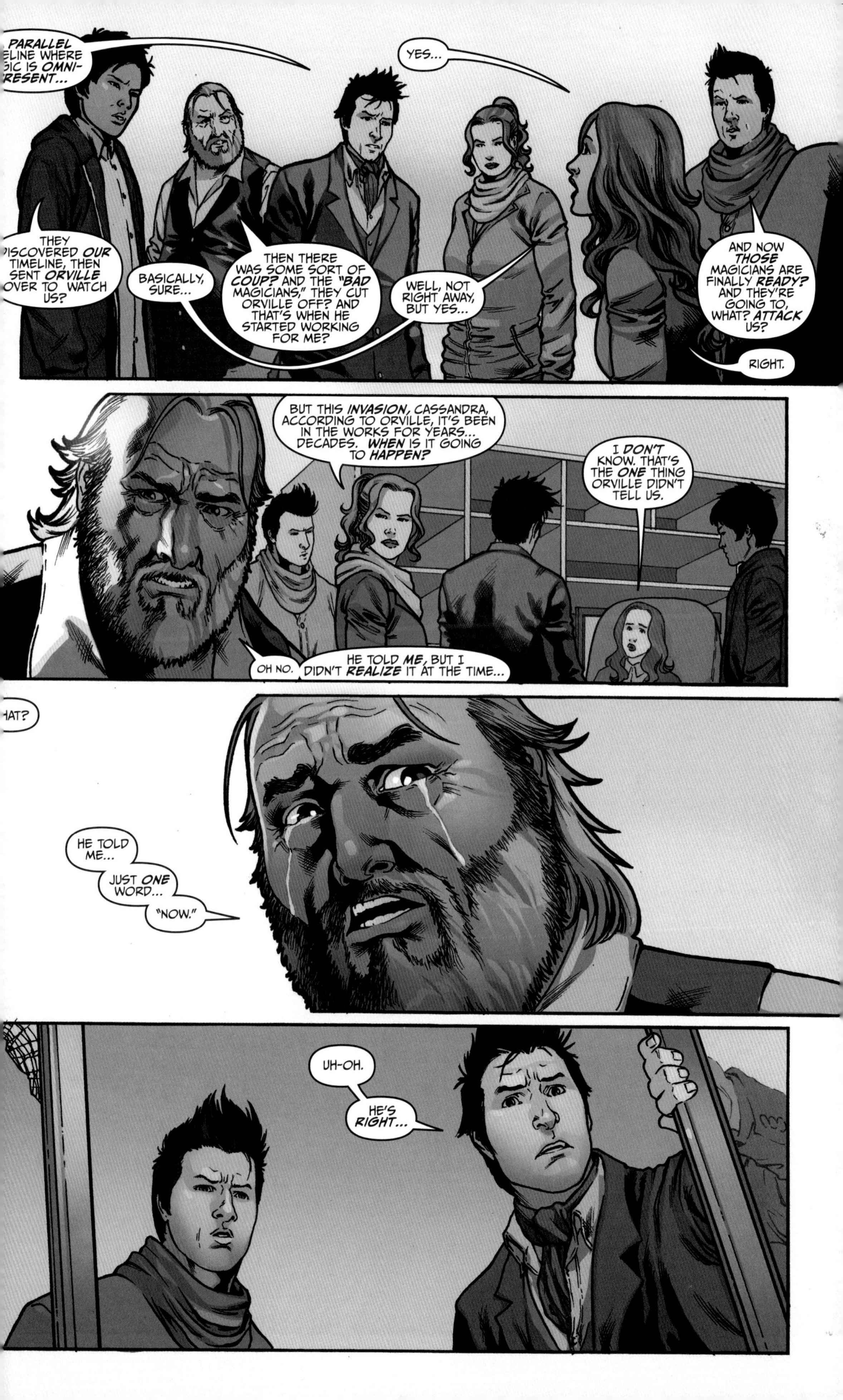
PARALLEL
ELINE WHERE
GIC IS OMNI-
RESENT...
YES...
THEY DISCOVERED OUR TIMELINE, THEN SENT ORVILLE OVER TO WATCH US?
BASICALLY, SURE...
THEN THERE WAS SOME SORT OF COUP? AND THE "BAD MAGICIANS," THEY CUT ORVILLE OFF? AND THAT'S WHEN HE STARTED WORKING FOR ME?
WELL, NOT RIGHT AWAY, BUT YES...
AND NOW THOSE MAGICIANS ARE FINALLY READY? AND THEY'RE GOING TO, WHAT? ATTACK US?
RIGHT.
BUT THIS INVASION, CASSANDRA, ACCORDING TO ORVILLE, IT'S BEEN IN THE WORKS FOR YEARS... DECADES. WHEN IS IT GOING TO HAPPEN?
I DON'T KNOW. THAT'S THE ONE THING ORVILLE DIDN'T TELL US.
OH NO.
HE TOLD ME, BUT I DIDN'T REALIZE IT AT THE TIME...
HAT?
HE TOLD ME...
JUST ONE WORD...
"NOW."
UH-OH.
HE'S RIGHT...

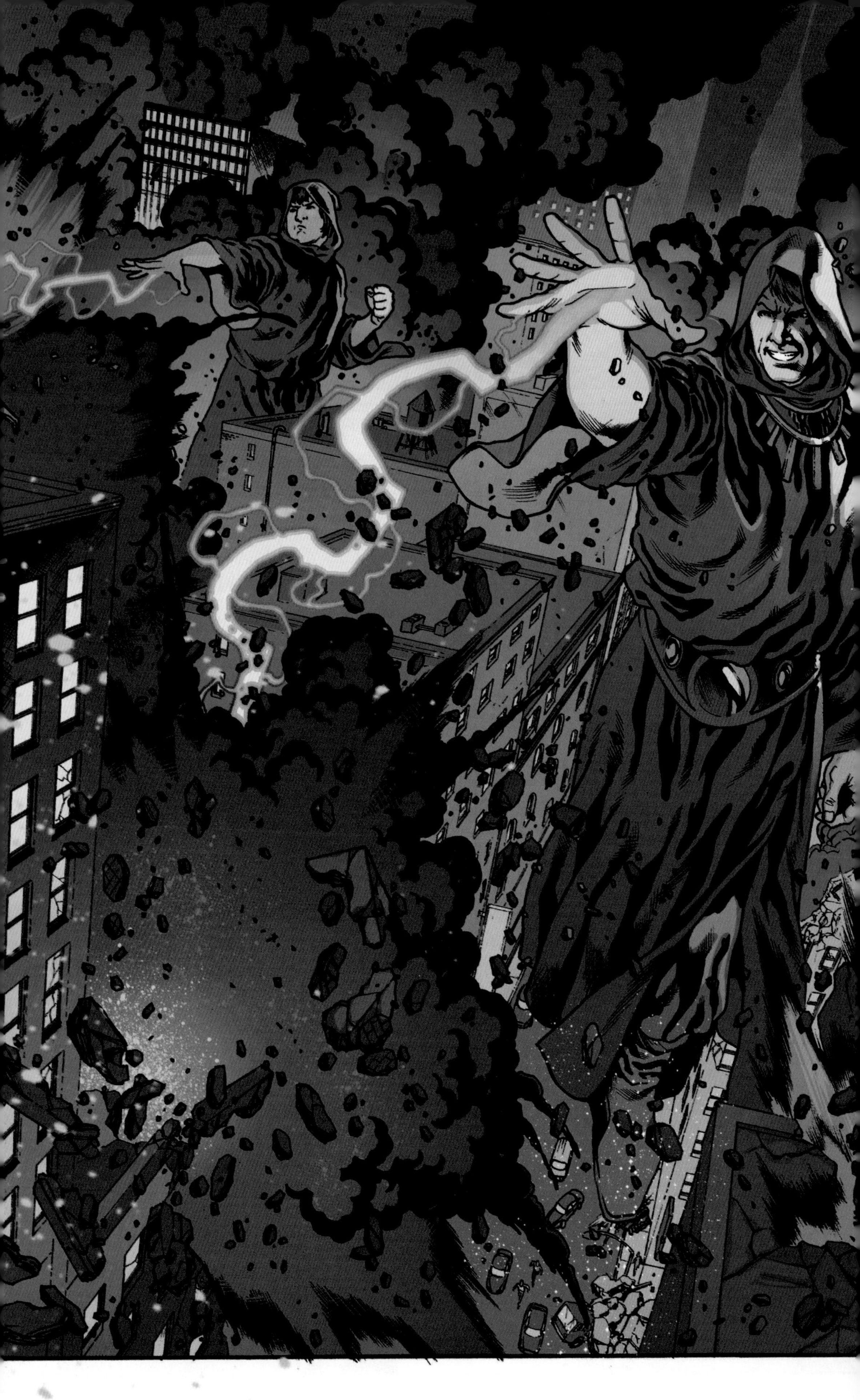

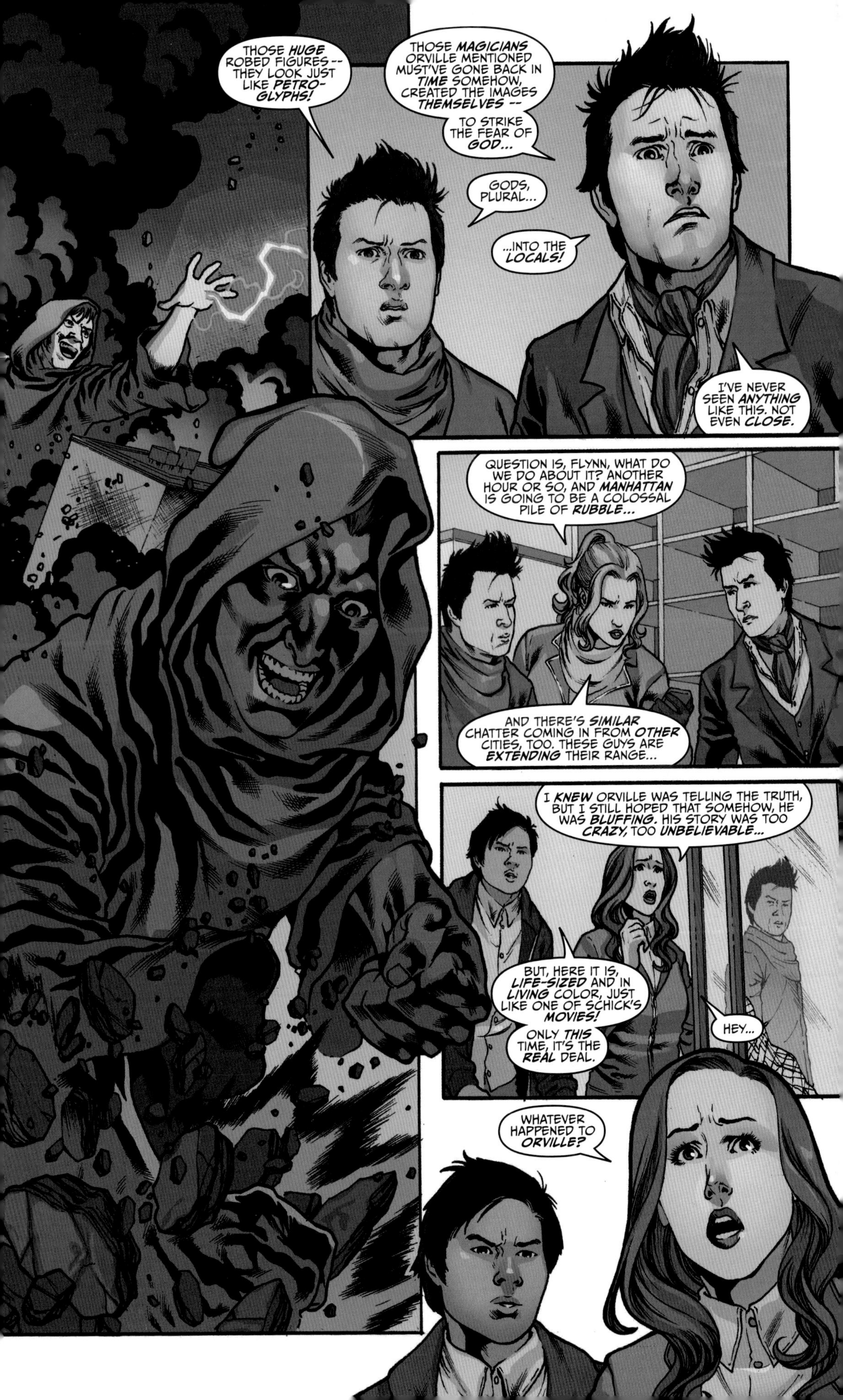
THOSE *HUGE* ROBED FIGURES -- THEY LOOK JUST LIKE *PETRO-GLYPHS!*
THOSE *MAGICIANS* ORVILLE MENTIONED MUST'VE GONE BACK IN *TIME* SOMEHOW, CREATED THE IMAGES *THEMSELVES* --
TO STRIKE THE FEAR OF *GOD*...
GODS, PLURAL...
...INTO THE *LOCALS!*
I'VE NEVER SEEN *ANYTHING* LIKE THIS. NOT EVEN *CLOSE.*
QUESTION IS, FLYNN, WHAT DO WE DO ABOUT IT? ANOTHER HOUR OR SO, AND *MANHATTAN* IS GOING TO BE A COLOSSAL PILE OF *RUBBLE*...
AND THERE'S *SIMILAR* CHATTER COMING IN FROM *OTHER* CITIES, TOO. THESE GUYS ARE *EXTENDING* THEIR RANGE...
I *KNEW* ORVILLE WAS TELLING THE TRUTH, BUT I STILL HOPED THAT SOMEHOW, HE WAS *BLUFFING.* HIS STORY WAS TOO *CRAZY,* TOO *UNBELIEVABLE*...
BUT, HERE IT IS, *LIFE-SIZED* AND IN *LIVING* COLOR, JUST LIKE ONE OF SCHICK'S *MOVIES!*
ONLY *THIS* TIME, IT'S THE *REAL* DEAL.
HEY...
WHATEVER HAPPENED TO *ORVILLE?*

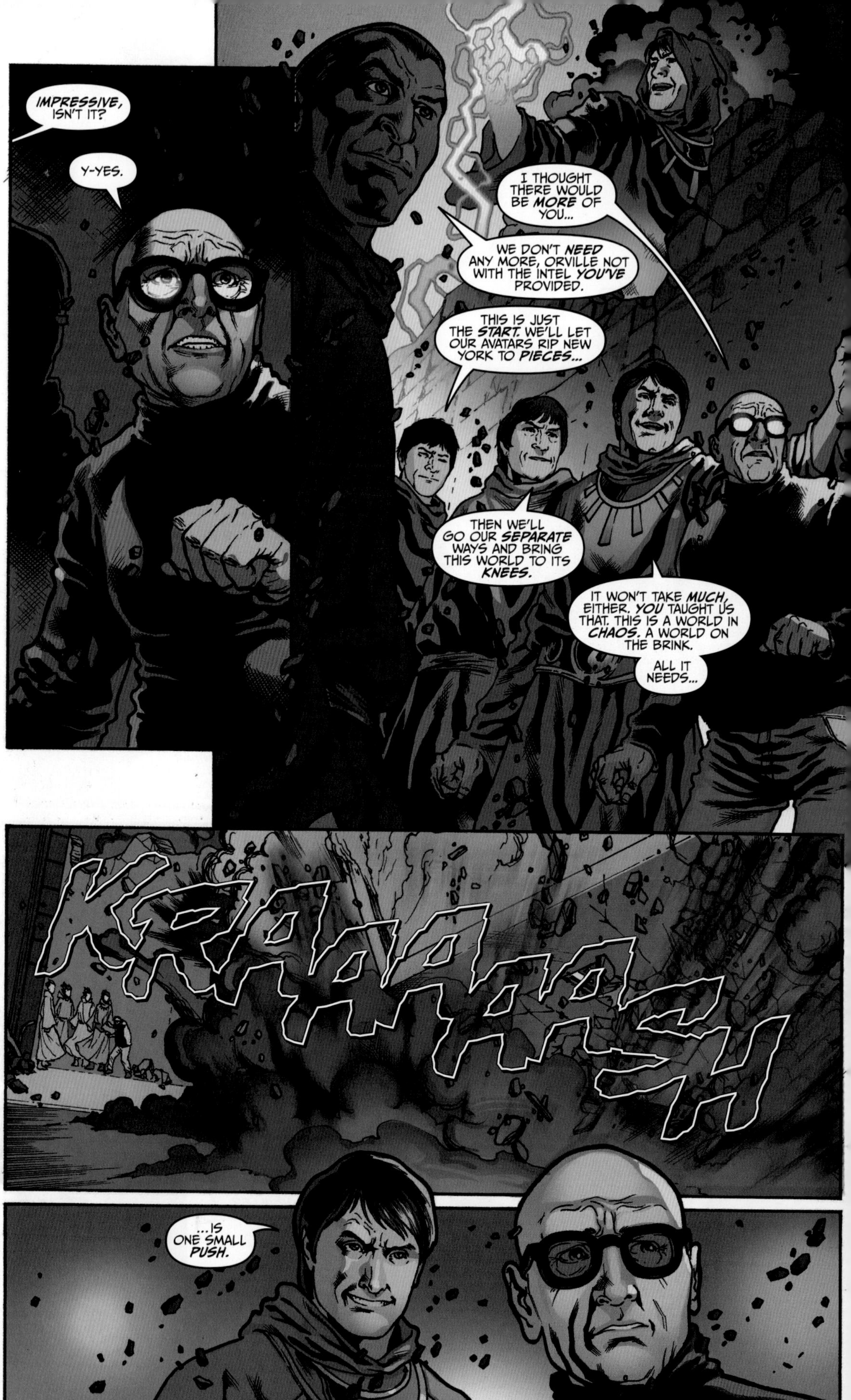
IMPRESSIVE, ISN'T IT?
Y-YES.
I THOUGHT THERE WOULD BE MORE OF YOU...
WE DON'T NEED ANY MORE, ORVILLE NOT WITH THE INTEL YOU'VE PROVIDED.
THIS IS JUST THE START. WE'LL LET OUR AVATARS RIP NEW YORK TO PIECES...
THEN WE'LL GO OUR SEPARATE WAYS AND BRING THIS WORLD TO ITS KNEES.
IT WON'T TAKE MUCH, EITHER. YOU TAUGHT US THAT. THIS IS A WORLD IN CHAOS. A WORLD ON THE BRINK.
ALL IT NEEDS...
KRAAAAASH
...IS ONE SMALL PUSH.

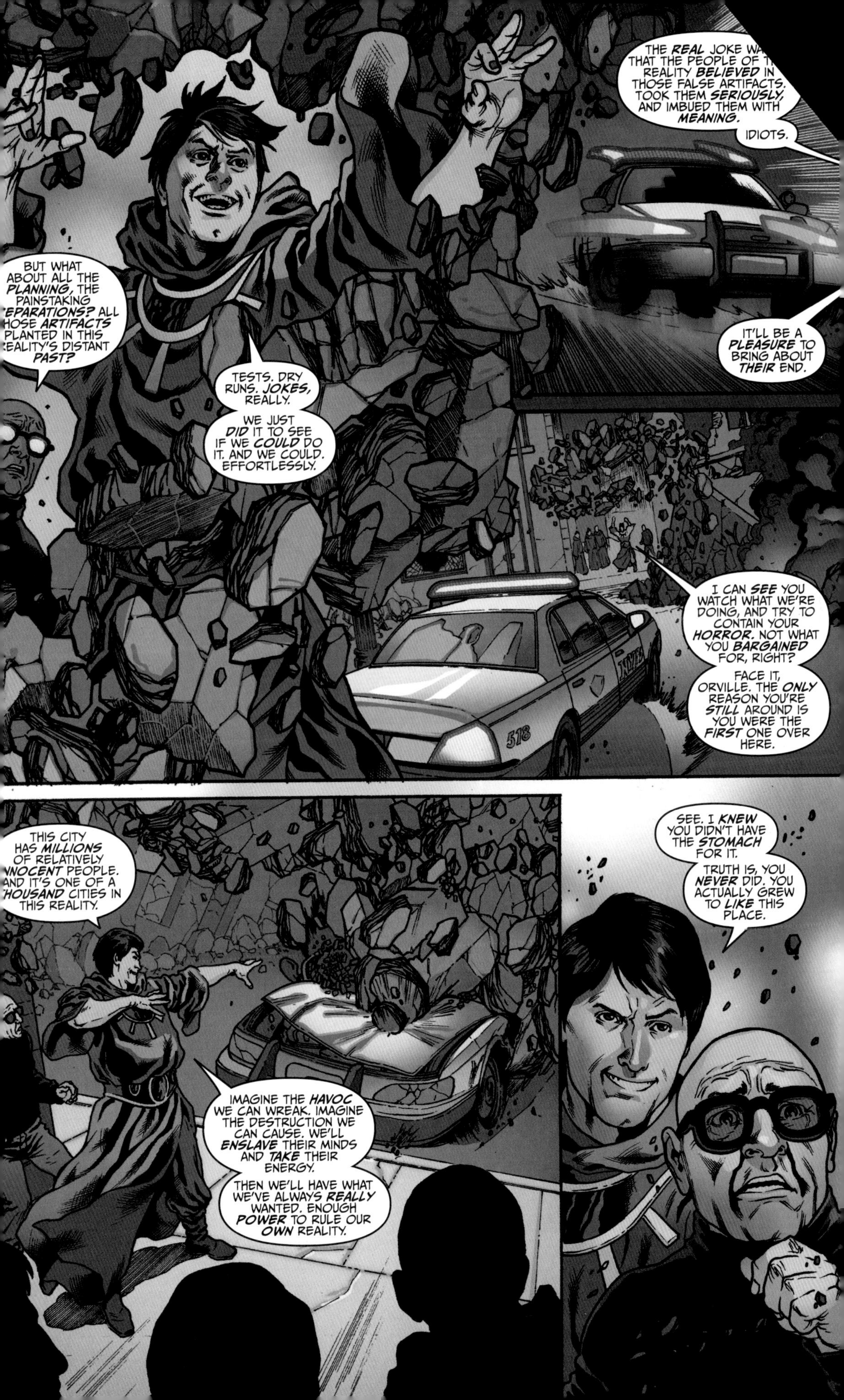
THE REAL JOKE WA[S] THAT THE PEOPLE OF T[HIS] REALITY BELIEVED IN THOSE FALSE ARTIFACTS. TOOK THEM SERIOUSLY, AND IMBUED THEM WITH MEANING.
IDIOTS.
BUT WHAT ABOUT ALL THE PLANNING, THE PAINSTAKING EPARATIONS? ALL HOSE ARTIFACTS PLANTED IN THIS EALITY'S DISTANT PAST?
TESTS. DRY RUNS. JOKES, REALLY.
WE JUST DID IT TO SEE IF WE COULD DO IT. AND WE COULD. EFFORTLESSLY.
IT'LL BE A PLEASURE TO BRING ABOUT THEIR END.
I CAN SEE YOU WATCH WHAT WE'RE DOING, AND TRY TO CONTAIN YOUR HORROR. NOT WHAT YOU BARGAINED FOR, RIGHT?
FACE IT, ORVILLE. THE ONLY REASON YOU'RE STILL AROUND IS YOU WERE THE FIRST ONE OVER HERE.
NYPD
518
THIS CITY HAS MILLIONS OF RELATIVELY NNOCENT PEOPLE. AND IT'S ONE OF A HOUSAND CITIES IN THIS REALITY.
IMAGINE THE HAVOC WE CAN WREAK. IMAGINE THE DESTRUCTION WE CAN CAUSE. WE'LL ENSLAVE THEIR MINDS AND TAKE THEIR ENERGY.
THEN WE'LL HAVE WHAT WE'VE ALWAYS REALLY WANTED. ENOUGH POWER TO RULE OUR OWN REALITY.
SEE. I KNEW YOU DIDN'T HAVE THE STOMACH FOR IT.
TRUTH IS, YOU NEVER DID. YOU ACTUALLY GREW TO LIKE THIS PLACE.

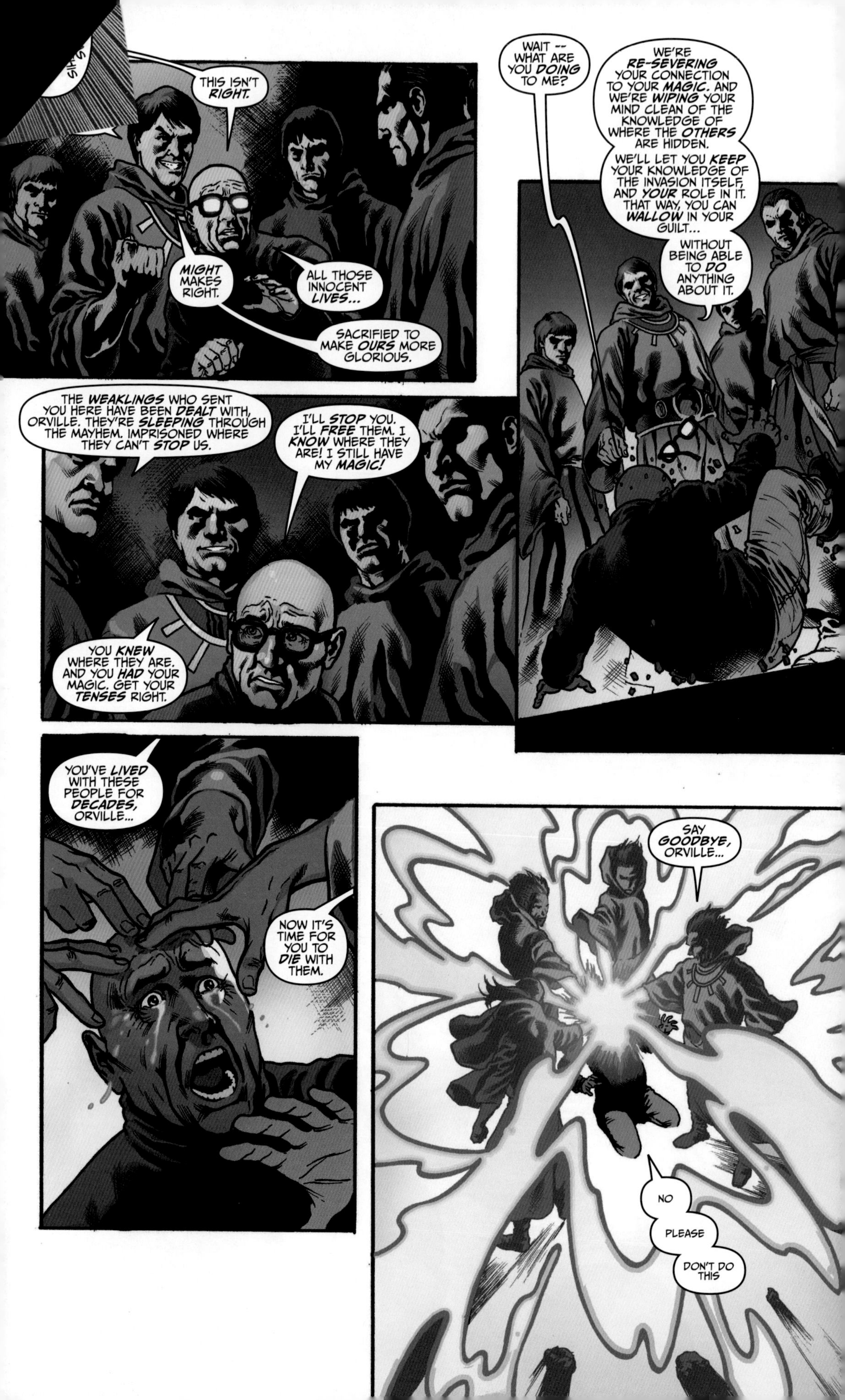

THIS ISN'T *RIGHT.*
MIGHT MAKES RIGHT.
ALL THOSE INNOCENT *LIVES...*
SACRIFIED TO MAKE *OURS* MORE GLORIOUS.
THE *WEAKLINGS* WHO SENT YOU HERE HAVE BEEN *DEALT* WITH, ORVILLE. THEY'RE *SLEEPING* THROUGH THE MAYHEM. IMPRISONED WHERE THEY CAN'T *STOP* US.
I'LL *STOP* YOU. I'LL *FREE* THEM. I *KNOW* WHERE THEY ARE! I STILL HAVE MY *MAGIC!*
YOU *KNEW* WHERE THEY ARE. AND YOU *HAD* YOUR MAGIC. GET YOUR *TENSES* RIGHT.
WAIT -- WHAT ARE YOU *DOING* TO ME?
WE'RE *RE-SEVERING* YOUR CONNECTION TO YOUR *MAGIC.* AND WE'RE *WIPING* YOUR MIND CLEAN OF THE KNOWLEDGE OF WHERE THE *OTHERS* ARE HIDDEN.
WE'LL LET YOU *KEEP* YOUR KNOWLEDGE OF THE INVASION ITSELF, AND *YOUR* ROLE IN IT. THAT WAY, YOU CAN *WALLOW* IN YOUR GUILT...
WITHOUT BEING ABLE TO *DO* ANYTHING ABOUT IT.
YOU'VE *LIVED* WITH THESE PEOPLE FOR *DECADES,* ORVILLE...
NOW IT'S TIME FOR YOU TO *DIE* WITH THEM.
SAY *GOODBYE,* ORVILLE...
NO
PLEASE
DON'T DO THIS

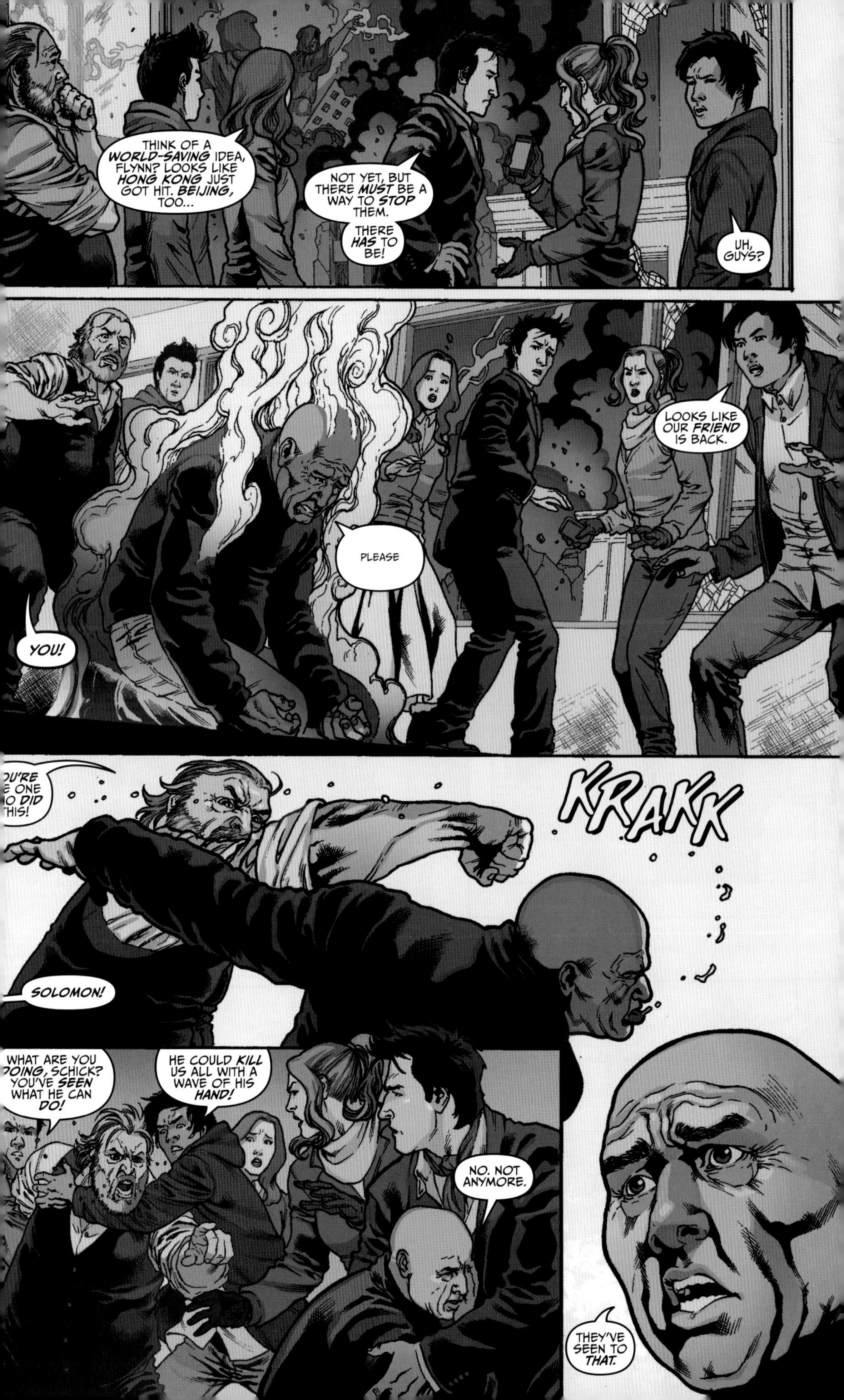
THINK OF A WORLD-SAVING IDEA, FLYNN? LOOKS LIKE HONG KONG JUST GOT HIT. BEIJING, TOO...
NOT YET, BUT THERE MUST BE A WAY TO STOP THEM.
THERE HAS TO BE!
UH, GUYS?
LOOKS LIKE OUR FRIEND IS BACK.
PLEASE
YOU!
OU'RE
E ONE
O DID
THIS!
KRAKK
SOLOMON!
WHAT ARE YOU OING, SCHICK? YOU'VE SEEN WHAT HE CAN DO!
HE COULD KILL US ALL WITH A WAVE OF HIS HAND!
NO. NOT ANYMORE.
THEY'VE SEEN TO THAT.

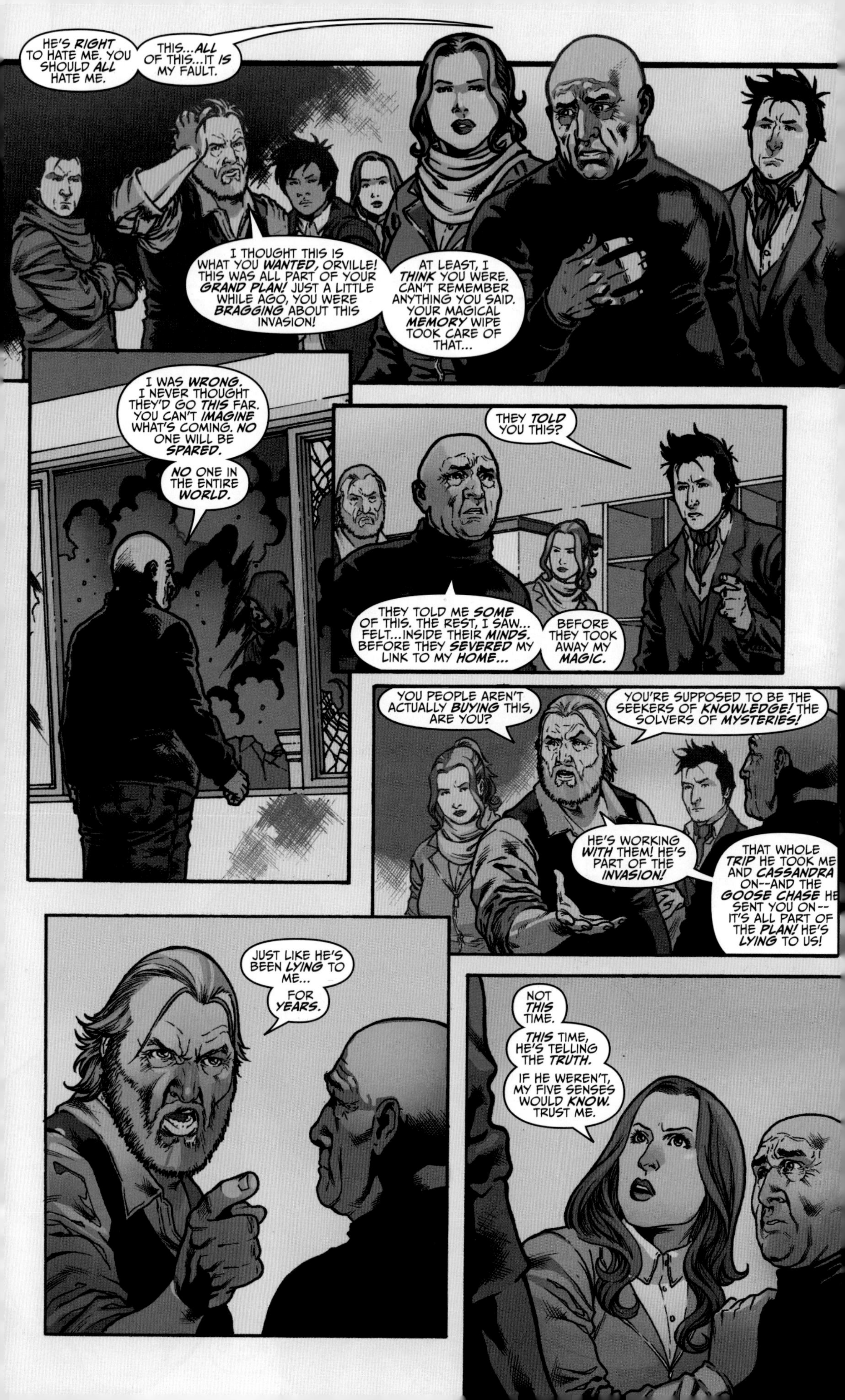
HE'S RIGHT TO HATE ME. YOU SHOULD ALL HATE ME.
THIS...ALL OF THIS...IT IS MY FAULT.
I THOUGHT THIS IS WHAT YOU WANTED, ORVILLE! THIS WAS ALL PART OF YOUR GRAND PLAN! JUST A LITTLE WHILE AGO, YOU WERE BRAGGING ABOUT THIS INVASION!
AT LEAST, I THINK YOU WERE. CAN'T REMEMBER ANYTHING YOU SAID. YOUR MAGICAL MEMORY WIPE TOOK CARE OF THAT...
I WAS WRONG. I NEVER THOUGHT THEY'D GO THIS FAR. YOU CAN'T IMAGINE WHAT'S COMING. NO ONE WILL BE SPARED.
NO ONE IN THE ENTIRE WORLD.
THEY TOLD YOU THIS?
THEY TOLD ME SOME OF THIS. THE REST, I SAW... FELT...INSIDE THEIR MINDS. BEFORE THEY SEVERED MY LINK TO MY HOME...
BEFORE THEY TOOK AWAY MY MAGIC.
YOU PEOPLE AREN'T ACTUALLY BUYING THIS, ARE YOU?
YOU'RE SUPPOSED TO BE THE SEEKERS OF KNOWLEDGE! THE SOLVERS OF MYSTERIES!
HE'S WORKING WITH THEM! HE'S PART OF THE INVASION!
THAT WHOLE TRIP HE TOOK ME AND CASSANDRA ON--AND THE GOOSE CHASE HE SENT YOU ON-- IT'S ALL PART OF THE PLAN! HE'S LYING TO US!
JUST LIKE HE'S BEEN LYING TO ME...
FOR YEARS.
NOT THIS TIME.
THIS TIME, HE'S TELLING THE TRUTH.
IF HE WEREN'T, MY FIVE SENSES WOULD KNOW. TRUST ME.

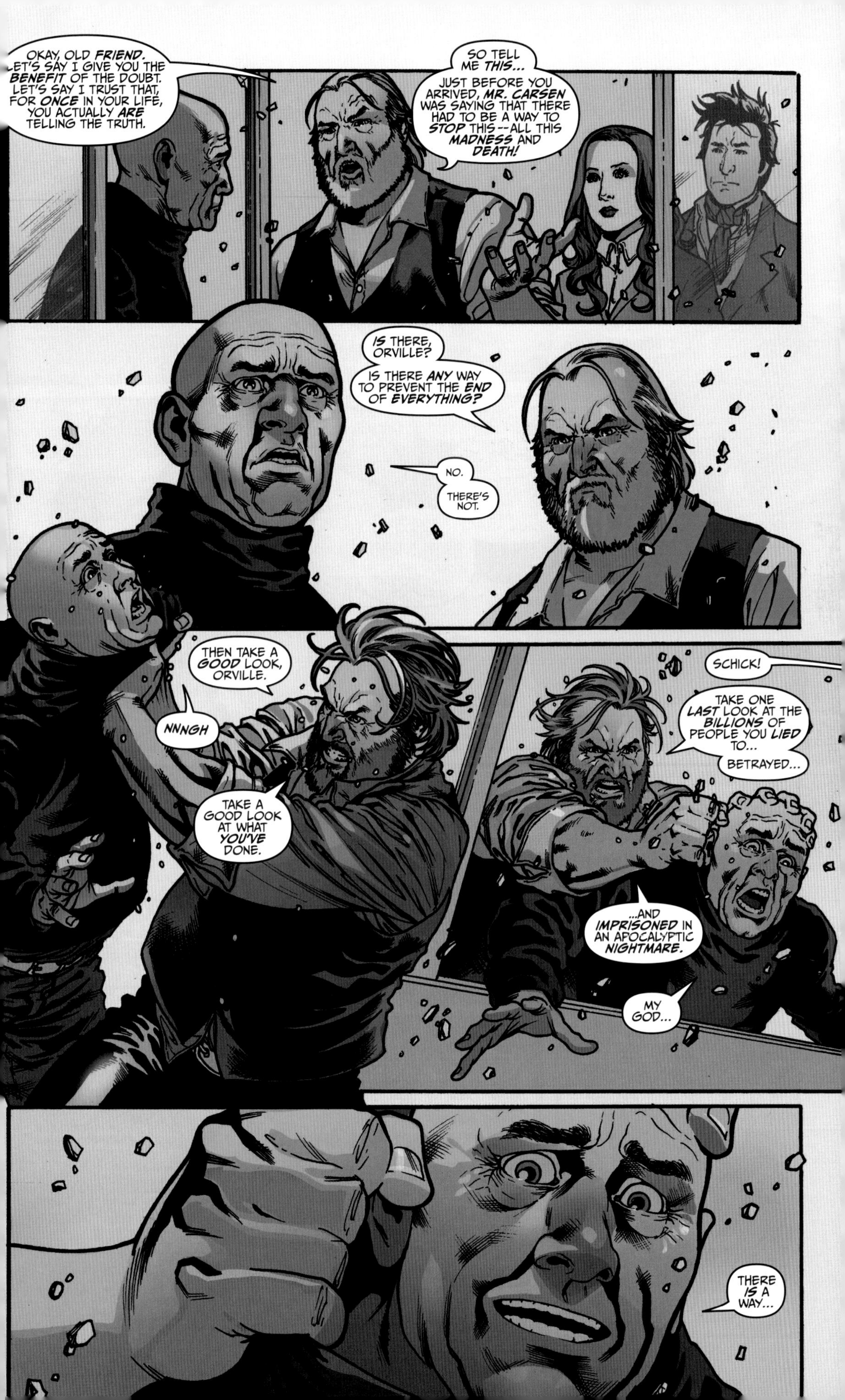
OKAY, OLD FRIEND. LET'S SAY I GIVE YOU THE BENEFIT OF THE DOUBT. LET'S SAY I TRUST THAT, FOR ONCE IN YOUR LIFE, YOU ACTUALLY ARE TELLING THE TRUTH.
SO TELL ME THIS...
JUST BEFORE YOU ARRIVED, MR. CARSEN WAS SAYING THAT THERE HAD TO BE A WAY TO STOP THIS--ALL THIS MADNESS AND DEATH!
IS THERE, ORVILLE?
IS THERE ANY WAY TO PREVENT THE END OF EVERYTHING?
NO.
THERE'S NOT.
THEN TAKE A GOOD LOOK, ORVILLE.
NNNGH
TAKE A GOOD LOOK AT WHAT YOU'VE DONE.
SCHICK!
TAKE ONE LAST LOOK AT THE BILLIONS OF PEOPLE YOU LIED TO...
BETRAYED...
...AND IMPRISONED IN AN APOCALYPTIC NIGHTMARE.
MY GOD...
THERE IS A WAY...

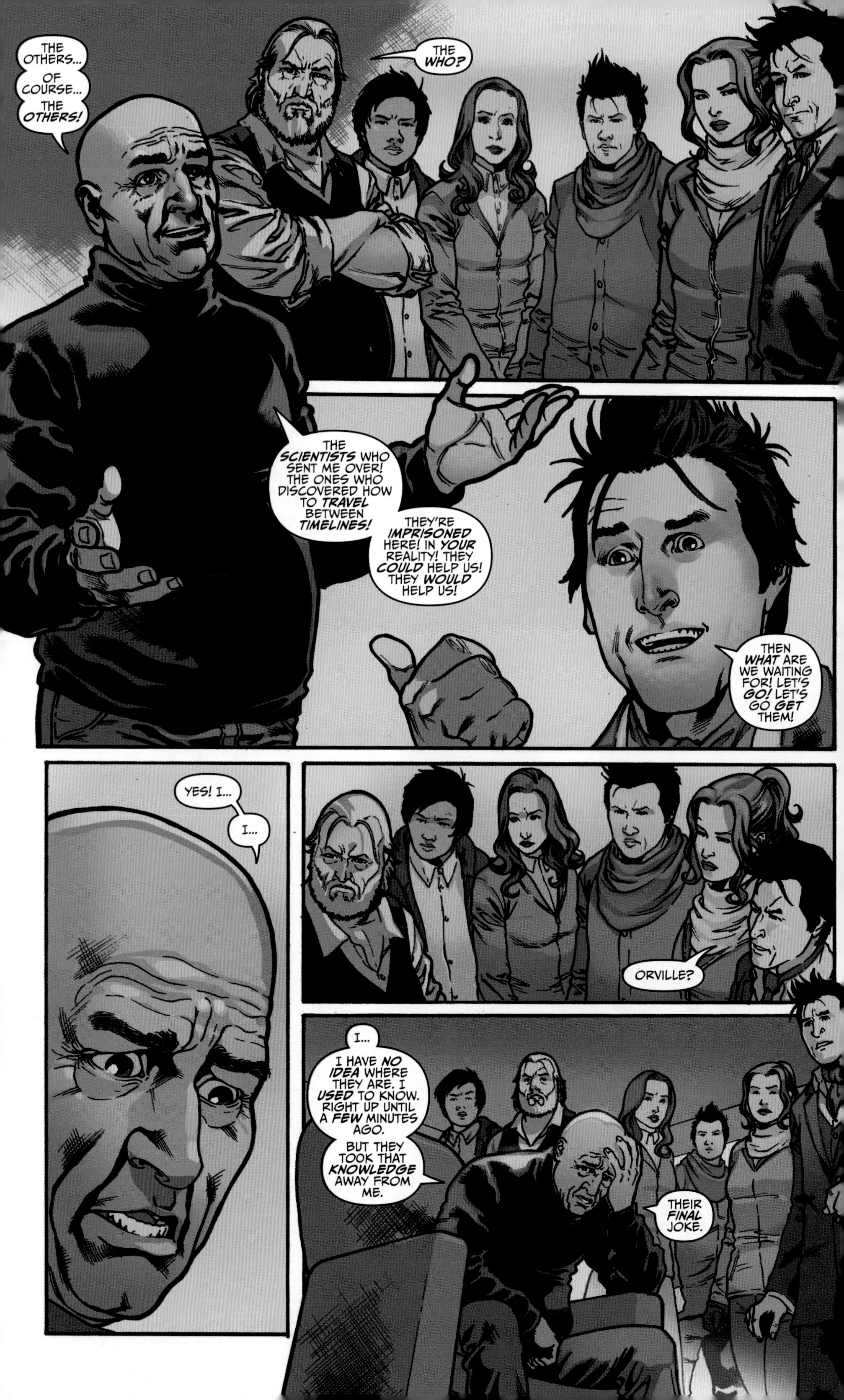
THE OTHERS... OF COURSE... THE OTHERS!
THE WHO?
THE SCIENTISTS WHO SENT ME OVER! THE ONES WHO DISCOVERED HOW TO TRAVEL BETWEEN TIMELINES!
THEY'RE IMPRISONED HERE! IN YOUR REALITY! THEY COULD HELP US! THEY WOULD HELP US!
THEN WHAT ARE WE WAITING FOR! LET'S GO! LET'S GO GET THEM!
YES! I...
I...
ORVILLE?
I...
I HAVE NO IDEA WHERE THEY ARE. I USED TO KNOW. RIGHT UP UNTIL A FEW MINUTES AGO.
BUT THEY TOOK THAT KNOWLEDGE AWAY FROM ME.
THEIR FINAL JOKE.

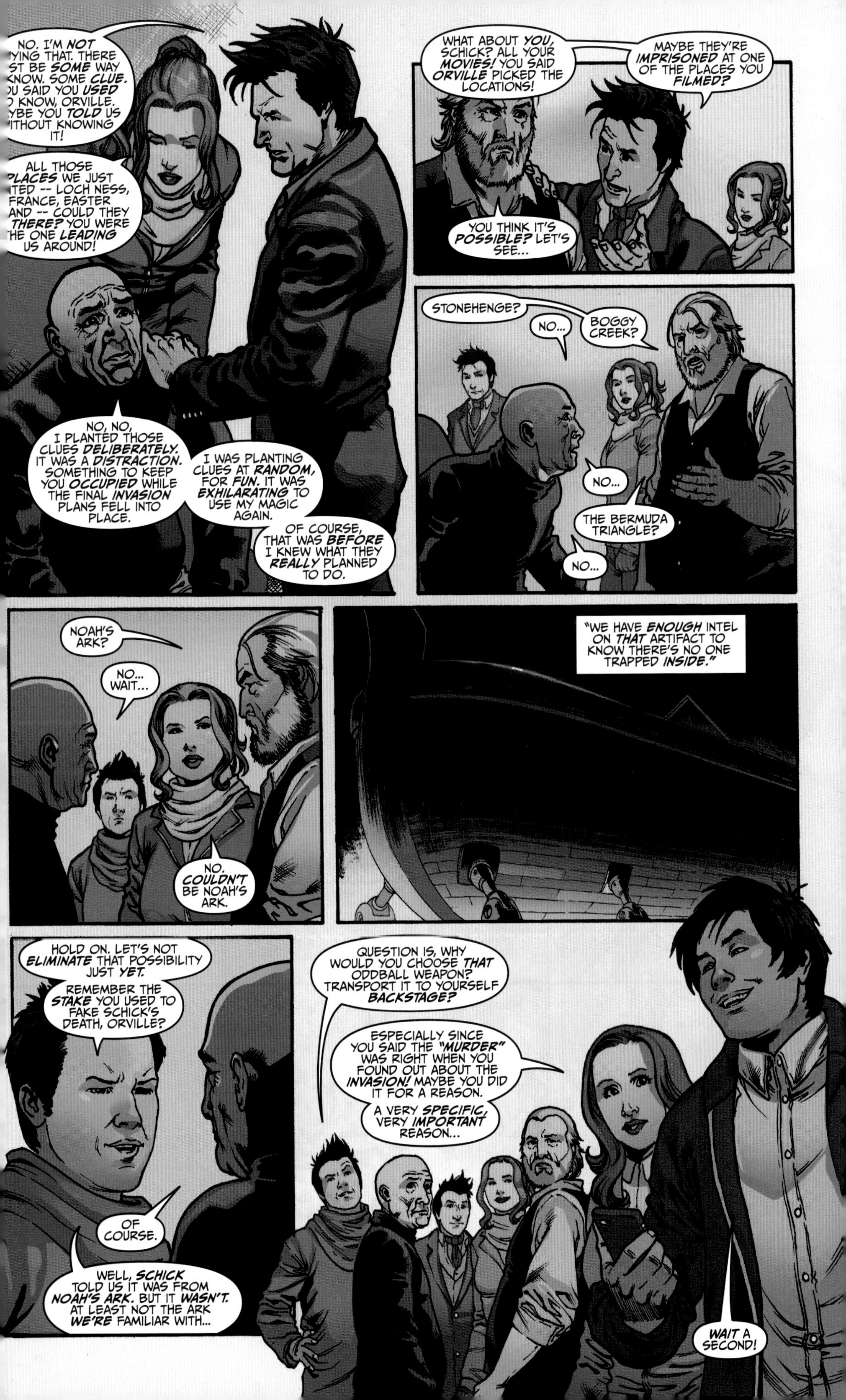

NO. I'M NOT
YING THAT. THERE
ST BE SOME WAY
KNOW. SOME CLUE.
OU SAID YOU USED
O KNOW, ORVILLE.
YBE YOU TOLD US
VITHOUT KNOWING
IT!
ALL THOSE
PLACES WE JUST
TED -- LOCH NESS,
FRANCE, EASTER
AND -- COULD THEY
THERE? YOU WERE
HE ONE LEADING
US AROUND!
NO, NO, I PLANTED THOSE CLUES DELIBERATELY. IT WAS A DISTRACTION. SOMETHING TO KEEP YOU OCCUPIED WHILE THE FINAL INVASION PLANS FELL INTO PLACE.
I WAS PLANTING CLUES AT RANDOM, FOR FUN. IT WAS EXHILARATING TO USE MY MAGIC AGAIN.
OF COURSE, THAT WAS BEFORE I KNEW WHAT THEY REALLY PLANNED TO DO.
WHAT ABOUT YOU, SCHICK? ALL YOUR MOVIES! YOU SAID ORVILLE PICKED THE LOCATIONS!
MAYBE THEY'RE IMPRISONED AT ONE OF THE PLACES YOU FILMED?
YOU THINK IT'S POSSIBLE? LET'S SEE...
STONEHENGE?
NO...
BOGGY CREEK?
NO...
THE BERMUDA TRIANGLE?
NO...
NOAH'S ARK?
NO... WAIT...
NO. COULDN'T BE NOAH'S ARK.
"WE HAVE ENOUGH INTEL ON THAT ARTIFACT TO KNOW THERE'S NO ONE TRAPPED INSIDE."
HOLD ON. LET'S NOT ELIMINATE THAT POSSIBILITY JUST YET.
REMEMBER THE STAKE YOU USED TO FAKE SCHICK'S DEATH, ORVILLE?
OF COURSE.
WELL, SCHICK TOLD US IT WAS FROM NOAH'S ARK. BUT IT WASN'T. AT LEAST NOT THE ARK WE'RE FAMILIAR WITH...
QUESTION IS, WHY WOULD YOU CHOOSE THAT ODDBALL WEAPON? TRANSPORT IT TO YOURSELF BACKSTAGE?
ESPECIALLY SINCE YOU SAID THE "MURDER" WAS RIGHT WHEN YOU FOUND OUT ABOUT THE INVASION! MAYBE YOU DID IT FOR A REASON.
A VERY SPECIFIC, VERY IMPORTANT REASON...
WAIT A SECOND!

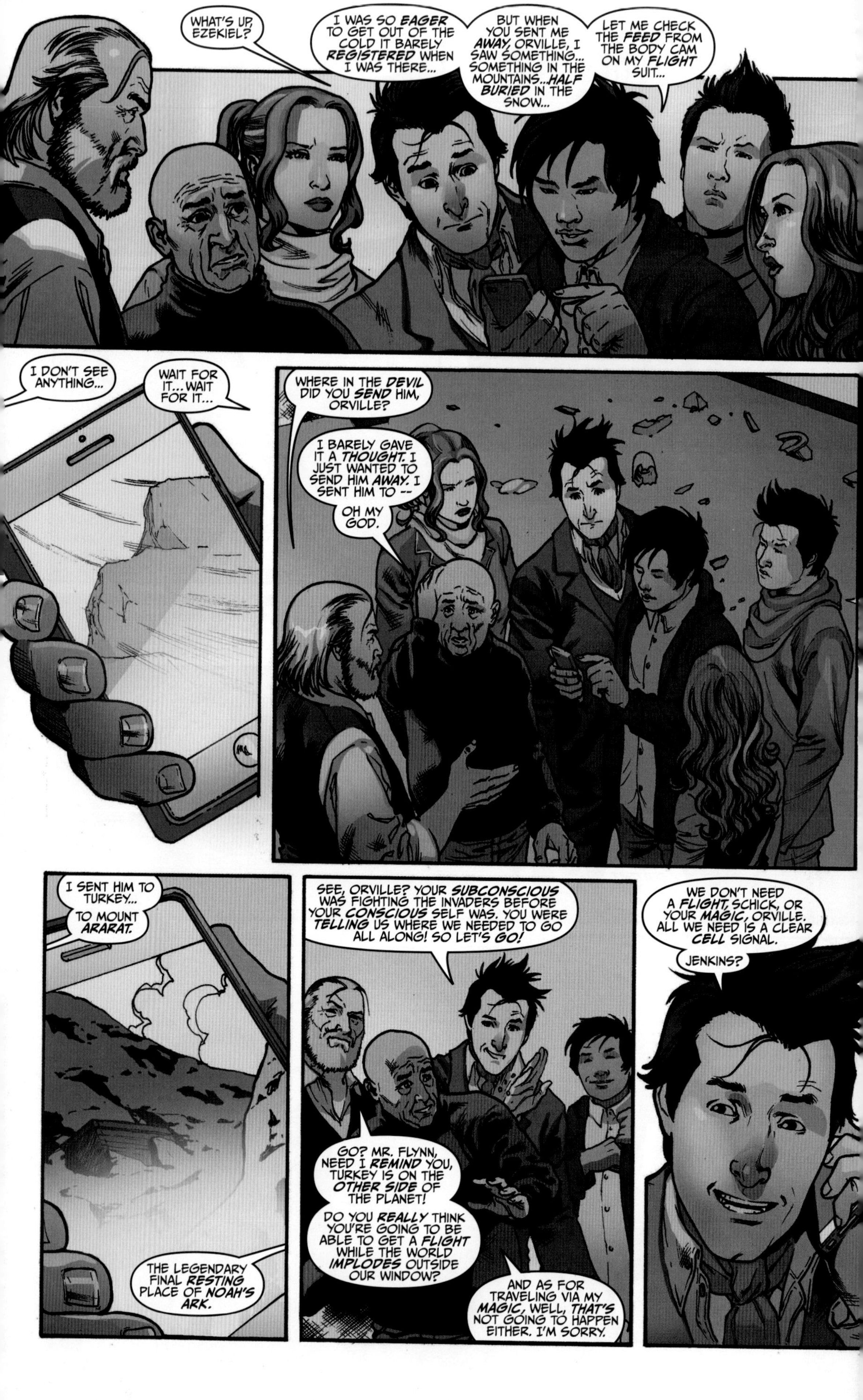
WHAT'S UP, EZEKIEL?
I WAS SO EAGER TO GET OUT OF THE COLD IT BARELY REGISTERED WHEN I WAS THERE...
BUT WHEN YOU SENT ME AWAY, ORVILLE, I SAW SOMETHING... SOMETHING IN THE MOUNTAINS...HALF BURIED IN THE SNOW...
LET ME CHECK THE FEED FROM THE BODY CAM ON MY FLIGHT SUIT...
I DON'T SEE ANYTHING...
WAIT FOR IT...WAIT FOR IT...
WHERE IN THE DEVIL DID YOU SEND HIM, ORVILLE?
I BARELY GAVE IT A THOUGHT. I JUST WANTED TO SEND HIM AWAY. I SENT HIM TO --
OH MY GOD.
I SENT HIM TO TURKEY...
TO MOUNT ARARAT.
THE LEGENDARY FINAL RESTING PLACE OF NOAH'S ARK.
SEE, ORVILLE? YOUR SUBCONSCIOUS WAS FIGHTING THE INVADERS BEFORE YOUR CONSCIOUS SELF WAS. YOU WERE TELLING US WHERE WE NEEDED TO GO ALL ALONG! SO LET'S GO!
GO? MR. FLYNN, NEED I REMIND YOU, TURKEY IS ON THE OTHER SIDE OF THE PLANET!
DO YOU REALLY THINK YOU'RE GOING TO BE ABLE TO GET A FLIGHT WHILE THE WORLD IMPLODES OUTSIDE OUR WINDOW?
AND AS FOR TRAVELING VIA MY MAGIC, WELL, THAT'S NOT GOING TO HAPPEN EITHER. I'M SORRY.
WE DON'T NEED A FLIGHT, SCHICK, OR YOUR MAGIC, ORVILLE. ALL WE NEED IS A CLEAR CELL SIGNAL.
JENKINS?

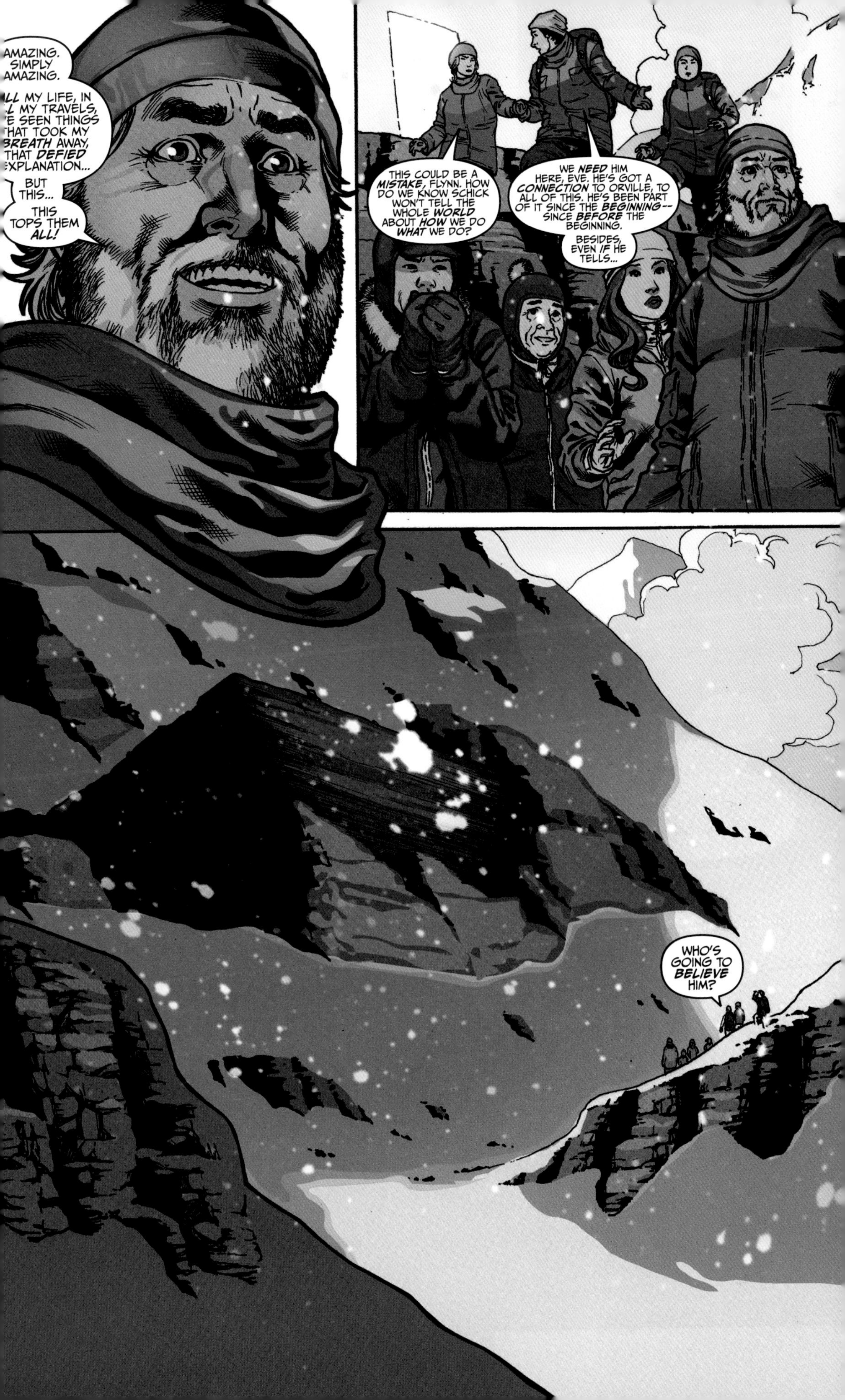
AMAZING. SIMPLY AMAZING.
LL MY LIFE, IN L MY TRAVELS, 'E SEEN THINGS THAT TOOK MY BREATH AWAY, THAT DEFIED EXPLANATION...
BUT THIS...
THIS TOPS THEM ALL!
THIS COULD BE A MISTAKE, FLYNN. HOW DO WE KNOW SCHICK WON'T TELL THE WHOLE WORLD ABOUT HOW WE DO WHAT WE DO?
WE NEED HIM HERE, EVE. HE'S GOT A CONNECTION TO ORVILLE, TO ALL OF THIS. HE'S BEEN PART OF IT SINCE THE BEGINNING-- SINCE BEFORE THE BEGINNING.
BESIDES, EVEN IF HE TELLS...
WHO'S GOING TO BELIEVE HIM?

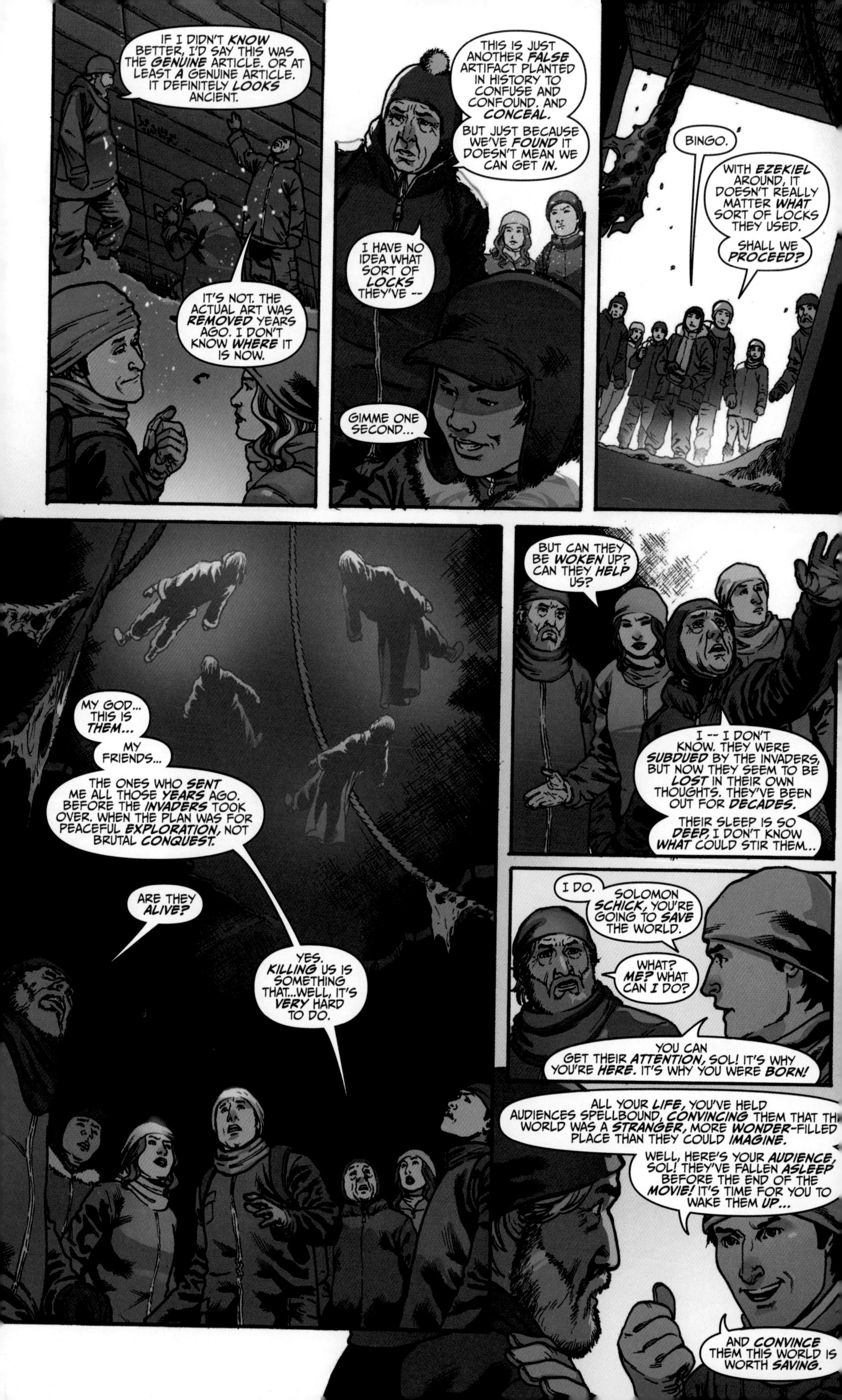
IF I DIDN'T KNOW BETTER, I'D SAY THIS WAS THE GENUINE ARTICLE. OR AT LEAST A GENUINE ARTICLE. IT DEFINITELY LOOKS ANCIENT.
IT'S NOT. THE ACTUAL ART WAS REMOVED YEARS AGO. I DON'T KNOW WHERE IT IS NOW.
THIS IS JUST ANOTHER FALSE ARTIFACT PLANTED IN HISTORY TO CONFUSE AND CONFOUND. AND CONCEAL.
BUT JUST BECAUSE WE'VE FOUND IT DOESN'T MEAN WE CAN GET IN.
I HAVE NO IDEA WHAT SORT OF LOCKS THEY'VE --
GIMME ONE SECOND...
BINGO.
WITH EZEKIEL AROUND, IT DOESN'T REALLY MATTER WHAT SORT OF LOCKS THEY USED.
SHALL WE PROCEED?
MY GOD... THIS IS THEM...
MY FRIENDS...
THE ONES WHO SENT ME ALL THOSE YEARS AGO. BEFORE THE INVADERS TOOK OVER. WHEN THE PLAN WAS FOR PEACEFUL EXPLORATION, NOT BRUTAL CONQUEST.
ARE THEY ALIVE?
YES. KILLING US IS SOMETHING THAT...WELL, IT'S VERY HARD TO DO.
BUT CAN THEY BE WOKEN UP? CAN THEY HELP US?
I -- I DON'T KNOW. THEY WERE SUBDUED BY THE INVADERS, BUT NOW THEY SEEM TO BE LOST IN THEIR OWN THOUGHTS. THEY'VE BEEN OUT FOR DECADES.
THEIR SLEEP IS SO DEEP, I DON'T KNOW WHAT COULD STIR THEM...
I DO.
SOLOMON SCHICK, YOU'RE GOING TO SAVE THE WORLD.
WHAT? ME? WHAT CAN I DO?
YOU CAN GET THEIR ATTENTION, SOL! IT'S WHY YOU'RE HERE. IT'S WHY YOU WERE BORN!
ALL YOUR LIFE, YOU'VE HELD AUDIENCES SPELLBOUND, CONVINCING THEM THAT TH WORLD WAS A STRANGER, MORE WONDER-FILLED PLACE THAN THEY COULD IMAGINE.
WELL, HERE'S YOUR AUDIENCE, SOL! THEY'VE FALLEN ASLEEP BEFORE THE END OF THE MOVIE! IT'S TIME FOR YOU TO WAKE THEM UP...
AND CONVINCE THEM THIS WORLD IS WORTH SAVING.

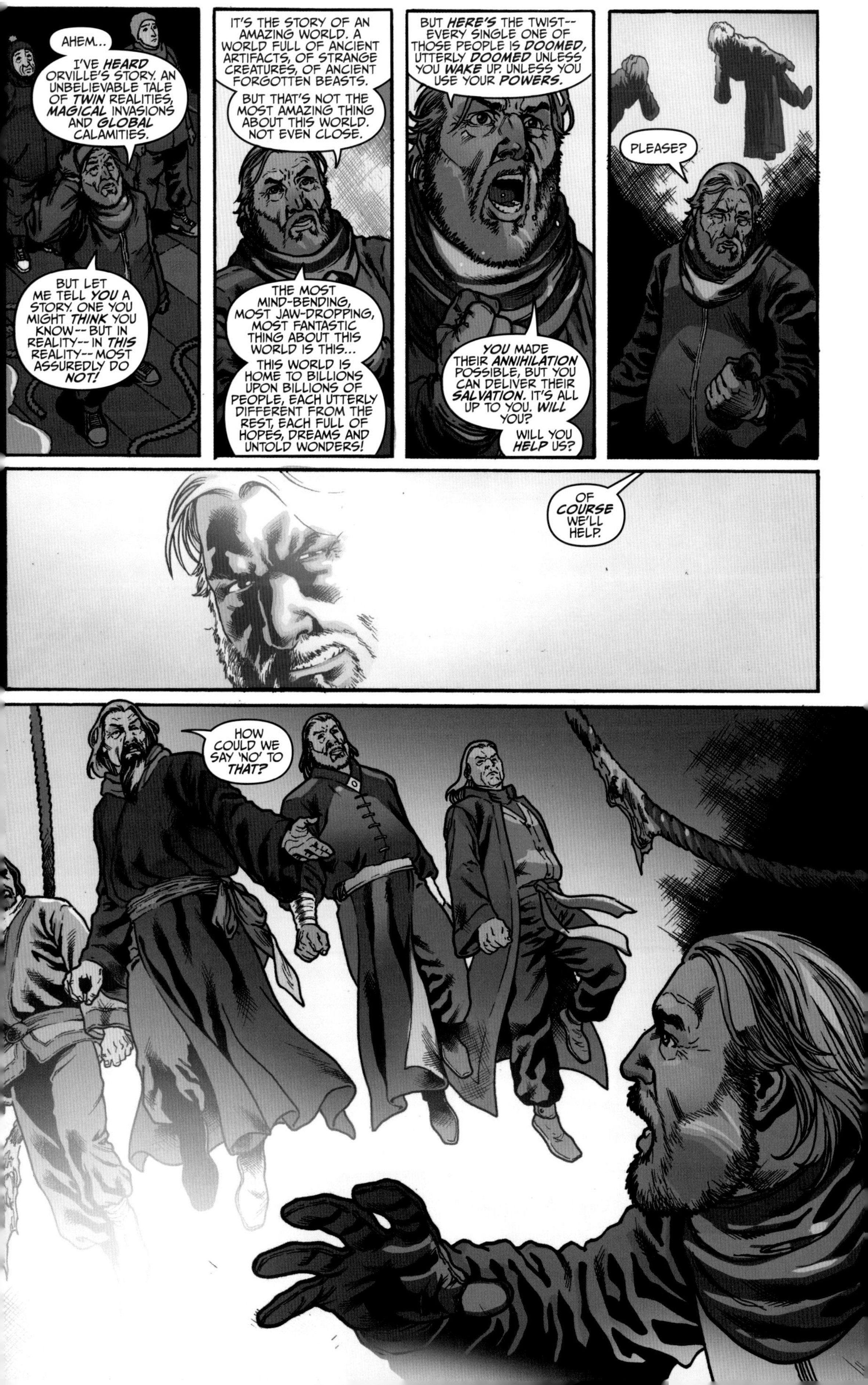
AHEM...
I'VE HEARD ORVILLE'S STORY. AN UNBELIEVABLE TALE OF TWIN REALITIES, MAGICAL INVASIONS AND GLOBAL CALAMITIES.
BUT LET ME TELL YOU A STORY. ONE YOU MIGHT THINK YOU KNOW-- BUT IN REALITY-- IN THIS REALITY-- MOST ASSUREDLY DO NOT!
IT'S THE STORY OF AN AMAZING WORLD. A WORLD FULL OF ANCIENT ARTIFACTS, OF STRANGE CREATURES, OF ANCIENT FORGOTTEN BEASTS.
BUT THAT'S NOT THE MOST AMAZING THING ABOUT THIS WORLD. NOT EVEN CLOSE.
THE MOST MIND-BENDING, MOST JAW-DROPPING, MOST FANTASTIC THING ABOUT THIS WORLD IS THIS...
THIS WORLD IS HOME TO BILLIONS UPON BILLIONS OF PEOPLE, EACH UTTERLY DIFFERENT FROM THE REST, EACH FULL OF HOPES, DREAMS AND UNTOLD WONDERS!
BUT HERE'S THE TWIST-- EVERY SINGLE ONE OF THOSE PEOPLE IS DOOMED, UTTERLY DOOMED UNLESS YOU WAKE UP. UNLESS YOU USE YOUR POWERS.
YOU MADE THEIR ANNIHILATION POSSIBLE, BUT YOU CAN DELIVER THEIR SALVATION. IT'S ALL UP TO YOU. WILL YOU?
WILL YOU HELP US?
PLEASE?
OF COURSE WE'LL HELP.
HOW COULD WE SAY 'NO' TO THAT?

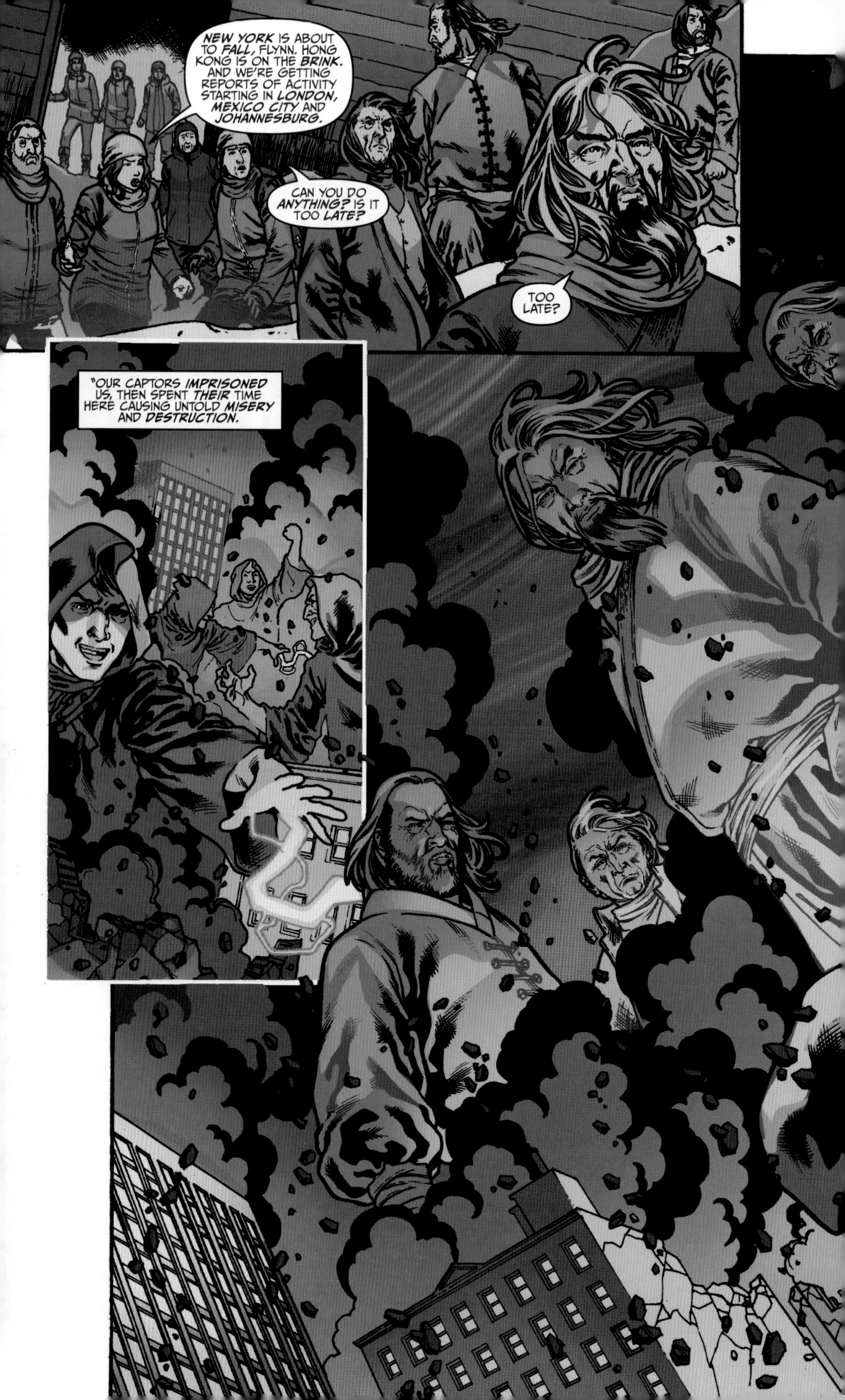
NEW YORK IS ABOUT TO FALL, FLYNN. HONG KONG IS ON THE BRINK. AND WE'RE GETTING REPORTS OF ACTIVITY STARTING IN LONDON, MEXICO CITY AND JOHANNESBURG.
CAN YOU DO ANYTHING? IS IT TOO LATE?
TOO LATE?
"OUR CAPTORS IMPRISONED US, THEN SPENT THEIR TIME HERE CAUSING UNTOLD MISERY AND DESTRUCTION.

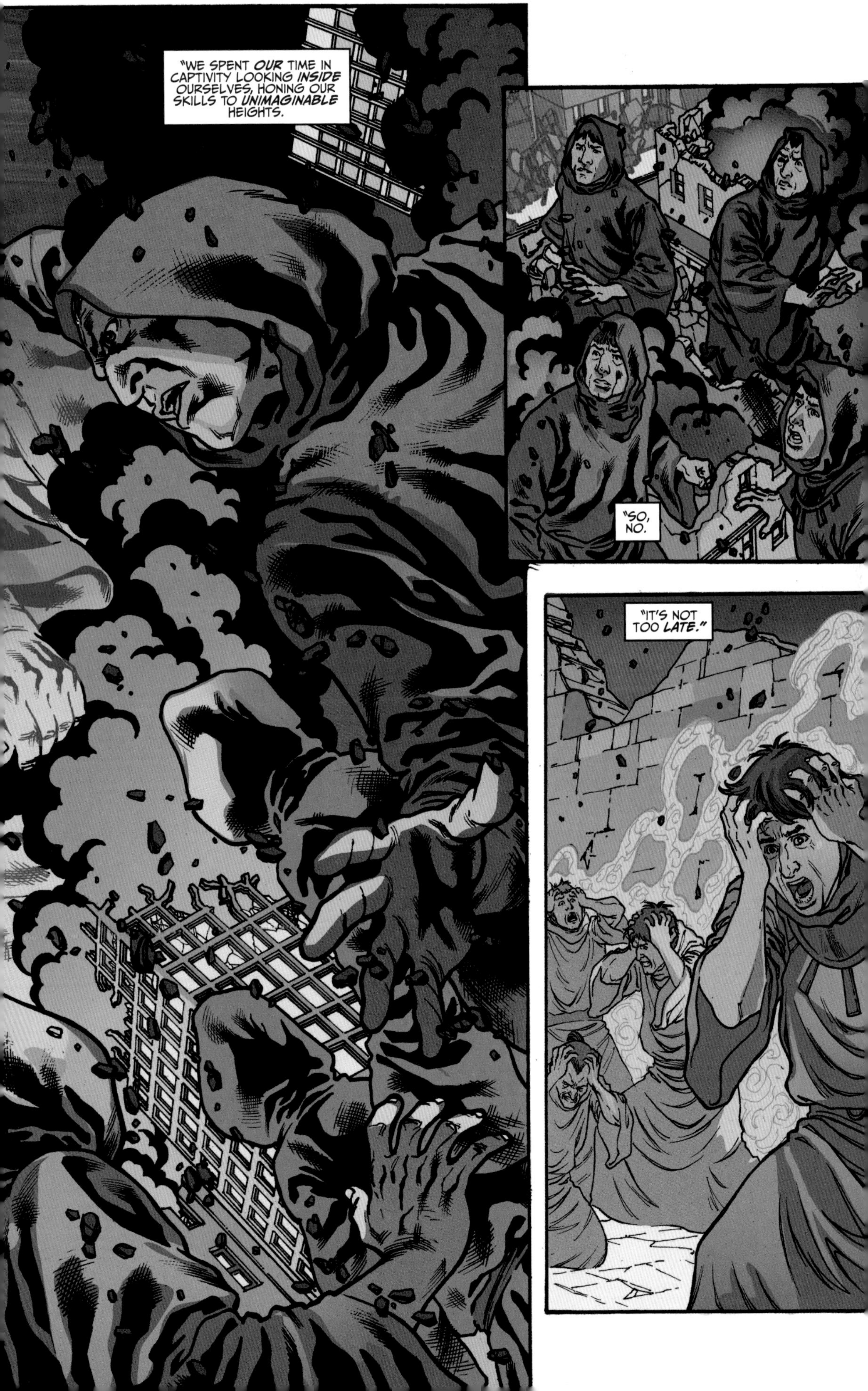
"WE SPENT OUR TIME IN CAPTIVITY LOOKING INSIDE OURSELVES, HONING OUR SKILLS TO UNIMAGINABLE HEIGHTS.
"SO, NO.
"IT'S NOT TOO LATE."

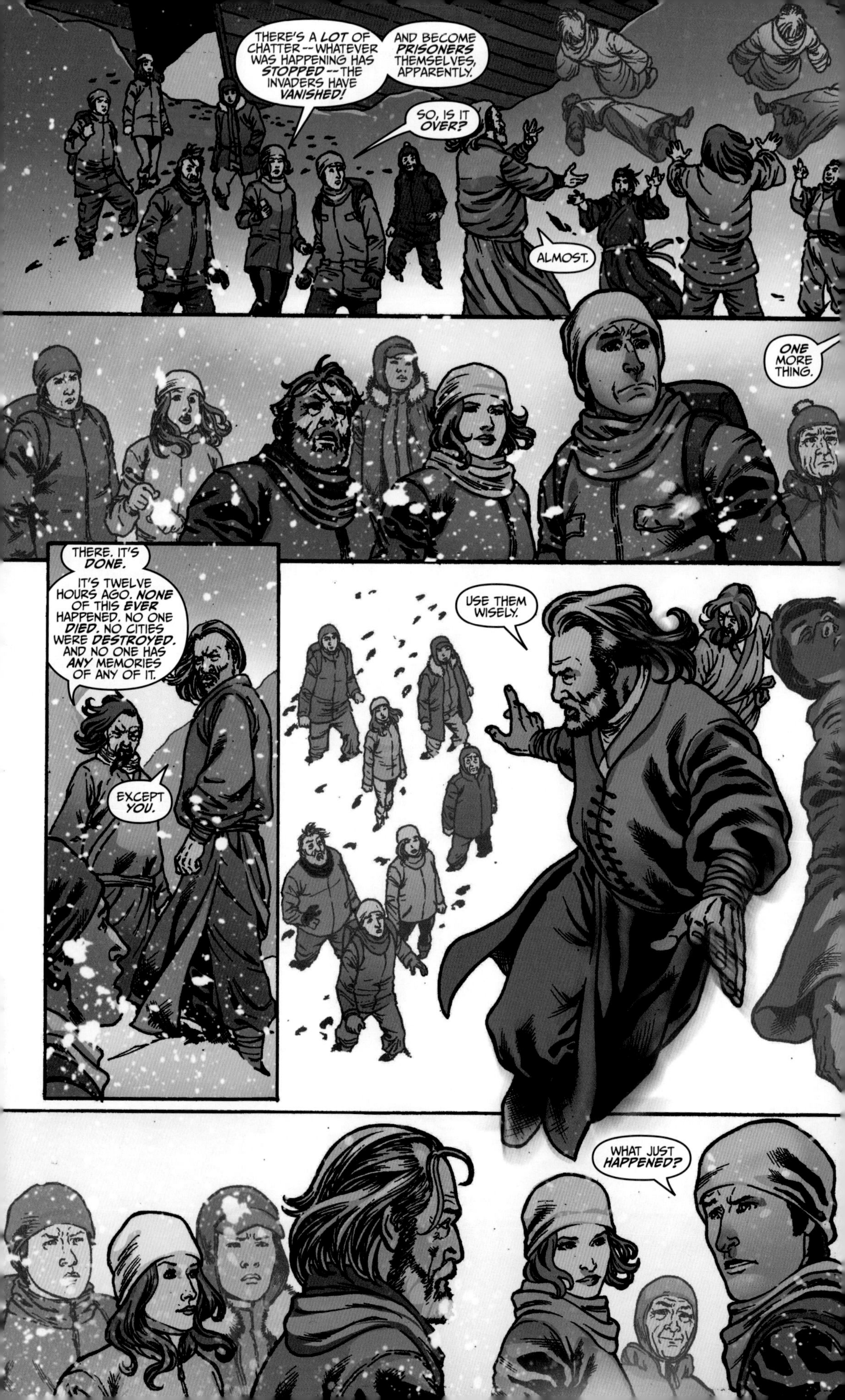
THERE'S A LOT OF CHATTER--WHATEVER WAS HAPPENING HAS STOPPED--THE INVADERS HAVE VANISHED!
AND BECOME PRISONERS THEMSELVES, APPARENTLY.
SO, IS IT OVER?
ALMOST.
ONE MORE THING.
THERE. IT'S DONE.
IT'S TWELVE HOURS AGO. NONE OF THIS EVER HAPPENED. NO ONE DIED. NO CITIES WERE DESTROYED. AND NO ONE HAS ANY MEMORIES OF ANY OF IT.
EXCEPT YOU.
USE THEM WISELY.
WHAT JUST HAPPENED?

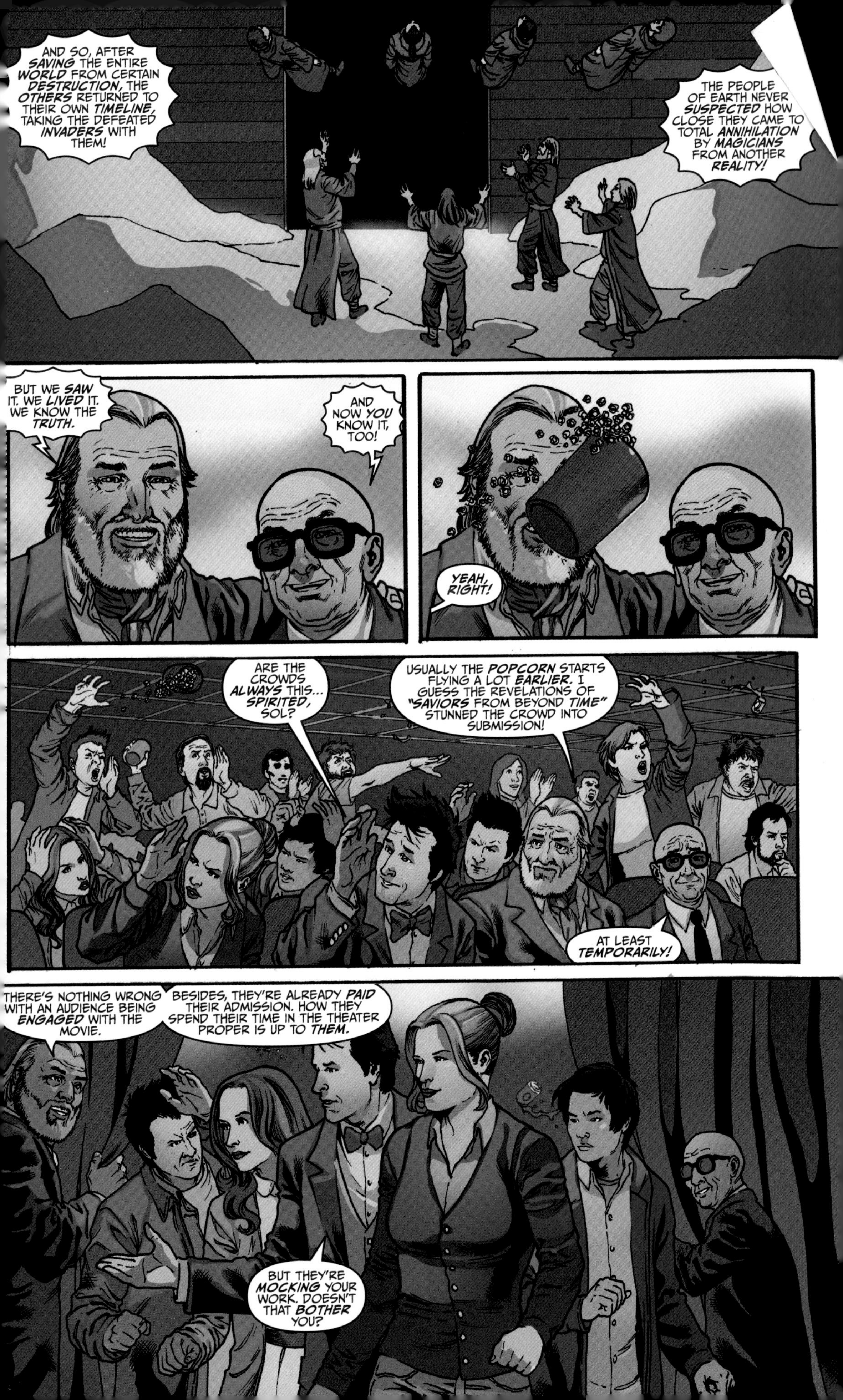

AND SO, AFTER SAVING THE ENTIRE WORLD FROM CERTAIN DESTRUCTION, THE OTHERS RETURNED TO THEIR OWN TIMELINE, TAKING THE DEFEATED INVADERS WITH THEM!
THE PEOPLE OF EARTH NEVER SUSPECTED HOW CLOSE THEY CAME TO TOTAL ANNIHILATION BY MAGICIANS FROM ANOTHER REALITY!
BUT WE SAW IT. WE LIVED IT. WE KNOW THE TRUTH.
AND NOW YOU KNOW IT, TOO!
YEAH, RIGHT!
ARE THE CROWDS ALWAYS THIS... SPIRITED, SOL?
USUALLY THE POPCORN STARTS FLYING A LOT EARLIER. I GUESS THE REVELATIONS OF "SAVIORS FROM BEYOND TIME" STUNNED THE CROWD INTO SUBMISSION!
AT LEAST TEMPORARILY!
THERE'S NOTHING WRONG WITH AN AUDIENCE BEING ENGAGED WITH THE MOVIE.
BESIDES, THEY'RE ALREADY PAID THEIR ADMISSION. HOW THEY SPEND THEIR TIME IN THE THEATER PROPER IS UP TO THEM.
BUT THEY'RE MOCKING YOUR WORK. DOESN'T THAT BOTHER YOU?

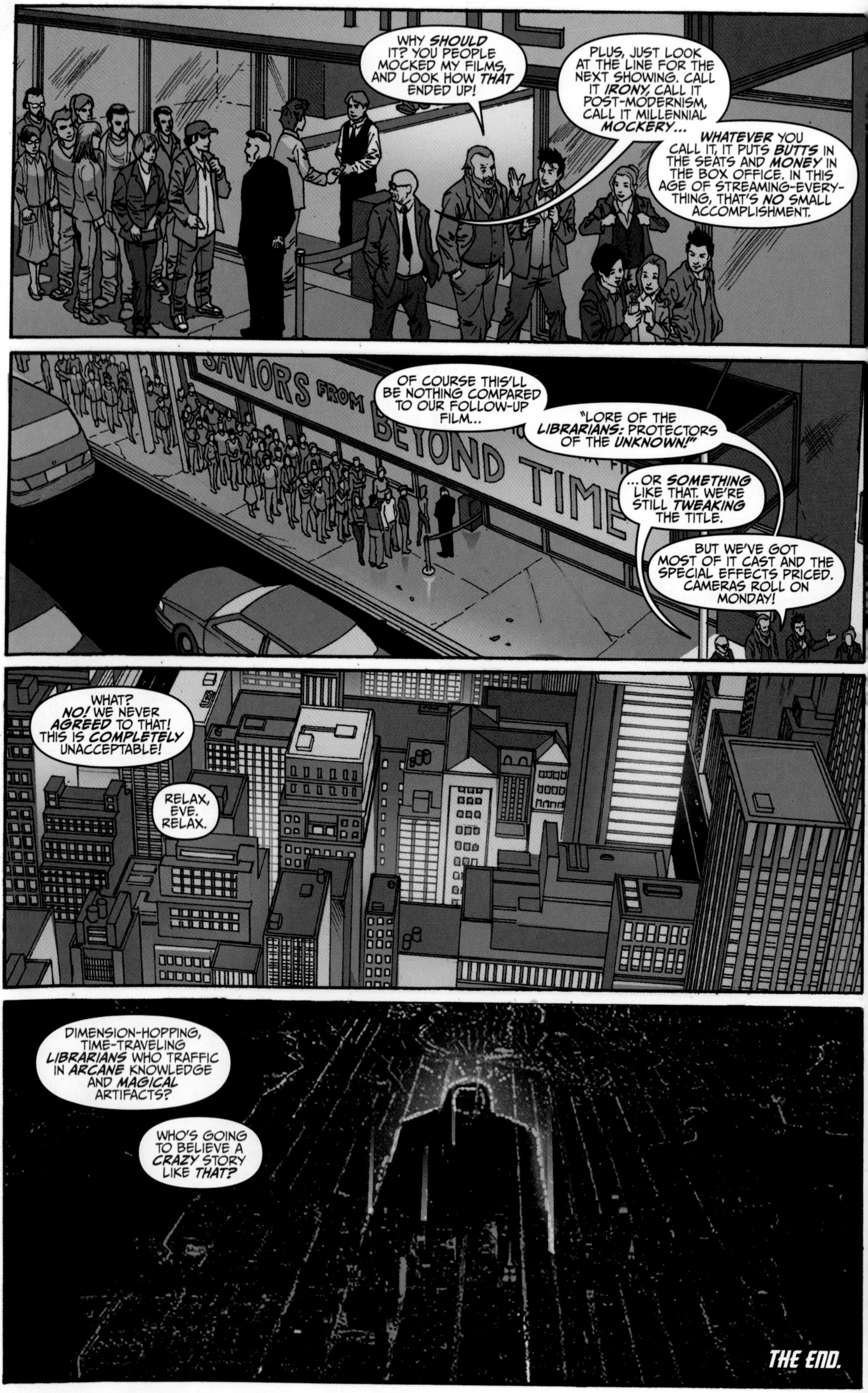
WHY SHOULD IT? YOU PEOPLE MOCKED MY FILMS, AND LOOK HOW THAT ENDED UP!
PLUS, JUST LOOK AT THE LINE FOR THE NEXT SHOWING. CALL IT IRONY, CALL IT POST-MODERNISM, CALL IT MILLENNIAL MOCKERY...
WHATEVER YOU CALL IT, IT PUTS BUTTS IN THE SEATS AND MONEY IN THE BOX OFFICE. IN THIS AGE OF STREAMING-EVERYTHING, THAT'S NO SMALL ACCOMPLISHMENT.
SAVIORS FROM BEYOND TIME
OF COURSE THIS'LL BE NOTHING COMPARED TO OUR FOLLOW-UP FILM...
"LORE OF THE LIBRARIANS: PROTECTORS OF THE UNKNOWN!"
...OR SOMETHING LIKE THAT. WE'RE STILL TWEAKING THE TITLE.
BUT WE'VE GOT MOST OF IT CAST AND THE SPECIAL EFFECTS PRICED. CAMERAS ROLL ON MONDAY!
WHAT? NO! WE NEVER AGREED TO THAT! THIS IS COMPLETELY UNACCEPTABLE!
RELAX, EVE. RELAX.
DIMENSION-HOPPING, TIME-TRAVELING LIBRARIANS WHO TRAFFIC IN ARCANE KNOWLEDGE AND MAGICAL ARTIFACTS?
WHO'S GOING TO BELIEVE A CRAZY STORY LIKE THAT?
THE END.

BONUS MATERIAL

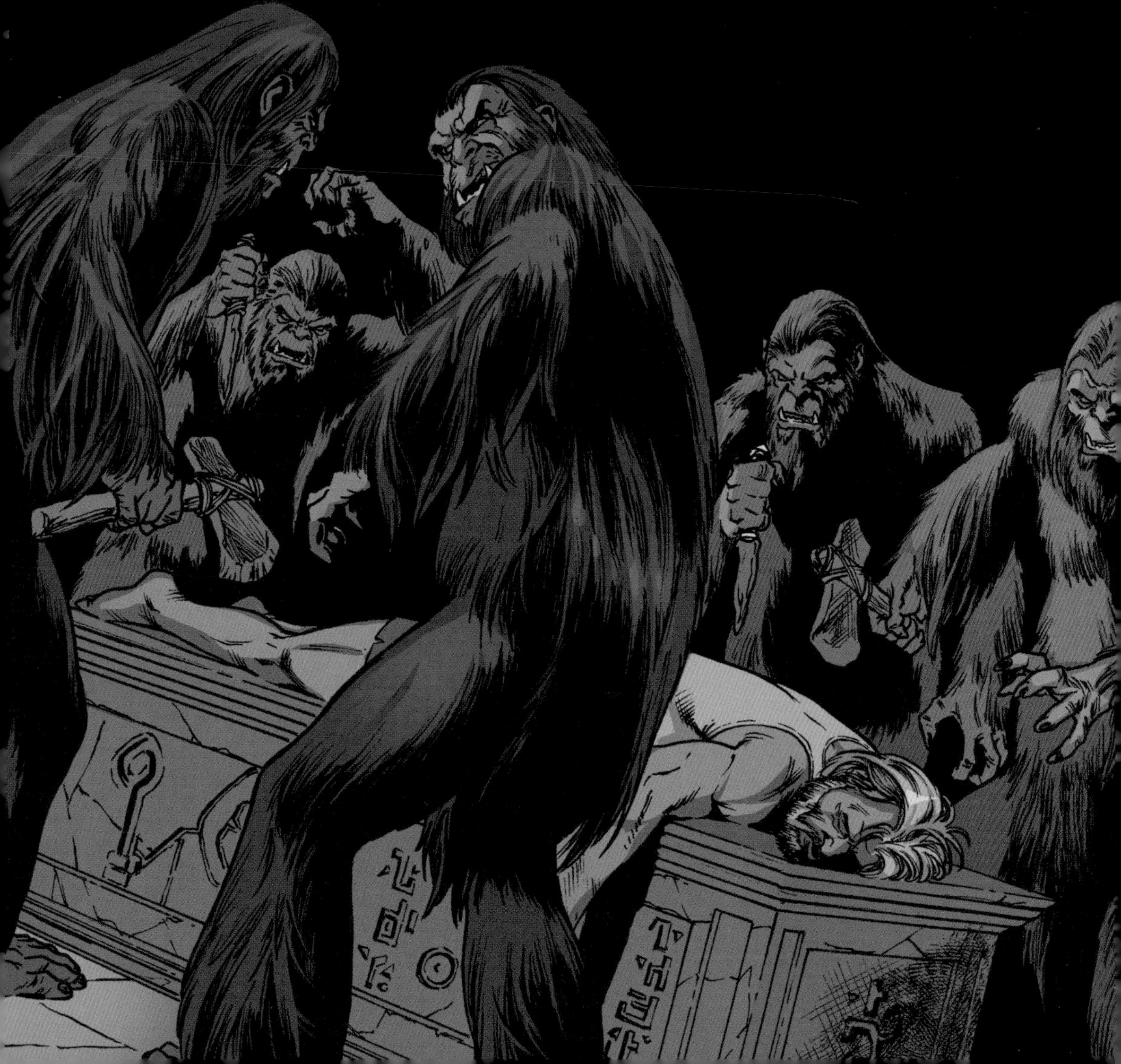

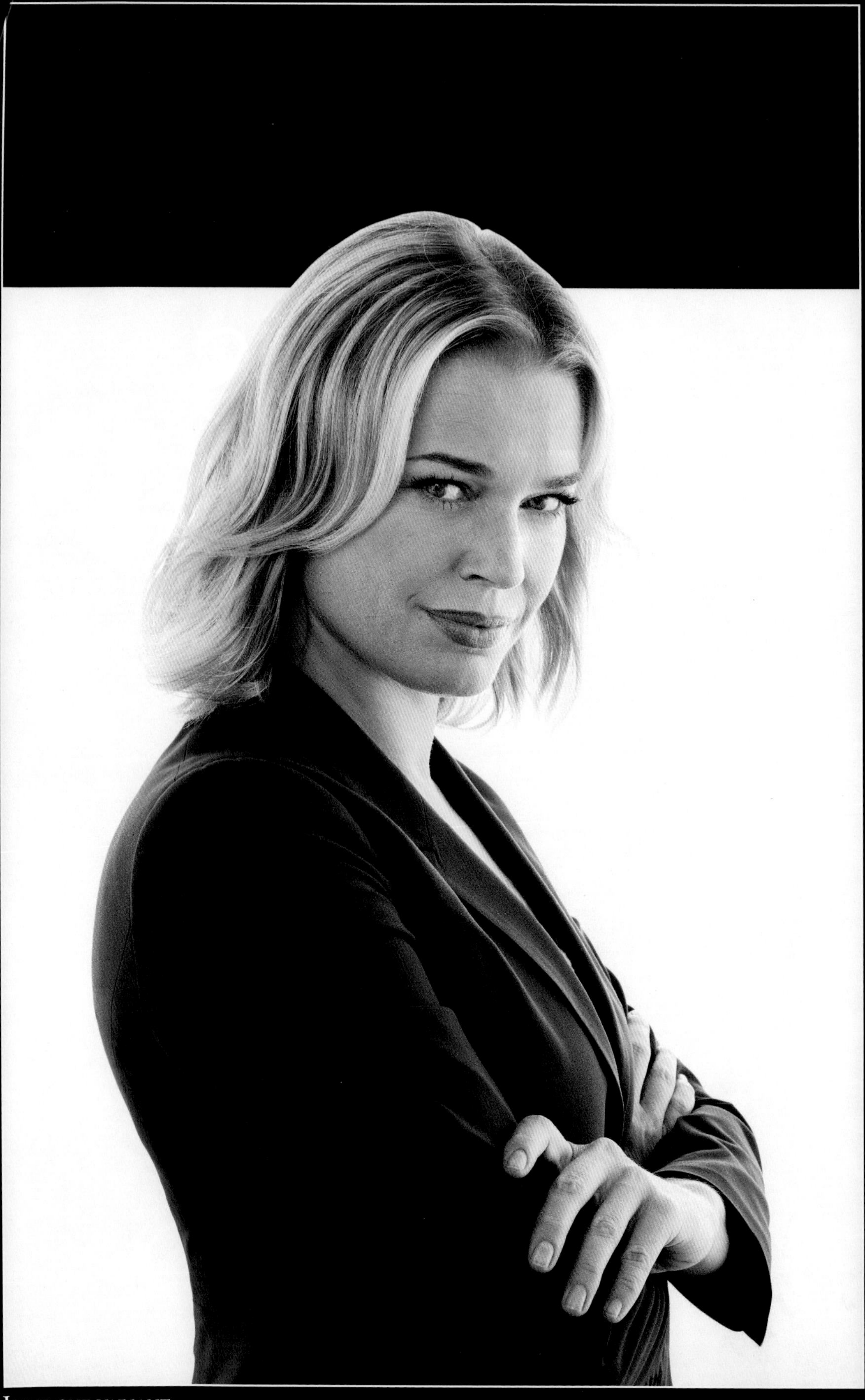

ISSUE ONE VARIANT
EVE BAIRD PHOTO COVER

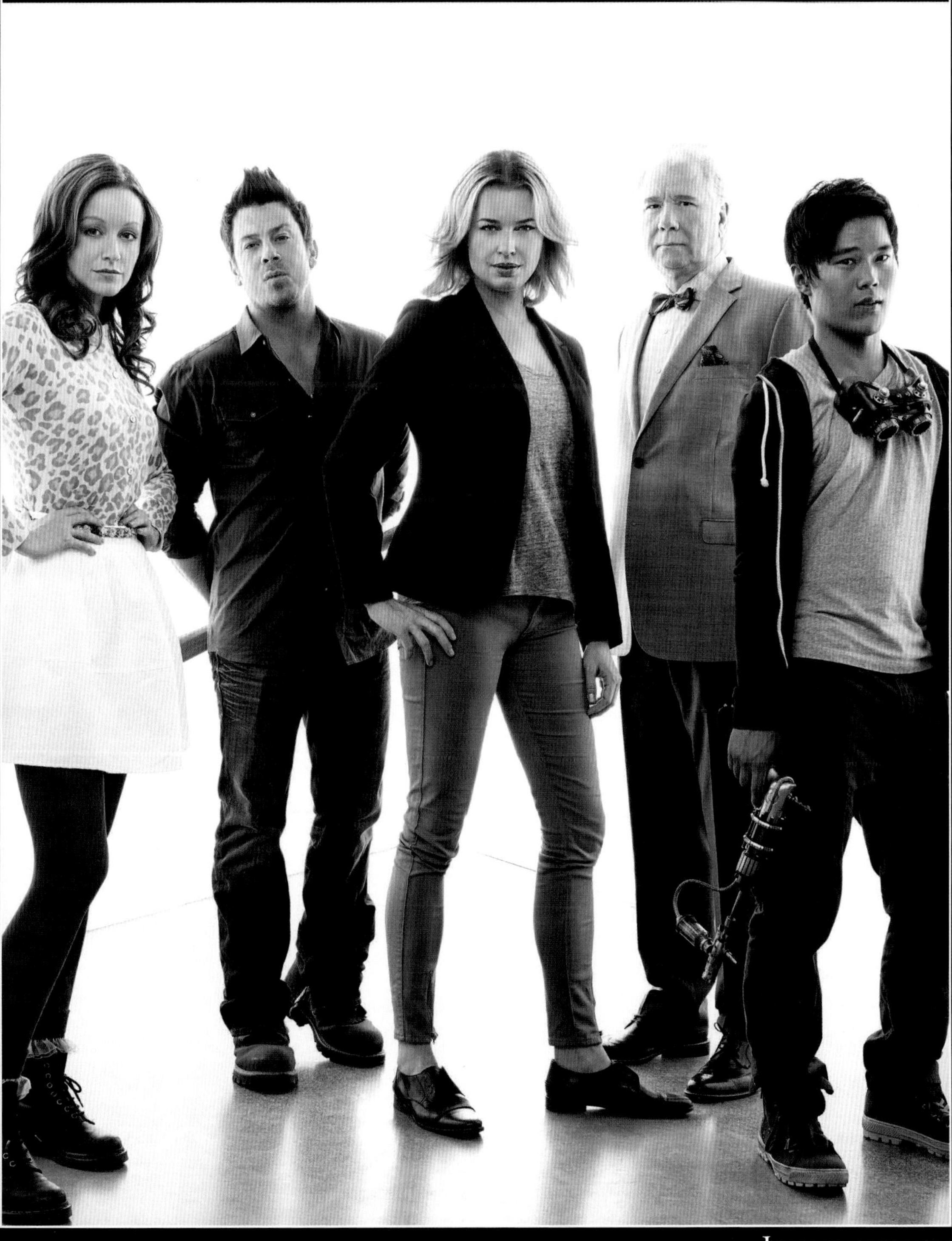

ISSUE ONE VARIANT
GROUP PHOTO COVER

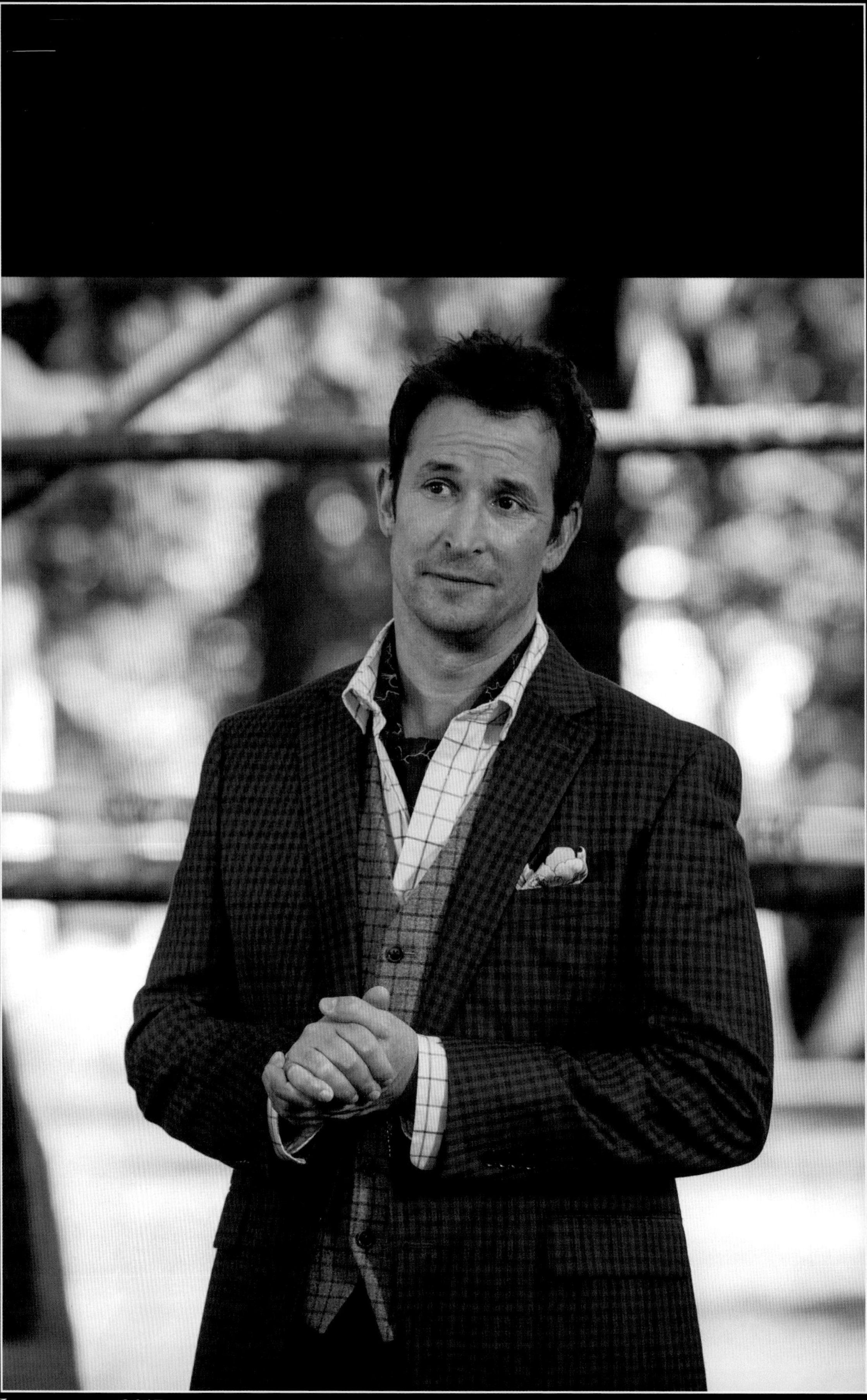

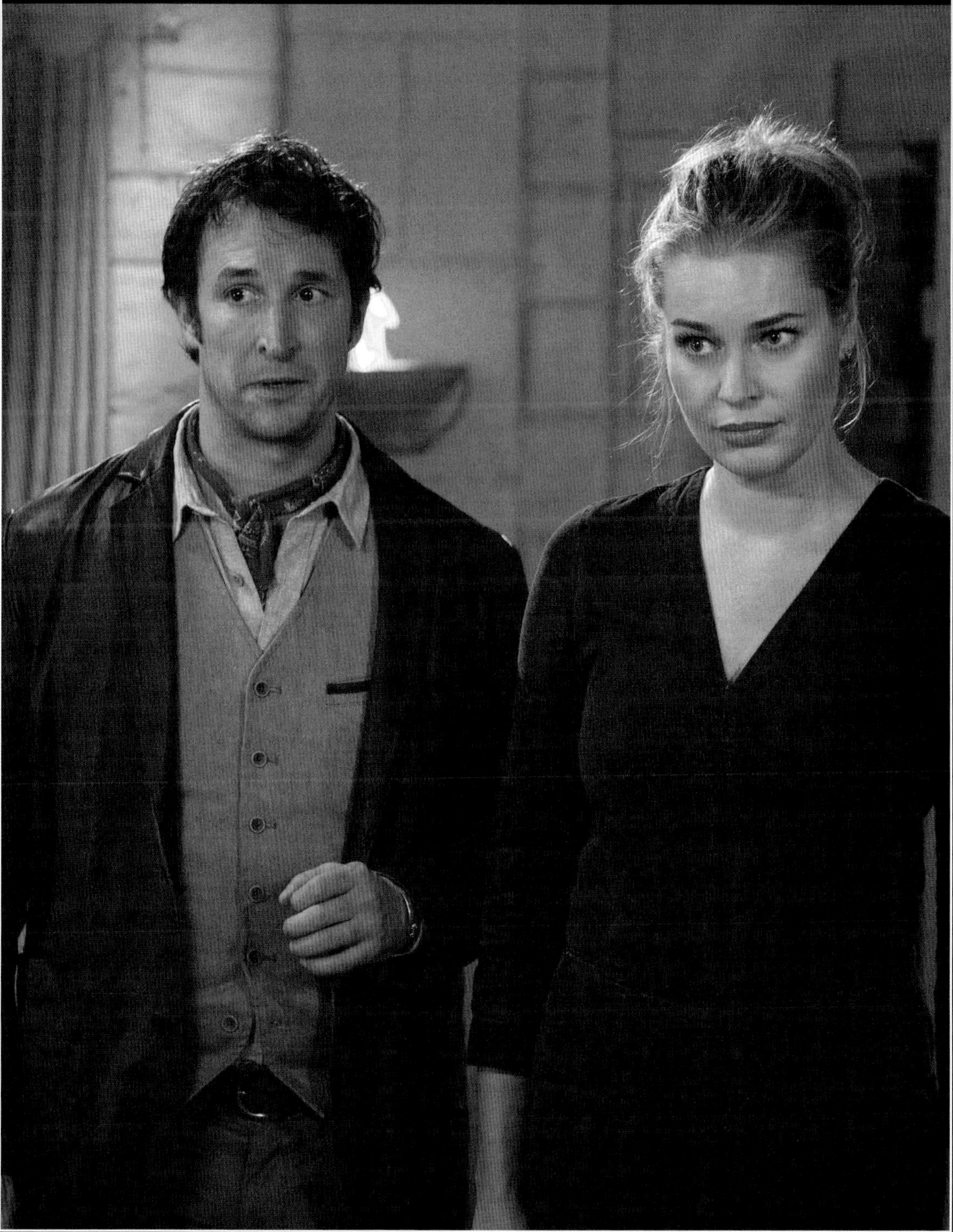

ISSUE ONE • BALTIMORE COMIC-CON EXCLUSIVE

FLYNN CARSON & EVE BAIRD PHOTO COVER

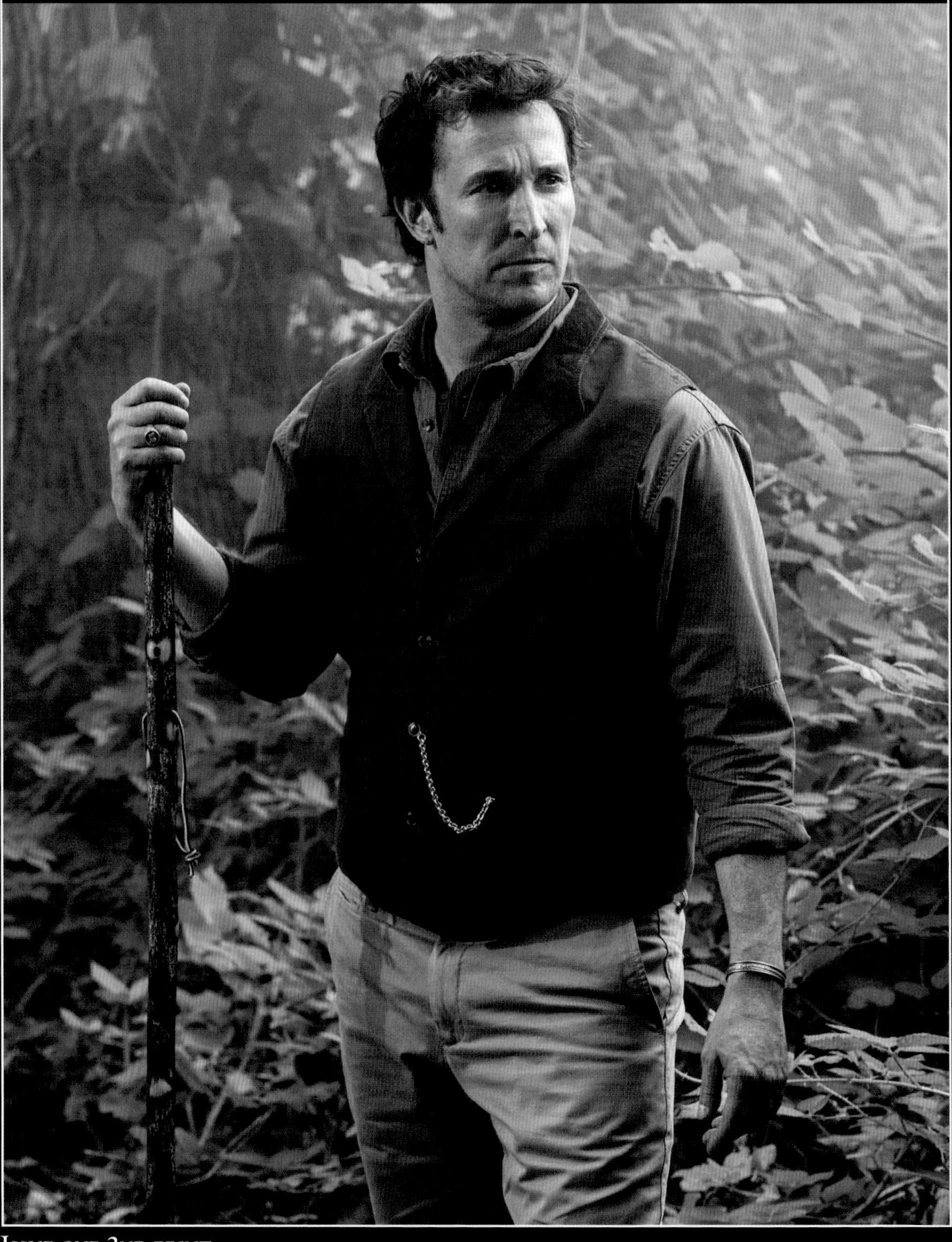

ISSUE ONE 2ND PRINT
FLYNN CARSON PHOTO COVER

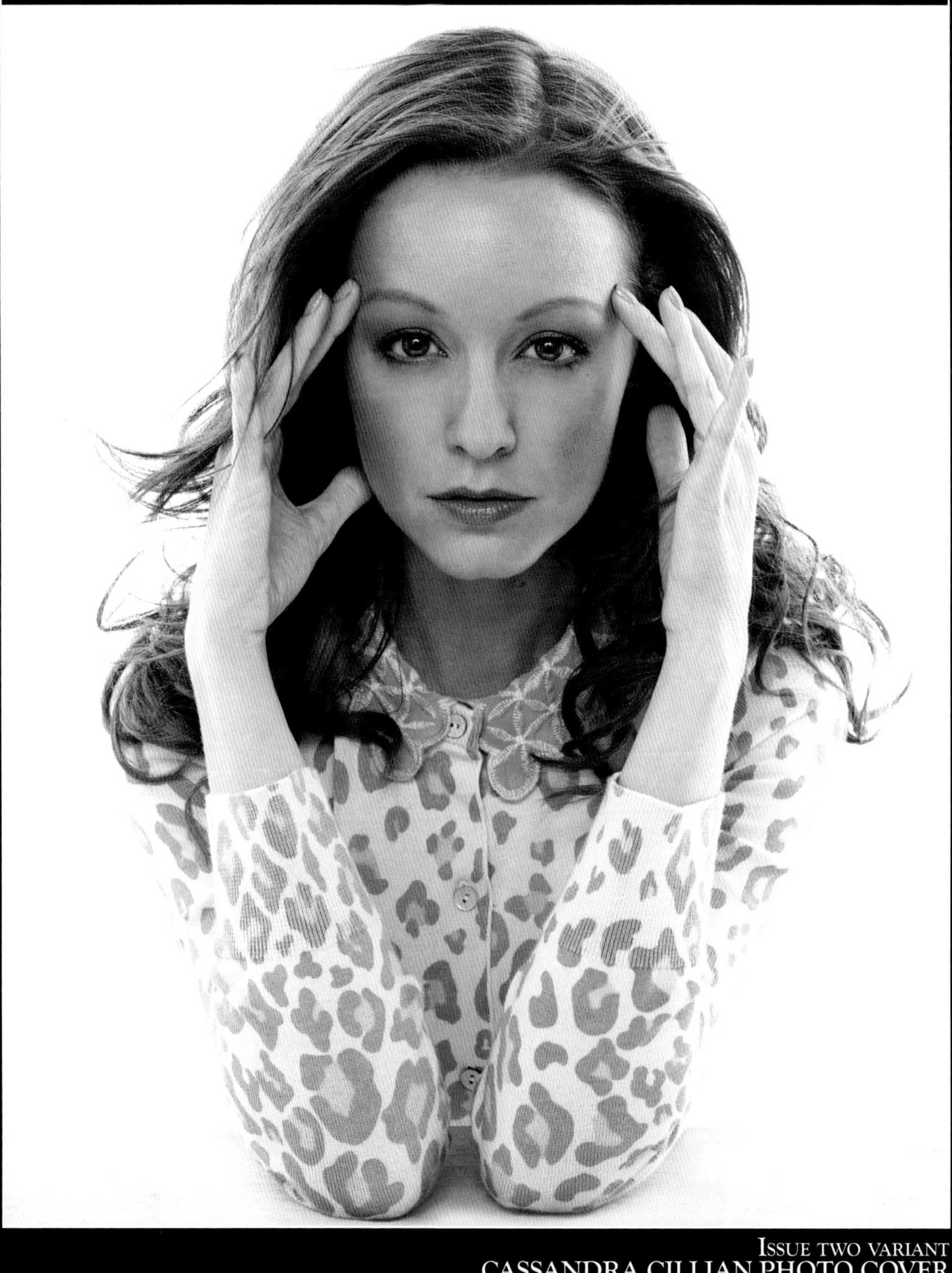

Issue two variant
CASSANDRA CILLIAN PHOTO COVER

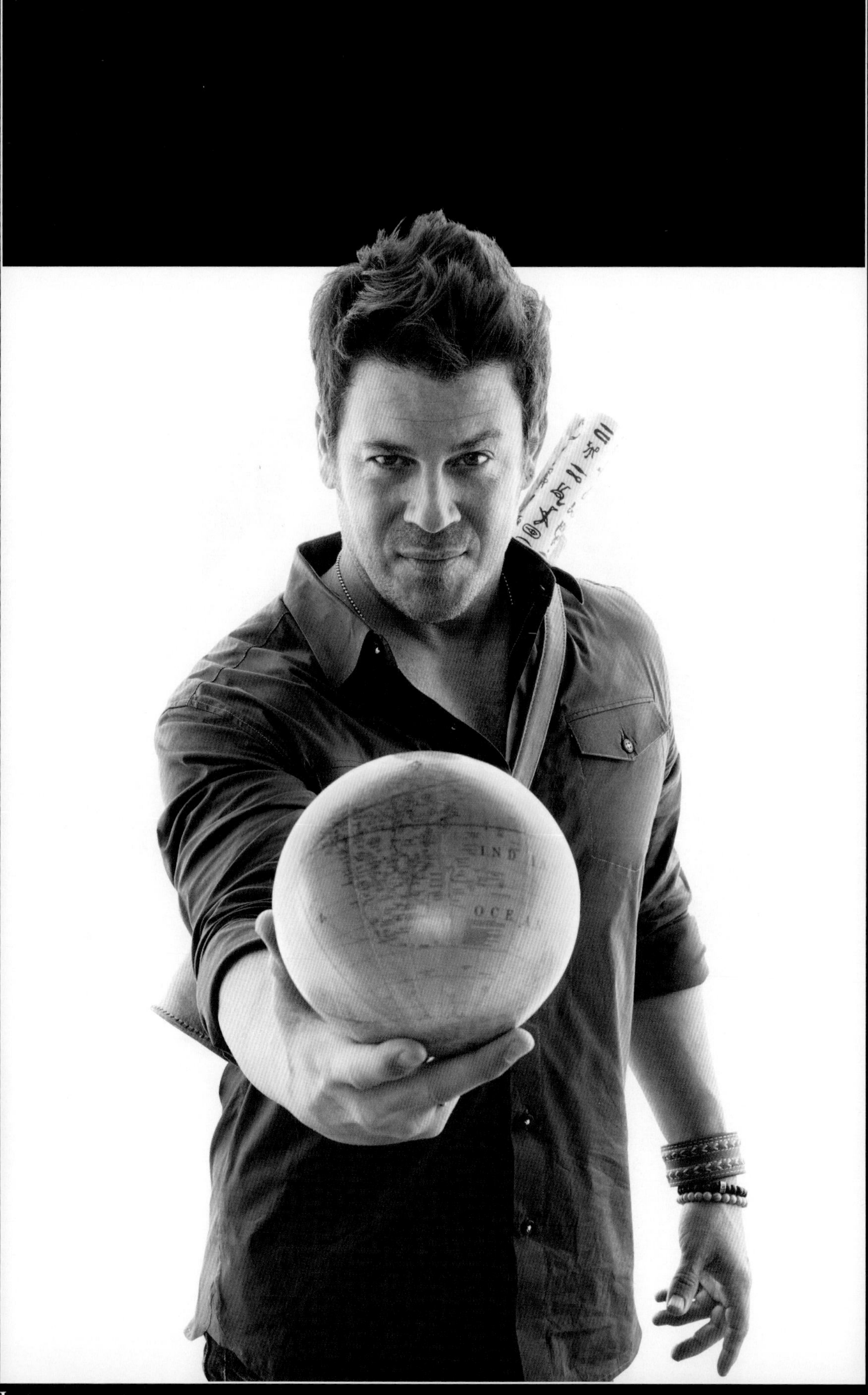

ISSUE THREE VARIANT
JAKE STONE PHOTO COVER

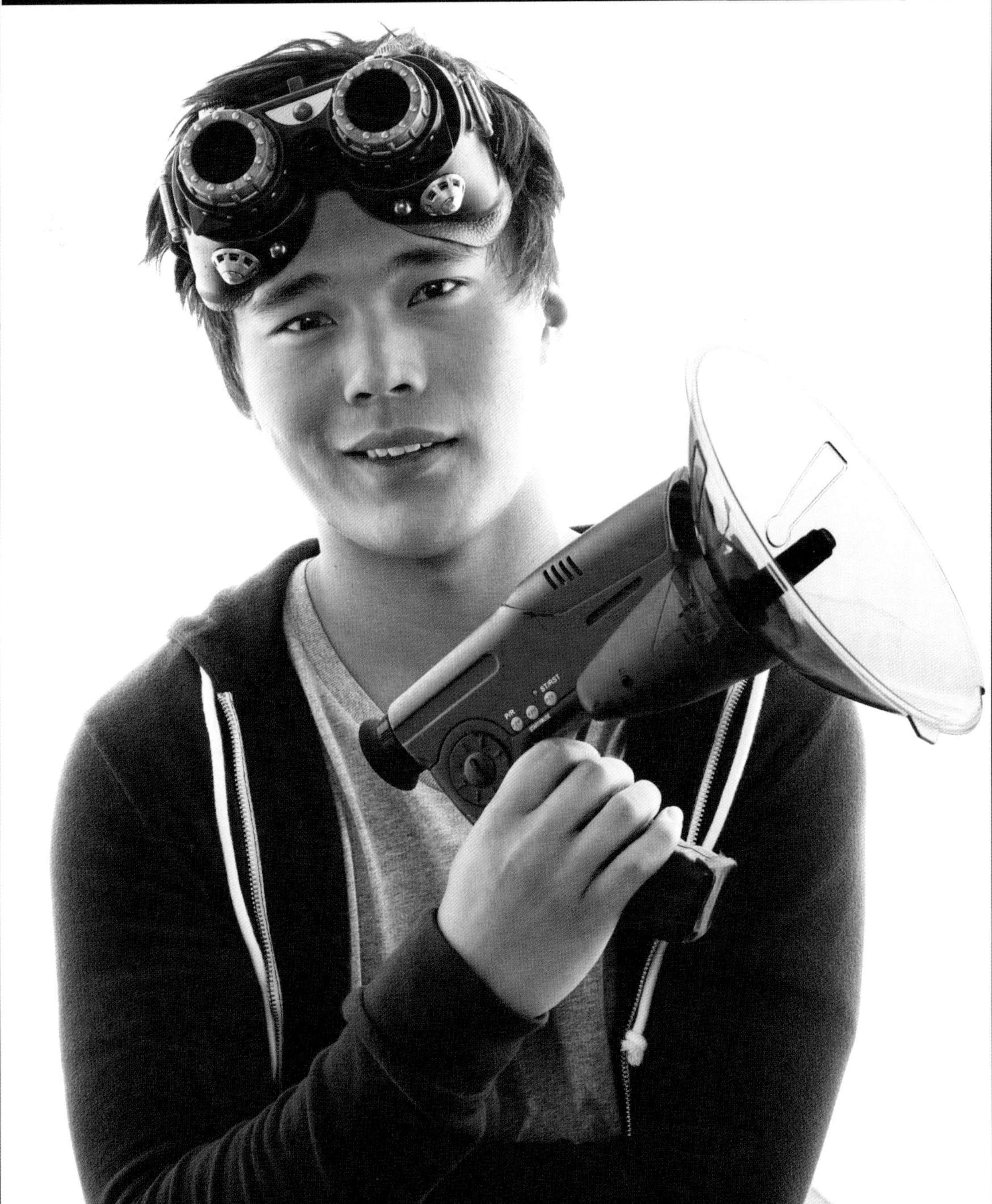

ISSUE FOUR VARIANT
EZEKIEL JONES PHOTO COVER

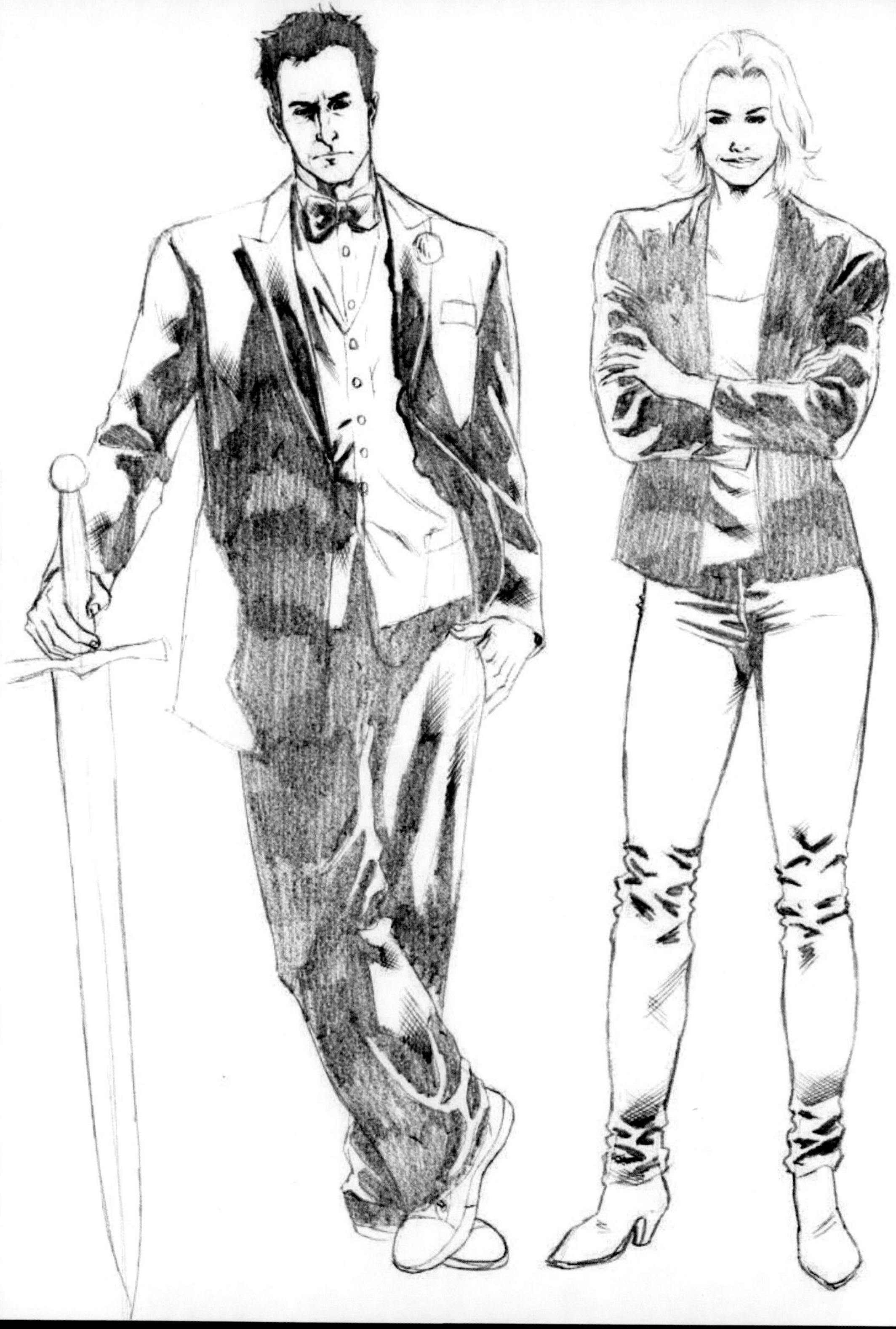

CHARACTER STUDIES AND SKETCHES BY RODNEY BUCHEMI

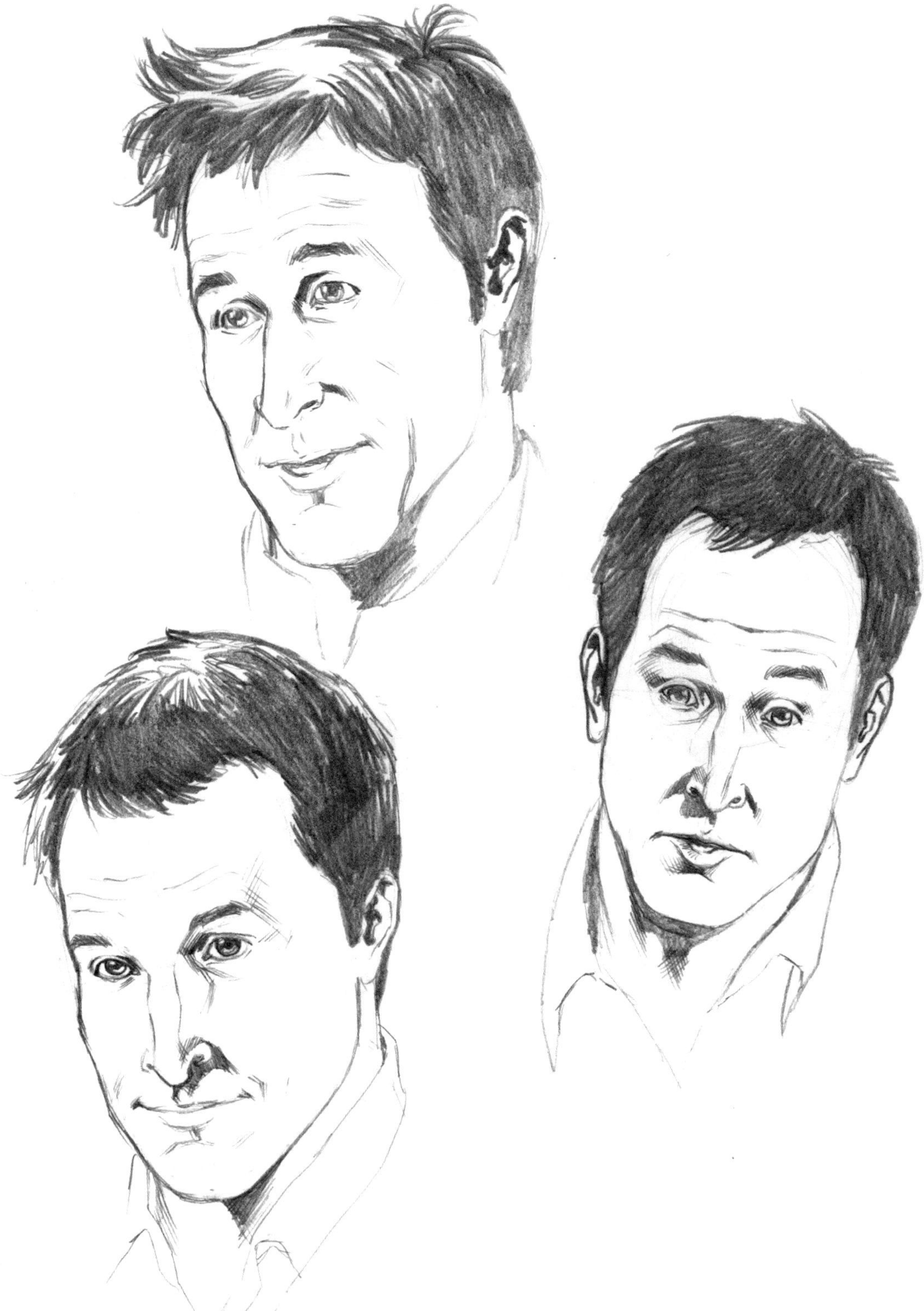

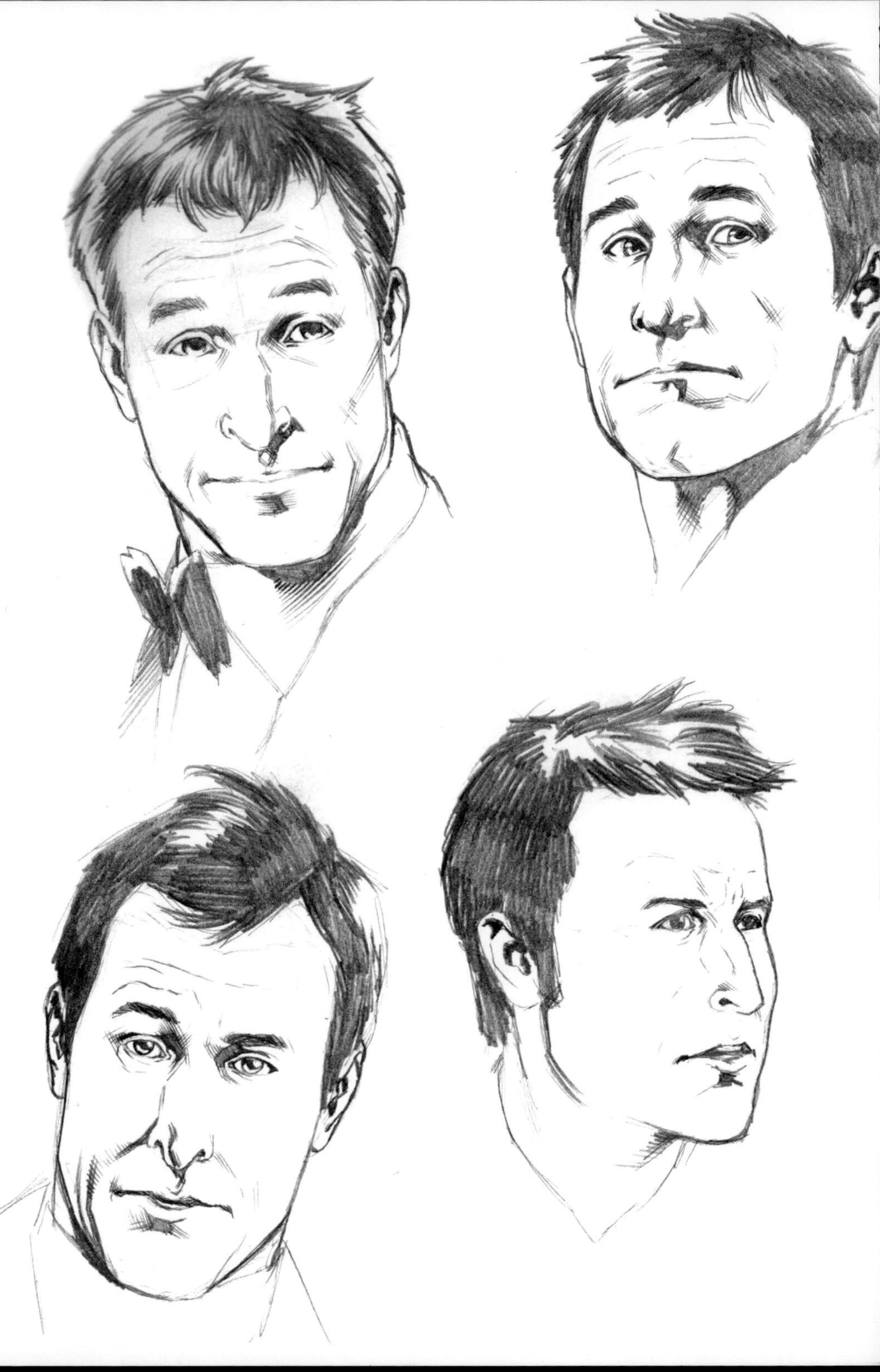

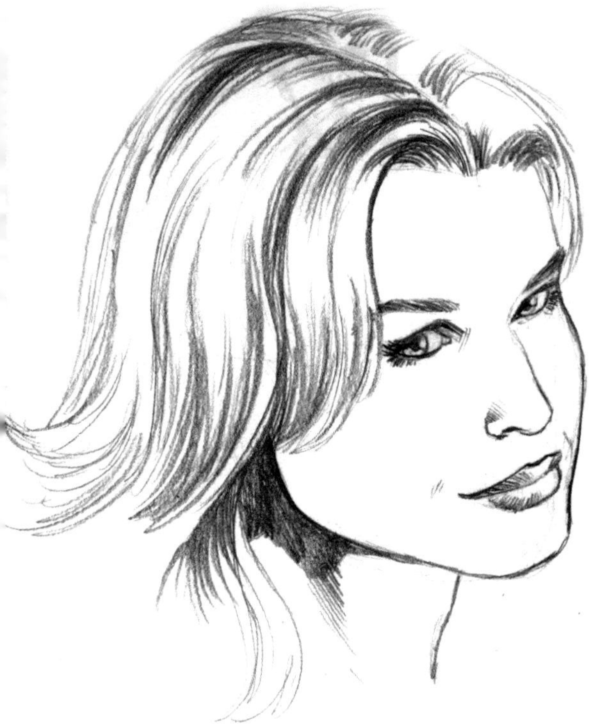

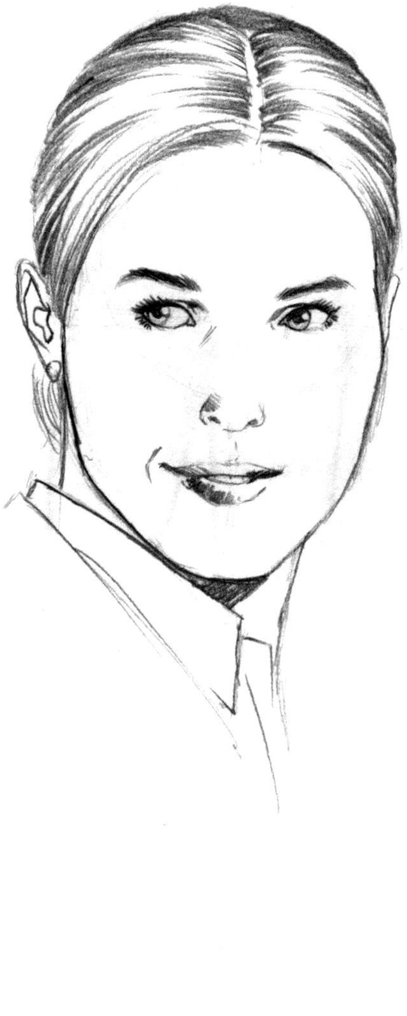

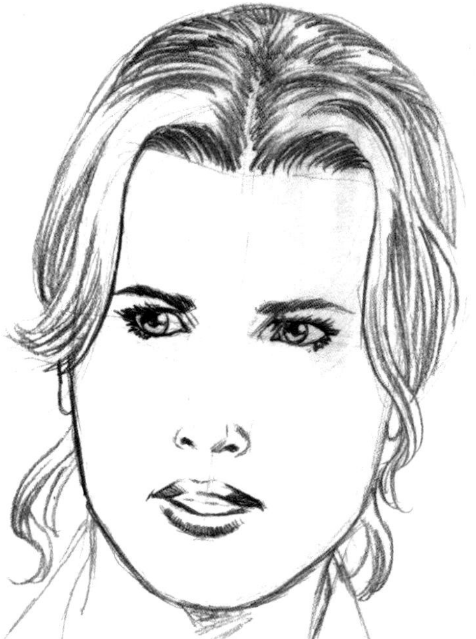

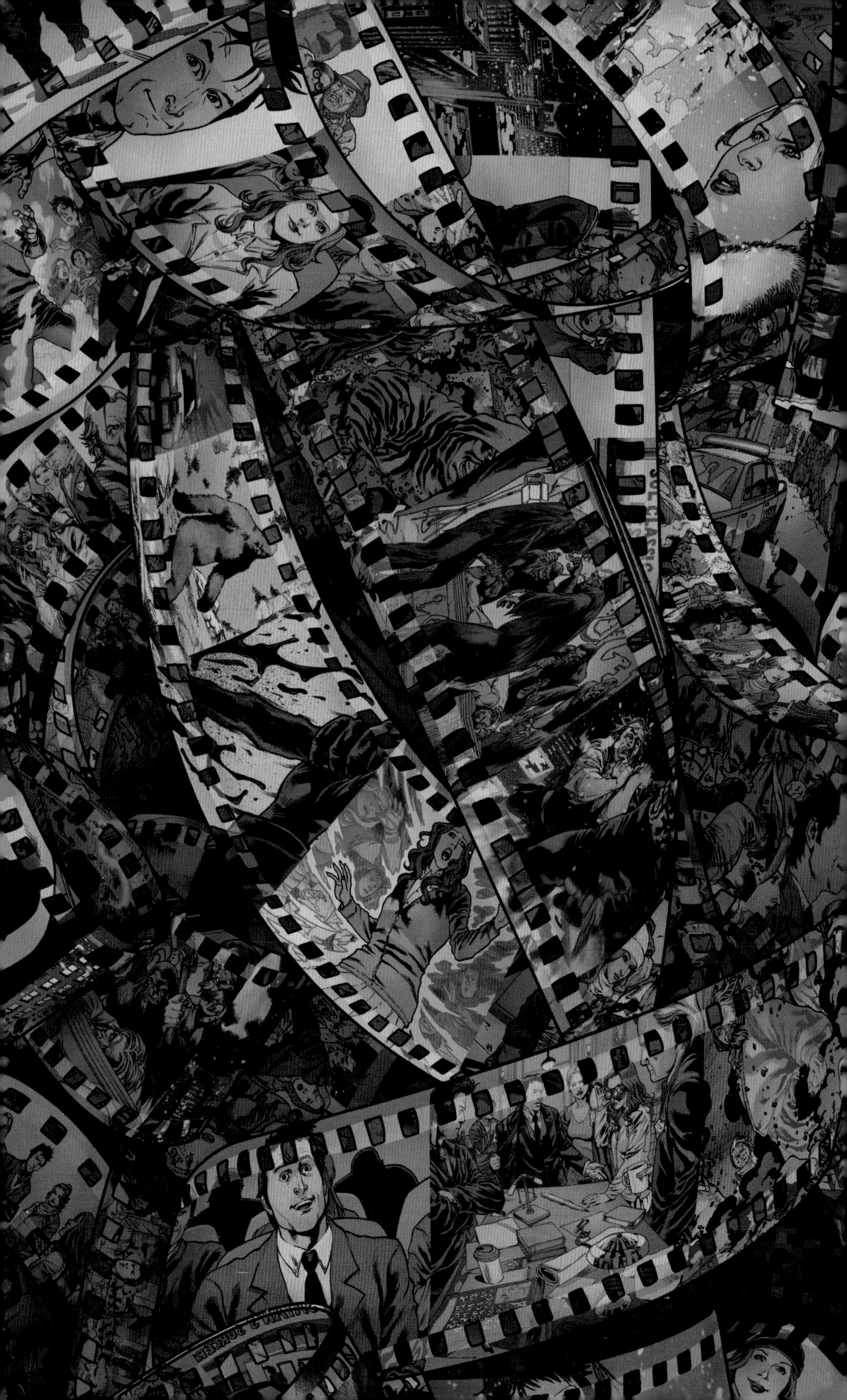